BEARING TRUE WITNESS

THE EERDMANS EKKLESIA SERIES

Editors

Michael L. Budde
Stephen E. Fowl

The Eerdmans Ekklesia Series explores matters of Christianity and discipleship across a wide expanse of disciplines, church traditions, and issues of current and historical concern.

The Series is published in cooperation with the Ekklesia Project, a network of persons for whom "being a Christian" is seen to be the primary identity and allegiance for believers — superseding and ordering the claims on offer by the modern state, market, racial and ethnic groups, and other social forces. The Ekklesia Project emphasizes the importance of the church as a distinctive community in the world, called to carry into contemporary society the priorities and practices of Jesus Christ as conveyed in the Gospels.

The Ekklesia Series will draw from the broad spectrum of the Christian world — Protestantism of many traditions, Roman Catholicism, Anabaptism, Orthodoxy — in exploring critical issues in theology, history, social and political theory, biblical studies, and world affairs. The Series editors are Stephen E. Fowl, Professor and Chair, Department of Theology at Loyola College in Baltimore; and Michael L. Budde, Professor of Political Science and Catholic Studies and Chair, Department of Political Science, at DePaul University in Chicago.

Additional information about the Ekklesia Project, including submission guidelines for the Eerdmans Ekklesia book series, may be found at www.ekklesiaproject.org.

BEARING TRUE WITNESS

Truthfulness in Christian Practice

Craig Hovey

WILLIAM B. EERDMANS PUBLISHING COMPANY

GRAND RAPIDS, MICHIGAN / CAMBRIDGE, U.K.

Published 2011 by
Wm. B. Eerdmans Publishing Co.
2140 Oak Industrial Drive N.E., Grand Rapids, Michigan 49505 /
P.O. Box 163, Cambridge CB3 9PU U.K.

Printed in the United States of America

17 16 15 14 13 12 11   7 6 5 4 3 2 1

Library of Congress Cataloging-in-Publication Data

Hovey, Craig, 1974-
Bearing true witness: truthfulness in Christian practice / Craig Hovey.
p.   cm. — (The Eerdmans Ekklesia series)
Includes bibliographical references and index.
ISBN 978-0-8028-6581-6 (pbk.: alk. paper)
1. Witness bearing (Christianity) 2. Truth — Religious aspects —
Christianity. 3. Knowledge, Theory of (Religion)
I. Title.   II. Title: Truthfulness in Christian practice.

BV4520.H68   2011

248′.501 — dc22

2011005894

www.eerdmans.com

To Kimberly

Contents

Preface

This book began life as a doctoral thesis at the University of Cambridge, where, under the direction of my advisor, Janet Soskice, I was consistently and graciously pressed to deepen the way that the study presents a theological response to the inadequacies, false starts, and at times outright contradictions of modern habits of knowing. After several years of letting the essay sit, during which I worked on a couple of books that elaborate on themes that I began thinking about while at Cambridge, I returned to it to discover, to my delight, how much my thinking truly has continued to develop on trajectories I had earlier encountered.

I treasure an interview with Michel Foucault in 1984 in which his questioner, François Ewald, asked why Foucault had not kept to an earlier writing plan that he had made public. Foucault confesses that he had become bored with his topic, which, in his arrogance, he had assumed was sufficiently complete in his mind and only required him to put it to paper. "It was," he says, "both a form of presumption and an abandonment of restraint. Yet to work is to undertake to think something other than what one has thought before."[1] Foucault was an extraordinarily gifted and free-ranging thinker, and I cannot help but imagine that his phenomenal career owed a lot to what is true about his comments in this interview. The best reason to bother to write something is to give yourself the freedom to think differently. I do not mean to compare myself with Foucault; I only mean to express how the task of theology is itself a journey of discovering things that

---

1. Michel Foucault, *Foucault Live (Interviews, 1961-1984)*, ed. Sylvere Lotringer, trans. Lysa Hochroth and John Johnston (New York: Semiotext[e], 1989), p. 455.

would remain hidden without genuinely embarking on the way. I consider it a great gift that I am able to attribute whatever is enlightening in this book to the courage of others who have preceded me in doing so.

I would not have been able to write this book without the support of many others. Ashland University provided a writing grant to aid in the final preparation of the manuscript, and my colleagues in the department of religion have generously indulged my needs. The friendship and generosity of those who indefatigably read portions of the manuscript and offered invaluable insights and suggestions have made the finished product something that would have been impossible otherwise. Specifically, I thank Jonathan Tran, Stanley Hauerwas, Jeff Bailey, David Cunningham, Peter Ochs, and Glen Stassen. Others have been unfailingly big-hearted in their encouragement and valuable conversation: John Kiess, Peter Slade, John Perry, Stephen Plant, Bill Cavanaugh, Charlie Pinches, David Ford, and Michael Northcott. I owe abundant thanks to Sam Wells, who not only believed in me and my intuitions for this project long before I was able to, but also refused to let me make Christian ethics an academic exercise separable from my love of God and the church. To my supervisors, Janet Soskice and Chris Insole, I owe appreciation for their gentle and perspicacious nudging when I was unsure how to say what I thought and, almost certainly worse, unsure how to think what I was saying. The community of St. Mark's Church, Cambridge, was a constant reminder that many of God's gifts come in the struggle to be what we are together. I am thankful for the generosity of the Bethune-Baker Fund, the Trinity Hall Chapel Council, and the Miller-Trayhern Fund. Finally, Kimberly Hovey has more than once courageously taken unpredictable steps with her husband in the confidence that doing so might constitute faithfulness rather than recklessness. Perhaps on some occasions they were both.

*   *   *

Some parts of this book have appeared elsewhere, either as conference presentations or in print, although I have reworked all of them for their present context. I presented parts of chapters 4 and 5 at a conference on "Faith's Public Role," sponsored by the Von Hügel Institute, St. Edmund's College, Cambridge (2005), the systematic theology seminar in the Faculty of Divinity, University of Cambridge (2006), and the McMenemy Seminar at Trinity Hall, Cambridge (2006); these parts were published as "Free Christian Speech: Plundering Foucault," *Political Theology* 8, no. 1 (January

2007): 63-81 (© Equinox Publishing Ltd. 2007). I presented parts of chapter 7 in Oxford at the Society for the Study of Christian Ethics (2005). Parts of chapter 8 appeared as "Narrative Proclamation and Gospel Truthfulness: Why Christian Testimony Needs Speakers," in *The Gift of Difference: Radical Orthodoxy, Radical Reformation,* edited by Chris K. Huebner and Tripp York (Winnipeg: CMU Press, 2010), 87-103. I presented parts of chapter 9 at a conference on "Research as a Theological Undertaking," convened by Susan Parsons and sponsored by the Society for the Study of Christian Ethics at the University of Birmingham (2005), and published as "Putting Truth to Practice: MacIntyre's Unexpected Rule," *Studies in Christian Ethics* 19, no. 2 (August 2006): 169-86. I am grateful to these journals and publishers for their kind permission to reprint this material.

Christ and Reality

> It is possible to think of the Gospel and our preaching of it as, above all and at no matter what risk, a speaking of the truth about the way things are.
>
> Frederick Buechner, *Telling the Truth*

I would like to think of this book as an extended commentary on these words by Frederick Buechner. If he is right that proclaiming the gospel is at root a matter of telling the truth about the way things are, then Christian witnesses are the paradigmatic truth-tellers. In this book I aim to take this claim as seriously as possible, and I think through how knowing the truth about the way things really are is inescapably bound up with knowing the truth about Christ. I investigate the risks involved in facing and declaring the truth about ourselves and the world, and how this is a function of overcoming the obstructions of power that attend to making Christ known to the world. I explore how the proclamation of the gospel is central to telling the truth about reality. A people possessed of the skills required for Christian witness will have learned to be a truthful people. In these pages, therefore, I study the particularity of these truth-tellers: their particular skills and the particular truth they tell.

Pursuing these issues requires operating on a field occupied by both theological ethics and philosophical theology. I have found it neither necessary nor desirable to differentiate between the two since neither label refers to a discrete or pure discipline. Nevertheless, I face the challenge of showing how the theological nature of both descriptions makes a difference to the enterprise it describes. How does bearing true witness to Christ impinge on the ordinary, everyday human contests with knowing, desiring, and speaking what is true? In response to this question, I have sought first to display the importance of what Christians *do,* that they are a people who are obliged to bear witness; second, I have found it necessary to show how it is that *what* Christians claim — their testimony — exhibits and demands a particularly theological approach. Because I have attempted, so far as possible, to hold together the medium and message of the gospel, I use theological claims as premises and proceed from them in arguments. Not to do so would suggest that what Christians proclaim only constitutes *content* within a practice that could be understood in other terms. But because I have wanted to argue that Christians learn what it means to tell the truth by bearing witness to Christ, the substance of that witness — and not just the report of a phenomenon — bears on that central claim.

I do not assume that Christian ethics is for anyone other than Christians. I do not claim any insight into how others might become truthful people, what this would mean, or whether they possess the necessary resources for doing so. To be sure, the Christian hope is that all of creation will worship God in the truth of Christ. Until that time, many who engage in reflection about how to live will take the refusal to worship God as a premise. This reflection may go on to specify the shape of national or international unity, enumerate rights, demand justice, enjoin virtues, and recommend culture. Though this kind of reflection will no doubt persist, I do not think we should consider it theological. Where it is concerned with knowledge and being, we may call it philosophy. Where it is concerned with how we are to live, we may call it ethics. But so long as the truth made known in Christ does not bear on the way such reflection proceeds, what it strives for, and how it understands itself, we will not properly call it Christian or theological in any ordinary senses of these words. We may speak of philosophy but not philosophical *theology;* we may speak of ethics but not *theological* or *Christian* ethics. I do not make these comments in order to clear the space for these nontheological discourses; I do so only to acknowledge that they exist and, even assuming I would know how to engage in them, I nevertheless have chosen not to do so.

Yet my skepticism is deeper than this. An unqualified ethic and an unqualified philosophy may not only be self-consciously nontheological, but they are generally hiding something that a qualifier would simply make explicit. They may even disguise how their own pseudotheological commitments are designed precisely to leave little room for other particu-

2

lar accounts. However, saying this is not primarily by way of accusation but by way of offering clarification. If I hold to my claims about the Christian nature and purpose of Christian ethics, not to mention the theological nature and purpose of philosophical theology, why, then, have I engaged to so great an extent with nontheological philosophers in the following pages?

My response to this question will be to adhere closely to the subject matter of this book and make plain how such philosophical engagements arise from it. Rather than departing from the claims in these pages, we can best see the engagements with philosophers in the light of these claims. Even though God's truth is found in Jesus Christ, seeing everything else in the light of Christ changes how everything else looks. Having seen Christ, his disciples do not consequently look at nothing else; but as witnesses, they are positively entreated to look at everything else in a new way. Therefore, theological reflection is free to plunder every resource available to it. For example, while it is important to read Nietzsche and Foucault, in a sense, on their own terms, we need not also assume that "their own terms" must be the final word. If Christian theology can make use of Nietzsche and Foucault in pursuit of better ways of expressing the reality of the world in the light of Christ, it is because such use exemplifies the conviction that Christ is lord of all things. As I argue in the first section, a witness trains her eyes to look for Christ in the unexpected, not out of uncertain doubt, but because a certainly risen Christ is already an unexpected reality and will be found in unexpected places.

By *witness,* I mean the ecclesially embodied process, activity, and task of making Christ known by word. Witness is the work of the church for declaring to the world that salvation is in Christ, that the world belongs to him, and that his works are good.

The material here comprises three sections that correspond to three moments of witness: seeing, coming forward, and testifying. While I believe that the structure is part of the argument, there can be a strong temptation to make the structure take the place of the argument. Given the antitheoretical nature of much of what I say here about Christian witness, the structure must be permitted to do very little work indeed. Therefore, it is no small point that I do not treat various aspects of witness — or principles of witness. Rather I hope that *moments* will reflect for readers the way that witness extends in ways that are irreducibly temporal. Witness happens in time. More specifically, as I argue in these pages, it is itself a way of referring to events within the gospel's history, which in turn is nothing other than the history of Christ. That we can speak about such temporal phases indicates that witness is a *practice,* not a theory.

The three movements I identify find their places within a juridical idiom that is profoundly biblical and that was used in early martyrologies. The New Testament themes of judgment, witness, truth, advocacy, and testimony not only convey the truth of the gospel by reporting information; they also extend the mission of Jesus in a way that involves readers and hearers in the trial itself. And the nature of their inclusion in it means that they cannot summarily evade the truth of the testimonies about Jesus by which they are included. Their status as witnesses (rather than simply readers) depends on the testimony they read being true (e.g., in the form of John's Gospel), which is only to say that they are ones who are able to claim that this is part of *our Scripture.* In the trial, their responses constitute judgments of the central claims, penultimately set against the final judgment of God.[1] (It is important that the judgments of witnesses are penultimate, since witnesses are never expected to be judges in any final sense, but must remain open to countertestimony.[2])

In this motif, moreover, the witnesses are not only called forward on behalf of the defendant, but are also themselves put on trial for their involvement in the testimonies they bear. Readers and hearers whose judgments accord with the judgment of God — that Jesus is Lord — themselves become witnesses and are subsequently put on trial before the world. What kind of court puts the *witness* on trial? It could only be a court devoid of justice, one that in actions like these is actually involved in condemning justice itself. Those who are called on as witnesses and who tell the truth are thus condemned.[3] By persisting in speaking truthful testimony, the faithful witness rebuffs the condemnation of the unjust trial, thereby testifying to the ultimacy of divine justice over worldly power at the risk of death. Their very noncompliance disputes the authority of those who exercise abused power and ersatz justice. The death of martyrs is recast in light of the life, death, and resurrection of Jesus Christ. No lon-

---

1. Andrew T. Lincoln, *Truth on Trial: The Lawsuit Motif in the Fourth Gospel* (Peabody, MA: Hendrickson, 2000), pp. 170, 141.

2. Walter Brueggemann prefers the provisional nature of testimony to a settled certainty that constitutes hegemonic theological systems of former generations. He constructs his *Theology of the Old Testament* (Minneapolis: Fortress, 1997) according to the movements of testimony, dispute, and advocacy.

3. Paul Ricoeur, "The Hermeneutics of Testimony," in *Essays in Biblical Interpretation* (London: SPCK, 1981), p. 128.

ger must death be understood as punishment for sin; it may now be a positive act of faith that shares in the glory of the Son of God. Martyrs do not die joyfully in order to expose the pretence of the city of man, but because they do not share the pagan worshipers' fear that their gods cannot grant eternal life.[4]

*   *   *

While I was initially working on this project as a doctoral dissertation, I had no idea that it would later lead me to write a book on martyrdom.[5] My interests at the time had to do with knowledge and truth-telling, and I simply did not grasp the full significance of how the theme of martyrdom was right in the middle of these things. But I believe my instincts eventually served me well and directed me toward what I was bound to see with greater clarity sooner or later. Martyrs are the paradigmatic witnesses of the gospel because their obedience and faith unto death speak something that words alone cannot. Even more, their being silenced by death may itself become a word so penetrating that nothing can be done to rob it of its truth. The martyr freely forsakes control over the message on which he stakes his life. He even blesses and forgives his killers in confidence that violence cannot negate God's peace, just as hatred cannot overturn God's goodness. The martyr is utterly at home in the world, at ease with God's gifts and reign, and perfectly unmoved by power that knows only its own ostentation.

Even so, I am now yet more haunted by the need to recognize in these things the fragility and vulnerability of martyrdom. The deaths of martyrs are very often not the straightforward witness implied by words that paint an ideal picture. Martyrs cannot declare their own deaths to be martyr-deaths, and thus their ultimate risk is perhaps dying without any guarantee about how they will be remembered or whether they will be remembered at all. In death, martyrs submit to the collective judgment of the church and put their own contribution to that judgment on the line. This is because silenced martyrs are not only unable to speak to their killers the testimony for which they died; they also are unable to speak within the church in ways that would help secure the significance of their own

---

4. Augustine, *City of God*, VI.1.

5. Craig Hovey, *To Share in the Body: A Theology of Martyrdom for Today's Church* (Grand Rapids: Brazos, 2008).

deaths. But even to acknowledge this is still to paint an ideal picture. In fact, Christians often do not know what to make of the deaths of their fellows; they do not know — and cannot know — how to think about what kind of witness this is. Is this someone who wrongly courted death and failed to embrace the difficulty and goodness of God's gift of life? Is this a death that witnesses in its faith the faithfulness of Christ's own death? Was this person killed for proclaiming the gospel in a way that the church endorses? And what is "the church" anyway? Where is this collective body of discernment into whose hands the Christian thrusts himself in his dying, his only hope being that God's justice vindicates the weak and faithful? Is not the church just as likely to betray God's justice as to represent and enact it in how it remembers?

These are haunting questions because they do not have easy or clear answers. One thing they do is force the difficulty of Christian living, proclaiming, and dying back onto the field of actual history and within the reality of the broken and imperfect community of believers. I do not know whether we should make a virtue out of this as such. But I am convinced that the skills that will enable us to put the focus of these difficulties back onto the rough ground of living draw us further into God's history with creatures rather than lead us away from it. And since this history has in Christ become nothing other than the history of Christ himself, when it looks forward and homeward, its looking actually draws us deeper into the heart of things. If these are genuine Christian skills, then they are also the same skills that are at the core of this book and that both derive from and enable the practices of proclaiming the gospel in a world beyond our control. I believe that it is no coincidence that the skills necessary to speak of the ambiguities of Christian living in such a world are the same as those that will be called on by the living itself. We are namers and livers, describers and agents within a world in which our authentic existence will continually discover that there is more than we first thought.

As a result, it is not merely autobiographical to acknowledge that I am now more convinced that martyrdom is best approached obliquely rather than directly. I have come to a greater appreciation of the fact that, because martyrdom, if it is to be Christian, must be something that happens to one rather than something one seeks, paradoxically one will be best prepared for it by focusing on other things. In particular, one should focus on developing the virtues that I discuss in this book: how to have a will that insists on the truth even at great cost; how to persist in desiring what is true even when it looks like doing so will not get one anywhere —

immediately, at least — and when desiring less than the truth does get one somewhere; how to refuse the lure of such places, especially when everything about them seems good and beautiful.

It is only right to be forthcoming about what this book is not. For one thing, I make no promise to settle Pilate's enduring and stirring question, What is truth? That is no doubt an important question, and it is certainly one that will outlive this book — and all books. Nevertheless, I do think that the shift in emphasis that I counsel is one that Christians should embrace for reasons that have their own integrity: away from the truth itself and toward the virtues, desires, and will to embrace the truth wherever it is found. Of course, truth is important. But even if it presented itself bald-faced and prominent among us with no hint of ambiguity, if it were shown to us uncomplicated, clear, and polished, we still might not embrace it. I am not convinced that we really want to hear the truth about the world, about ourselves, or about God. Nietzsche wondered how we might remain faithful to the earth. We are, after all, constantly tempted to transcend it and to see in it something other than what really is. In doing so, we sin against the earth.[6] Nietzsche not only insisted that our knowing must be human but, by affirming our humanity, he sought to impress on us that any knowing that seems to exceed it really denies it. In these pages, I seek to understand the humanness of knowledge as organic and integral to the work of Christian witness, rather than as limitation.

Of course, we want to see things become better and see ourselves taking part in making them better. Nietzsche did, too, in his own ways. For Christianity, this is clearly a salutary form of transcendence that is just as properly eschatological as it is metaphysical. But I believe Christianity can still learn much from Nietzsche's disdain for metaphysics, which was primarily motivated by his worry that metaphysics easily converts into — or derives from — a hatred of life and contempt for what is merely human. His disdain instructs Christians not to allow their ideas about Christ to take flight into the inviolability of eternity. God's creatures never cease being God's creatures. The Son of God is not a creature, of course; but in Christ, God the Son is a man. We might, in the spirit of Nietzsche, fault much of Christian thought for ignoring the simple fact that the incarnation is not over. The Son of God is still incarnate in history and is materially and sacramentally present within the church. Christ is still a Jew. The

---

6. Friedrich Nietzsche, *Thus Spoke Zarathustra,* in *The Portable Nietzsche,* ed. and trans. Walter Kaufmann (London: Viking Penguin, 1968), prologue, sec. 3.

Son's eternal future is the future of creation rather than his own removal — and rescue of others — from it. Every careful refutation of Gnosticism, old and new, will conclude as much.

Nevertheless, it is easier to dismiss this Gnosticism than genuinely to inhabit this dismissal. I suspect that part of the reason is that it forces us to confront one of the greatest human fears: that we will find ourselves unable to talk about what is most important, our intimacy with and vulnerability to loss. What we "have" is always precarious and easily lost, particularly in death. But our coming to terms with loss without attempting to overcome our status as creatures is a worthy Christian work in which we are preceded by Christ himself. After all, the cross and resurrection of Jesus are not an action and its inverse. The cross's loss is a human death that meets God three days later with a human rebirth, another creative act of giving *into* creation *as* a new creation. Our loss, in other words, is not "solved" through being rescued into the inalienable life of the uncreated God; instead, it is met with God's "more" of resurrection. This means that Christ shares in our loss, even preceding us in it, while also going before humanity in God's more — indeed, *as* God's more.

Even the love of justice, Nietzsche thought, tempts us away from embracing the world as it is inasmuch as such love tames the wildness of life and overwhelms the contingent reality of things. Where justice is a way to explain suffering and loss, it will always fail. Nietzsche admired those Greek tragedians who were best able to keep from explaining the suffering they portrayed since explained suffering has already removed itself from the lives of those who suffer, betraying in its alienation a loss of commitment to what is real. The noblest tragedians have no place for an overweening justice: "Whatever exists is both just and unjust, and equally justified in both."[7] And, of course, justifying what is just and unjust is not the point either, since justification is itself a distancing technique of those who are unprepared to suffer as humans. Nietzsche's is a severe embrace of reality in which every explanation risks being an elaborate dodge. What passes for understanding can come at a very great cost — a determined refusal to allow the object of understanding to live in me, to penetrate my own life.[8] On the other hand, one need not absorb the world in defiance of every dis-

7. Friedrich Nietzsche, *The Birth of Tragedy* (with *The Genealogy of Morals*), trans. Francis Golffing (Garden City, NY: Doubleday, 1956), sec. 9.

8. Rowan Williams, "What Does Love Know? St. Thomas on the Trinity," *New Blackfriars* 82 (2001): 260-72.

tinction in order to claim to know it; this merely repeats in different form the enactment of distance from objects, in this case eliminating what is other rather than keeping it at arm's length. But the loss is the same: I lose recognition that I live in the same world as the objects of my thinking, that they are fellow creatures, and that I cannot both know them and evade them at the same time. Even when I incline toward justice, I risk unknowing unjust things when I look for a future justice to invade the reality of my present circumstance. I will inevitably wipe away some things that nonetheless exist. This is the thrust of Nietzsche's severe formula, "Whatever exists is both just and unjust, and equally justified in both," and he is exuberant over it, exclaiming, "What a world!"[9] Severe indeed. But he was determined not to let even our salutary longings subvert our devotion to what is real.

Christianity has not always and everywhere cultivated an appropriate love of our creaturely status. It has very often fostered the opposite sentiments: despair for human limitation, impatience with immanence, yearning after the pure contemplation of ideas. I do not think such sentiments are unconnected with what is right about the human longing for deliverance and salvation. But I do think that we are almost always in danger of wanting to be delivered from the wrong things. Human is not the problem; *sin* is. "Deliver us from evil" is Christian; "deliver us from earth" is not. Even so, I believe that Christianity can actually outdo Nietzsche. At its best, it stretches to transcend a sin-marked world in a way that is also internal to the world, true to our humanity and creatureliness, and thus refuses to take immaterial flights of soul or to beat a hurried retreat of repudiation and fantasy.[10]

So the primary questions this book asks are ones that are prior to Pilate's question about truth itself. Rather, how do Christians go about cultivating a deep desire for truth that does not betray the love they should feel toward God's creatures, especially when that includes themselves as humans? To be human is to be vulnerable to surprises and subject to connections that we did not see at first. It is also to be beset by the reality of things that exert themselves against our vulnerability in ways that may never allow us to come to understand what is going on. How can even our un-

---

9. Nietzsche, *Birth of Tragedy*, sec. 9.

10. I am partly dependent, in these remarks, on language used by Martha C. Nussbaum in *Love's Knowledge: Essays on Philosophy and Literature* (Oxford: Oxford University Press, 1990).

knowing be marked by the grace and patience necessary to live in a world beyond our control? How can both our knowing and our unknowing be truthful? What would it mean to be free from needing to control things in order to make peace with them? How can Christianity welcome the contingency entailed in what it means to be humans in the world? What does it take — which virtues are required — to greet what is true, particularly in advance of knowing what it is, what it will entail, how it will change us, and what demands it will make? All of this is involved in what I refer to as witness.

However, someone may object that putting things this way nearly paints one into a corner. It at least is attended by some very great paradoxes. After all, a book devoted to the contingency of reality, particularly one that commends ways of uniting words with life, seems inherently ill-suited to the task simply because it is a book. Must it repeatedly and tediously claim that it is not entitled to the sense-making in which it is engaged? Is it possible to explain with sufficiency why explanation is not sufficient? I admit that I simply do not know how to respond to such things. I certainly do not think that being silent is always the best option. Certainly there are times when the only way to be truthful is to say nothing at all. The death of martyrs may be a truthful witness despite their being silenced in death: their dying, in fact, can be *more* true than anything they can say.

Nevertheless, I do not think that Christians, in order to be faithful to God and at ease with what God has created, need to refuse to talk about it out of fear that what we say will never be enough. The world is too big, things are too different, God is too God — but why should we despair over this? Why not rather be joyful? Why not throw our words into the *more* of God's creation, free from the anxiety that in doing so we are making it less? I believe that theology, when it strives to be truthful, will find itself edging closer to poetry than more analytical forms. Its relationship with the language in which it speaks will tend toward the provisional and ad hoc. It will not imagine that, just because it can say something precisely, it has said everything that needs to be said about it. Precision is important; but on its own it can distort the task of describing in a way that is appropriate to the excessiveness of things. In this regard, I confess to feeling as though much of what I say in this book could be said much better if it were said differently. Then again, it is characteristic of theology's provisional nature that it devote itself to looping back over itself again and again in new language, new contexts, and with new eyes in the hope that what we thought we were saying may surprise us by turning out to be deeper than we had imagined. Hoping in this way will not be a function of our confidence that we have said deep things, but quite the opposite: that the world belongs to an infinite God. In the end, I am content knowing that what I say here is not final, since the last word is not something we get to say.

It hardly needs mentioning that, empirically, Christians are not always the best truth-tellers. Worse than that, Christians may often be captivated by serious obstacles to seeing, knowing, and speaking the truth. Sometimes overzealous for God's truth, Christianity can breed its own tendency to outpace grasping after it and declaring it to others. I will not exonerate things that are clearly disreputable about Christian existence. Though it seems trite and tedious to point out that Christians are sinful and that they fail in faith, doing so at least presses theology to deal honestly with its limitations. Surely, part of the precariousness of Christian existence comes from an awareness that our seeing is, for now, partial. Stumbling and falling is not the *reason* that the Christian life is characterized by following; but worse than stumbling is stopping and standing still. The seeing and knowing that make Christian living possible is not only the outcome of the constant striving to follow Jesus Christ; but, crucial to the arguments that I develop in this book, they are themselves how Christians persevere in following and keep from settling for lesser — though more certain — forms.

Moreover, I believe that such failings put a finer point on what I aim to identify in these pages. It seems to me that theology, at its best, does not only disclose truths about God, but guides a much-needed human therapy. It is not first knowledge that can be possessed but a set of disciplines and corrective orientations. Foremost among them will be ways of chastening our God-talk in order to keep what we say and claim to know from hardening into an impervious formulation that edges out God's life and presence. This is not easily done. Theology can slip into attempting to be like the other disciplines whose objects submit to scrutiny and study. But where theology becomes system-building, it leaves an out for the church that some will always exploit. Who needs the church when a body of knowledge can exist independently of them, can be neatly packaged and stored for a future time?

What follows is one attempt to do theology in a way that is self-consciously precarious, vulnerable, and unsettled. I offer it in the spirit of gift and invitation, and thus my project strives to be true to what it presumes to address. I do not know whether I have succeeded in this. But when I write, I attempt to be of service to the church and to be true to the claim that the church is the first and often only legitimate generator and beneficiary of theology. This is because I think of theology as a subset of witness and therefore connected to prayer, praise, proclamation, and lament. I acknowledge that one of Christianity's greatest dangers lies in the temptation to set claims about God adrift to do on their own the work of witness: the faithful living, inhabiting, and persuading that theological claims must certainly produce if they are true. Our living, inhabiting, and persuading by no means *make* the claims true. But I have no interest in discussing how they might be true apart from this, because I cannot see how the conversation can then go in any directions that are not misguided. In fact, I do not think it is too strong to claim that this is the point at which theology becomes deeply sinful: it cannot help but make Christian existence redundant. Witness is not a strategy for transmitting knowledge and truth. Rather, it is the shape of living and speaking that God makes possible among a people who embrace Jesus Christ as the truth of God.

*   *   *

Part I, "Seeing," asks some closely related questions. What is the object of the witness's seeing? How does the nature of the object impinge on the skills we might name for what constitutes good, as opposed to bad, witness? I pursue these questions for their nonepistemological (even anti-epistemological) possibilities in light of the contingent nature of complex, created objects of chance and variety. I suggest that a witness's sight is clearest and, ironically, most correct when it is correctable, open to the freedom of contingent objects on account of love. The import of this for Christian witness is also the starting point, since bearing witness is both enabled and required by the resurrection of Christ. Building on critiques of the modern myth of objectivity, I show that the best way to come to terms with human limitations and fear of contingency is to acknowledge God's own freedom. A witness is first someone who sees Jesus. When we do not see Jesus, it is not only because of our sin, but also because we try to see him by grasping and controlling him. Insofar as Christian witness can come to terms with the freedom of Christ, it is more likely to accept and respect the contingency of other things without trying to overcome it.

Part II, "Coming Forward," discusses the moment of resistance, the moment of conflict in which resides the determination to testify, in Buechner's words, "at no matter what risk." Resisting is not the primary goal of coming forward, but it is located within the larger practice of bearing witness. The most effective way of resisting falsehood is already to be engaged in telling the truth, because the lies we believe to be true often simply have no competition. The Christian "no" to the falsehood of the world is not a first principle funding the perpetual rebellion of an antagonistic people. Rather, it is part of a concomitant "yes" that arises from having been trained in a relationship to the truth on account of a commission to speak it, and to speak it in a truthful way. In this part I show that the Christian practice of bearing true witness is a resource of resistance. In witness, the truth of God is beheld but not held, spoken but not controlled, and as such makes a people's life together depend on the love of truth, whose resistance to domination is a function of its love and mission. Witness is most effective in defiance exactly when it does not try to be, which is to say, when it remembers that its positive mission is so compelling that there are some things it simply cannot countenance.

The third part, "Testifying," takes up the moment of speaking the truth, of delivering testimony. It maintains that there can be no reason to testify to the truth of the gospel other than the gospel itself. It explicates errors in which controlling concepts (such as goodness and love) or institutions (such as oaths) are made to govern the giving of testimony. In the same way, truth-telling cannot be known without distortion on the basis of prior definitions of lying that begin with a natural law account (of a certain sort), nor on the basis of negative legal prohibitions. By locating truth-telling first within the mandate of Christian mission, I show how the positive nature of witness surmounts these problems. I postpone a discussion of lying until part III in order to emphasize that telling the truth involves more than not lying. Witness is itself a truth-telling practice that cannot be replaced by or even understood as the outcome of reasons or theories. This yields a paradox that I endeavor to sustain, urging that it is only able to be resolved in practice. Witness is necessary because of the uniqueness of its testimony, but it also cannot be necessary in any stronger sense that would imply that witness attempts to accomplish something. The paradox intimates that, after epistemology, truth is adjudicated by witness.

The gospel is a message about an appearance, a message about a message. It is about Jesus Christ appearing in the flesh, acting and speaking, dying and rising. The Christian confession is not only that the truth of the gospel is constituted by Jesus' speech but also that Jesus is himself the truth. "Truth is a person" is a conclusion arrived at without the use of a separate and prior definition of what it means for something to be true.[11] Indeed, like all theories, theories of truth cannot help but give a reductive account of the truth of Christ. Therefore, knowing the truth depends on knowing Christ. If the gospel were a proposition or a theory, one could argue for and defend it. But in these pages I follow Karl Barth in maintaining that this is not possible with the gospel:

> This is the truth speaking for itself. It is not an argument. It will thus prevent those who know and honor and love it as the truth from entering into argument or even the most laudable of exploitations. . . . As distinct from any theory or factual record, it can only be attested, known and proclaimed.[12]

Seeing, coming forward, and testifying — as three moments — constitute a single train of thought: the nonpossessive sight of witnesses is not only clear-sighted (part I) but also participates in a positive mission that issues in the most determinative resistance (part II) against falsehood and distortion (part III). Nevertheless, it is still possible to see clearly but not come forward. In the Gospel idiom, this is a light under a bushel; it is hiding "for fear of the Jews" (John 20:19[13]); it is not being available as an expert witness in Jesus' trial. Peter nearly comes forward as a witness, but he does not make it beyond the courtyard. Even so, the courtyard becomes the location of his false testimony, his denial. Though he does not come forward to present himself as a witness in the official trial by the high priest, he is nevertheless called on to testify to the high priest's maid (Mark 14:66-72). Jesus' other disciples fail to come forward, and Peter is made to testify against his will. He does so falsely, paralleling the false testimonies being given a short distance away. The latter testimonies were given by those who either failed to see clearly or committed perjury.

True witness is embodied in all three moments: seeing, coming forward, and testifying. Witnesses do not simply tell the truth about what they have seen in the past, but involve themselves in performing a speech-act in which their telling is a present-tense demonstration that these events

11. Bruce Marshall, *Trinity and Truth* (Cambridge: Cambridge University Press, 2000), p. 2.

12. Karl Barth, *Church Dogmatics,* trans. G. W. Bromiley et al. (Edinburgh: T. & T. Clark, 1956-1975), IV/3, p. 410.

13. Unless otherwise specified, Scripture quotations are from the Revised Standard Version.

in the past now also constitute a confession of faith for those who commit their lives and deaths to it. In the face of competing false witnesses, Christ's true witnesses narrate historical events that change the meaning of all history and the truth of all true things.

PART I

SEEING

Yet a little while, and the world will see me no more, but you will see me . . . . He who has my commandments and keeps them, he it is who loves me; and he who loves me will be loved by my Father, and I will love him and manifest myself to him.

John 14:19, 21

To see differently, and to *want* to see differently . . . is no small discipline.

Nietzsche, *On the Genealogy of Morality*

Certain things appear only in certain lights.

Wendell Berry, *Life Is a Miracle*

CHAPTER 1

Seeing God

There can never be a single story.
There are only ways of seeing.

Arundhati Roy, *War Talk*

Theologians are fond of talking about stories — and for good reason. The gospel is a story that witnesses to the real history of God with creatures and most acutely in Israel and Jesus. Theology rightly begins with this as the narrative that structures our seeing and living within the truth of God. But there are also always perils, especially that *story itself* will take the place of the specific story and stories that give form and shape to the world we see. Stories guide our vision; they guide what we see into their ongoing narrative flow; they make us notice what we might otherwise overlook; they make us overlook other things. Observing this on its own, however, is not only mildly uninteresting but it positively courts distortion if it only leaves us with these kinds of metalevel claims. The more urgent project will always be to attend to the particular stories that are true. My topic is the Christian story, though not simply in its most straightforwardly narrative sense. It is, instead, the way that Christianity as God's story with creatures is itself a story that Christian creatures tell by the very fact of their inclusion within it. If, as Arundhati Roy says, "there are only ways of seeing," then bearing witness is the Christian point of contact between its story and its vision.

Bearing witness is *speaking the truth* about what one sees and hears. This section concerns seeing and hearing. There are internal and peculiar reasons that these works of the senses are important to the Christian life and mission. As a witness to Christ, witness is concerned first with seeing Christ in order to deliver a testimony by speaking about what is seen, principally the resurrection: "That which we have seen and heard we proclaim also to you" (1 John 1:3). In this way, seeing serves testimony. The *delivery* of what is seen — giving testimony — will be the subject of section 3.

Before going further, though, let us inquire into these senses themselves. Why seeing and hearing? Or even, why seeing (since I will for convenience mostly abandon hearing) at the expense of the other human ways of making sensory contact? After all, humans have five senses, all of which are involved in our knowing what is real. When Augustine claimed that "every sense is a kind of sight," he was representing what some scholars have pointed out as the hegemony of vision in Western thought.[1] The history of this thinking has more closely associated knowledge with the surety of what is visible. Jacques Derrida notes how the senses of taste and smell have not been adequately explored because of the dominance of sight and sound metaphors.[2] Against an ancient historiographical tradition that was famously represented in Thucydides' and Polybius's citation of Heraclitus, which said that "eyes are surer witnesses than ears," Stephen H. Webb makes a case for the theological priority of hearing over vision.[3] The distinction turns on whether what is heard is itself a primary experience of the event or a secondary report of it. I will simply assert my view here and then move on: since Christianity attests to a Word that is both flesh (incarnation) and sound (proclamation), and consequently may both be seen and heard, making strong claims for one or the other sense does not seem to me particularly important. The eucharistic character of Christ's continual presence to the church includes the other three senses. There is, however, much less interest — historically, theologically, and otherwise — in questions of, say, right tasting, though one may point out how even biblical habits collapse one into the other: "O *taste* and *see* that the LORD is good!"

---

1. Augustine, *De Verbo Domini, Serm.* xxxiii. Quoted in Thomas Aquinas, *Summa Theologica,* trans. Fathers of the English Dominican Province (Allen, TX: Christian Classics, 1981), II-II.1.4 (this notation refers to the second part of the second part, question 1, article 4). Hereafter cited as *ST.* David Howes, *Sensual Relations: Engaging the Senses in Culture and Social Theory* (Ann Arbor: University of Michigan Press, 2003).

2. Jacques Derrida, "White Mythology: Metaphor in the Text of Philosophy," in *Margins of Philosophy,* trans. Alan Bass (Sussex, UK: Harvester, 1982), pp. 207-72.

3. Stephen H. Webb, *The Divine Voice: Christian Proclamation and the Theology of Sound* (Grand Rapids: Brazos, 2004), esp. chap. 2.

(Ps. 34:8). However, I acknowledge that this bias may exist for reasons that are not always altogether reputable.

Christian witness serves testimony and feels expansive pressures that owe to its mission. In addition, it is also concerned with the quality and faithfulness of the life of discipleship and so wants to see Christ in order to follow him. Disciples do not look on Christ with scientific detachment in order merely to report on him: the stakes of their devotion make demands on their seeing. The two aspects of seeing Christ cannot be separated; in fact, they depend on each other. Still, how many Christian movements have wanted the one without the other? How many have wanted to declare the truth about Christ without following Christ? How many have been attracted to the clear-sighted confidence of authoritative testimony with its convincing speeches while declining the uncertainty of chasing behind an uncontrollable God? True witness will not bear such a separation.

Witness begins with what we might call a hermeneutical practice of identifying Christ in order to follow him, and through this practice are issued the skills of vision appropriate to seeing him. This is not a universal strategy for seeing clearly, but a particular practice that Christians engage in by virtue of living the Christian life. Understood in this way, the Christian life is not an application of principles but a concrete, communal, hermeneutical process. Nevertheless, in what follows I hope to show that, in order to see anything clearly, we must necessarily first see Christ clearly, that is, see him as Lord. It is possible to cite either Karl Barth or Dietrich Bonhoeffer nearly at random on the idea that the proper starting point for thinking about reality is thinking about Christ. For example, Bonhoeffer writes:

> Any perception or apprehension of things or laws without Him is now abstraction, detachment from the origin and goal. Any enquiry about one's own goodness, or the goodness of the world, is now impossible unless enquiry has first been made about the goodness of God. . . . The point of departure for Christian ethics is not the reality of one's own self, or the reality of the world. . . . It is the reality of God as he reveals Himself in Jesus Christ.[4]

The subsequent apprehension of all other things in the illumination of Christ's lordship, in the light of vision redeemed and transformed by the

4. Dietrich Bonhoeffer, *Ethics*, trans. Neville Horton Smith (New York: Touchstone, 1995), pp. 187-88.

resurrection, is to see things for what they really are. This is, for Bonhoeffer, "seeing and recognizing the world in Christ."[5] Arguments of this kind depend on the indisputable substance of Christian witness, namely, that Jesus is Lord, a present, continuous reality who is not only to be seen in order to be followed, but is also followed in order to be seen. Here is where testimony and discipleship meet.

This section of the book considers some distinctive aspects of the Christian form of seeing appropriate to the Christian life as one of following Christ and also to the hope of beholding God in glory. I outline how appreciably different this kind of loving, seeing, and beholding is compared to the knowing and seeing prized by modernity. Modern habits have championed and perfected a separation that is parallel to seeing for testimony versus seeing for following because, as a strategy for avoiding the distortions of self-deception and fantasy, the modern knower is the one who is least involved in what is known. As a result, as I show in chapter 3 below, moral vision is eclipsed by modern epistemology — often ruinously. This section specifically explores how seeing clearly is confounded by a muted desire for the truth, weakened by self-deception and by the proclivity for mastering contingency.[6] The aesthetic and practical proposals it identifies for seeing clearly (that is, through love and with skill) are displayed in and challenged by how Christian discipleship relates to Christian testimony.

One feature of loving a living object is that it does not place a limit so much on knowledge of the loved one, but on anticipation.[7] A living person possesses an agency for free action that is not knowable simply by knowing the person. Christian witness is an attestation to the reality of the resurrection of Christ in that it maintains that Christ is not only knowable as a historical occurrence but as an abiding reality. Therefore, a consequence of the claim that Christ is risen and is thus alive is that he can surprise us, that he can be known but, because he is living and will act freely, he cannot be

---

5. Bonhoeffer, *Ethics,* p. 195.

6. Though I will not specifically refer to it at particular points, it will be evident how much my thinking about contingency has been influenced by Martha C. Nussbaum, *The Fragility of Goodness: Luck and Ethics in Greek Tragedy and Philosophy,* updated ed. (Cambridge: Cambridge University Press, 2001).

7. Wendell Berry accuses science of both mastering contingency by reducing observation to theory and mastering time by reducing anticipation to prediction. "A thing is true only if it is *predictably* true; a thing is true, not because it is true now, but because it is true always." Wendell Berry, *Life Is a Miracle* (Washington, DC: Counterpoint, 2000), p. 18.

anticipated or predicted. Our knowing cannot outpace genuine anticipation without undoing itself so long as we know what is really alive. The resurrected Christ must be attested by a people who expect him to exercise the freedom that comes with living. Moreover, since nonanticipation is the way that a lover affirms the freedom of the loved one, "it is the very substance of love to be full of surprises for the loved one."[8] Any practical reasoning appropriate to recognizing free acts of a resurrected Christ must have the form of love. Believing and attributing these acts to Christ is thus an accomplishment of faith in the resurrection. But it is shaped by love insofar as Christ is not known by being verified empirically, but in being avowed as living and free. The belief of "doubting" Thomas, who was so struck by the physical reality of the risen Christ's wounds that he declared, "My Lord and my God!" (John 20:28), was immediately displayed in worship, indicating to Aquinas that he "saw one thing and believed another."[9] He *saw* the wounds but *believed* that Christ is Lord. Love perfects the will that exercises faith, "since every right movement of the will proceeds from a right love."[10] Wittgenstein put it much more simply: "Only love can believe the Resurrection."[11]

Beholding discloses how an inability to see clearly does not derive only from the problem of God's transcendence over against the immanence of human creaturely being nor from some imagined conundrum having to do with God's universality and the particularity of human existence. We are unable to see God; and even though God has become particular, immanent, contingent, and human in Jesus Christ, we *still* do not see him. Christianity traditionally attributes the separation to our sin. Seeing is the consequence of a moral, rather than metaphysical or ontological, accomplishment. The Fall renders our vision opaque: it is blurred because we are sinners, not because we are humans. Athanasius counseled moral

---

8. Robert W. Jenson, *Systematic Theology: The Triune God* (Oxford: Oxford University Press, 1997), 1:198. David Burrell's focus on the analogical use of *actus* in Aquinas, where God is pure act, or "to-be," is a reminder that God's divinity is only grasped as act; but precisely because it is act, the divine nature cannot be "grasped" in the sense of tamed or anticipated. Instead, action is known by human beings through knowing and loving. See Burrell, *Aquinas: God and Action* (Notre Dame, IN: University of Notre Dame Press, 1979). This section presents this insight in a christological register.

9. Aquinas, *ST*, II-II.1.4. Aquinas cites St. Gregory here: *Homilies on the Gospels,* no. 26.

10. Aquinas, *ST*, I-II.65.4. Aquinas cites Augustine, from *City of God*, XIV.9.

11. Ludwig Wittgenstein, *Culture and Value* (Oxford: Basil Blackwell, 1980), p. 33e.

purity in order to come to understand the sacred writers of Scripture and the saints, because one comes closer to the meaning of what they wrote by imitating their lives of virtue.[12] After all, Jesus taught that, of all unlikely things, it would be the pure in heart who would see God (Matt. 5:8). (One of the great ironies of the synoptic Gospels is that even though the disciples are the most prominent eyewitnesses to Jesus, their lack of understanding is presented as a profound blindness [e.g., Mark 8:18].) The one who brings herself into conformity with virtue in God's service has her eye illuminated in righteousness to see heavenly things and to break through the darkness of ignorance. The conceit and indolence implied by modern scholarship's preoccupation with the science of meaning and critical tools for uncovering the intent of ancient authors surely contrast with the moral rigor of earlier theologians.

In this chapter I develop further the theme of seeing Christ. I do so according to a motif that I believe goes some way toward imposing on our imaginations an appropriate and salutary emphasis on the risen life of Christ. This means pursuing an aesthetic adapted to what is scandalously uncertain and unforeseeable apart from attachments formed by love. I want to allow the fact of the resurrection the freedom to press itself against our concepts of vision by simply asking about the association of vision to a Christ whose unrestricted movements make him difficult to see. For this motif, sight comes as it is exercised for the purpose of seeing where Christ goes in order to follow him there. Once one assumes that one is seeing adequately, Jesus withdraws again and we lose sight of him; he will not be subject to possessive logic. What we take as true can quickly become falsehood if our means of arriving at it are not disciplined by the skills necessary for belief in a God who surprises us. The five wise maidens watchfully trimmed their lamps because they did not know what the next moment would bring (Matt. 25). This is not first a remark about the nature of sight or even of knowledge generally, but of the movements of an unpredictable God.[13] The bridegroom goes ahead and bids us follow, meaning that we need to be able to see clearly. It is in the continual exercise of following Christ, then, and not only in the cultivation of clearsightedness for its own sake, that our vision is corrected; it is only being corrected in the course of following, and it certainly stops when we stop.

---

12. Athanasius, *On the Incarnation*, chap. 9, p. 57.

13. On the needful watchfulness of the sleepers in Gethsemane, see Karl Barth, *Ethics*, trans. G. W. Bromiley (Edinburgh: T. & T. Clark, 1992), pp. 75-76.

Two implications follow from this: Christ's showing himself and our seeing clearly are not two things but one; and witnesses are disciples before they are apostles.

Christian witness does not simply proclaim the truth *about* God, but proclaims God. Or better, it proclaims the truth about God, who is Christ himself, God's truth. Truth, in other words, is not prior to Christ the truth. This proclamation takes place according to the tempo of discipleship.[14] Saying that witnesses are disciples before they are apostles (i.e., followers before being the ones who are sent) retemporalizes the practice of witness and avoids rarefying it into an abstract principle. Attending to the detail of particulars is not a matter of securing the correct concepts — ones expansive enough to allow for contingency — but of encountering those particulars *in time* for the sake of an activity that requires their recognition as particulars. It is through practical engagement with a diversity of factors that attending to them becomes a habit. The activity of the disciple is temporally structured: it has a beginning (baptism perhaps, or a prior act of desire-generating grace[15]); it engages in choices, negotiations, and responses along the way; it raises objections, loses its way, and tries again to find it. These negotiations are the way the church's communal life reflects the ongoing attempt to follow Christ.

All of this is only to say that the Christian story is something that is in its temporal reality both told and inhabited, and telling it is partly how one goes about inhabiting it. Wolfhart Pannenberg says as much about the

14. It is unfortunate that discipleship is often taken to be a rather pedestrian and less than academically rigorous concept. However, I know of no better way to describe the continuous action of the Christian life as a response to Christ's continuous life and activity. Michel De Certeau offers a helpful image in *The Practice of Everyday Life,* trans. Steven F. Randall (Berkeley: University of California Press, 1984), chap. 7. City spaces only remain defined so long as there are people who move decisively within them, and even those definitions are fleeting, dependent as they are on those who walk the ground. In fact, the spaces are only make-believe; only the walkers are real. Christ's disciples do not follow predefined spaces, but only those paths made by walking — not their own walking, but that of Jesus, "who is going ahead of you into Galilee" (Mark 16:7). Perhaps just such a pedestrian concept is appropriate after all.

15. In *ST,* III.68.2, Aquinas argues that the sacramental effect of baptism may be had by one who desires it but who is killed before being able to receive it. Also, when discussing the Eucharist: "Before receiving a sacrament, the reality of the sacrament can be had through the very desire of receiving the sacrament. . . . A man can obtain salvation through the desire of receiving it, just as he can before baptism through the desire of baptism" (Aquinas, *ST,* III.73.3).

temporal aspect of theological knowledge: that this is part of what makes it limited and never complete. It is not only the case that, as is widely understood, theology is finite and its object (God) is infinite. It is that all knowledge of any kind is time-bound.[16] That God will finally be seen at the end of time, then, makes the difficulty of seeing God in the meantime a "limitation" only so long as we attempt to see him without following or within an academic modus that leaves little room for the churchly life of discipleship. (Pannenberg does not draw this same conclusion for reasons I identify in part III.)

When the witnessing community makes claims such as "Jesus is Lord," it is likewise attesting to and demonstrating its ability to perceive particulars. Its capacity for making such claims owes to the lordship of Christ over the community, not just the truth of a belief. To put it differently, proclaiming "Jesus is Lord" as true is not merely a way of assenting to a concept, but is a felicity with the language Christians use to describe how continual following not only makes possible the discovery of what it means for someone to be a lord, but for something to be true.[17] Continual following names such felicity, which may indicate that, at some level, "Jesus is Lord" and "we follow him" are saying the same thing.[18]

Consider how the witness is in a situation that is necessarily linguistically and logically circular. Theology owes a great debt to those postliberal thinkers who have rightly insisted that we do not see with our eyes but rather with our imaginations, which is to say that our seeing is always mediated through the images and language that fashion for us how the world looks. Whatever metaphors, images, and other linguistic associations most command and govern our thinking will do so by way of first shaping our vision. Our thinking will follow from what we perceive to be both real and possible, which are those things that pass through our linguistic ordering of the world. "Our ability to 'step-back' from our deceptions is dependent on the dominant story, the master image, that we have

16. Wolfhart Pannenberg, *Systematic Theology*, trans. Geoffrey W. Bromiley (Grand Rapids: Eerdmans, 1991), 1:54.

17. This is the point Stanley Hauerwas makes when he summarizes the third volume of James McClendon's systematic theology as showing how "issues of justification are, indeed, a subset of Christian witness" (Hauerwas, *With the Grain of the Universe: The Church's Witness and Natural Theology* [Grand Rapids: Brazos, 2001], p. 210).

18. To cite Wittgenstein again: "[If I do not believe,] I cannot utter the word 'Lord' with meaning. . . . And it could say something to me, only if I lived *completely* differently" (Wittgenstein, *Culture and Value,* p. 33e).

embodied in our character."[19] The dominant images and stories are the skills required to incorporate what is seen into a much larger framework for ordering things and making sense of them. Along these lines, Hauerwas and Burrell suggest what would be necessary for a story to be true:

> A true story could only be one powerful enough to check the endemic tendency toward self-deception, a tendency which inadequate stories cannot help but foster. Correlatively, if the true God were to provide us with a saving story, it would have to be one that we found continually discomforting. For it would be a saving story only as it empowered us to combat the inertial drift into self-deception.[20]

Given the weight of the subjunctives in these sentences, perhaps it is obvious that *if* we were handed a story by God, we could depend on that story to save us from our self-deception. A true story would function to limit the reign of fantasy, to check our unremitting and protracted slide into illusion, and to expose our tendencies absentmindedly to prefer self-serving chimeras. Now all of this may be the case. But simply pointing to a story's function for limiting fantasy does not constitute a claim that it is true.

Of course, our thirst for unbridled fantasies about ourselves funds our willing distortion of the world. But it would be a mistake to imagine that an alternative involves selecting the true story from among an array of false ones in order to keep ourselves in check. Our choosing will always already be a function of whatever story dominates. We cannot will ourselves out of fantasy's absurdity because, though it sounds as farcical as it does remorselessly bleak, our wills co-conspire within the fantasy world that offers up to us what seem to be the only available choices. This suggests that at some level the exercise of the will is more fundamental than its freedom. It is important not to allow the story solution to slip into abstraction apart from the specific story Christians tell. Put differently, if the story Christians proclaim does not check our tendency toward self-deception, should we look for another one? And how would we recognize one that accomplishes this? We cannot, obviously, and Hauerwas was right to abandon story-as-such in his later work for precisely this reason.[21] As Gerard Loughlin ob-

---

19. Stanley Hauerwas and David B. Burrell, "Self-Deception and Autobiography: Reflections on Spoer's *Inside the Third Reich*," in Hauerwas, *Truthfulness and Tragedy* (Notre Dame, IN: University of Notre Dame Press, 1977), p. 95.

20. Hauerwas and Burrell, "Self-Deception and Autobiography," p. 95.

21. "I think it is a mistake to try to do theology by basing the work theology is meant

serves, "Christian truth has never been a matter of matching stories against reality. It has always been a matter of matching reality-stories against the truth: Jesus Christ."[22] Story-as-such is a category that is only available as long as one refuses to inhabit any stories. And "I do not inhabit a story" is the ultimate self-deception, even on its own grounds. There can be no by-standers to all stories, because standing by as a strategy for achieving dis-passionate objectivity itself relies heavily on myths that are substitutes for love. Here is where the witness to Christ is in a circular situation: if Jesus is risen, then the proclamation "Jesus is risen" is part of the story in which Je-sus is risen.[23] In other words, the church does not simply tell a story *about* Christ, but its telling is part of the content of its proclamation insofar as the risen Christ is free to surprise the church in its own speech.

This does not mean that the church merely proclaims *itself* as good news to the world. But it does mean that an aspect of the fact that it is so proclaiming is precisely its conviction that the gospel is good — so good, in fact, that it willingly tells of the church's own founding and continued exis-tence in terms that are internal to the gospel message itself. The church, in effect, says: "Here is the news that we not only share with you, but our life as a people capable of so sharing stands or falls with whether that news is good and true." There can be no other possibility so long as the church insists on speaking of the resurrection in the present tense. This also goes for the church's reading of Scripture, since its reading of Scripture is an event within the story it reads. The Bible does not contain the complete story of God. Rather, it tells the story that God's people are invited to claim as their

---

to do on a literary type. . . . I simply quit writing about the importance of narrative for the-ology" (Stanley Hauerwas, *Performing the Faith: Bonhoeffer and the Practice of Nonviolence* [Grand Rapids: Brazos, 2004], p. 139). Similarly, Hauerwas says that he is no longer happy with the metaphor of "stepping back" (which originally came from Stuart Hampshire) on grounds that it is "a liberal presumption that whatever our engagement is, we should be able to step back from it. Stepping back is a correlative of the skills we've gained from certain nar-ratives" (Hauerwas, personal correspondence with the author, July 11, 2005). I would add that insofar as those skills allow one to step back from the narrative that engenders them, one is not really stepping back at all. Alasdair MacIntyre uses the language of "stepping back" to characterize the myth of objectivity in the search for universal foundations (MacIn-tyre, *After Virtue*, 2nd ed. [Notre Dame, IN: University of Notre Dame Press, 1984], p. 30).

22. Gerard Loughlin, *Telling God's Story: Bible, Church, and Narrative Theology* (Cambridge: Cambridge University Press, 1996), p. 23.

23. "[T]he telling of Jesus' Resurrection belongs itself to the narrative by which the resurrection proclamation establishes its own meaningfulness" (Jenson, *Systematic Theol-ogy,* 1:175).

own through faith: obedience, grace, and submission to the life of disciples. Therefore, in calling this book their Scripture, the church signals that the Bible's witness to the things of God is continuous with that of the church, not least in some very direct ways, such as determining to narrate what goes on in the contemporary world in terms of the biblical narrative. Proclaiming the resurrection is thus not separable from giving an account of how it is that Christ speaks now in this very proclamation, because anything less would demonstrate that the resurrection is not true. This is the way that witness and testimony are circularly related.[24]

I have just narrated how the practice of witness is self-involving: *that* it proclaims is part of *what* it proclaims. It does not attest to knowledge that somehow leaves things unchanged or makes no difference to how it knows what it knows. Instead, as Barth noted of the true hearer of the Word of God, "He does not hear it in the distraction, be it ever so profound and spiritual, in which he imagines that, while it may be true, it does not apply to him, the reference being to some other or others and not to himself."[25] The story that Christians tell is part autobiography, since it includes the claim that the church exists on account of the resurrection. And as Wittgenstein adduced, you cannot, in speaking about yourself, ever utter anything that is more truthful than you yourself are.[26] Accordingly, witnesses do not simply present God's evidence to the world; they are, in fact, *themselves* nothing less than God's evidence to the world.[27]

24. Jenson, *Systematic Theology,* 1:175: "This circularity is essential." In making this point, Jenson is arguing against the Bultmannians, who take proclamation of the resurrection to be a *response* to historical and existential realities. But insofar as it is a response, it is not part of them. Rowan Williams, like Jenson, wants to reconnect the *kerygma* with the narrative of Christ, and in this he is also critical of Bultmann, though he approaches the critique from the opposite direction. If, with Bultmann, we accept that "whatever we find to say [theologically] about the resurrection, it will not include anything that depends on the non-availability of Jesus' corpse," then the narratives of the Gospels are "pretty incidental to the substance of the proclamation itself" (Williams, "Between the Cherubim," in *On Christian Theology* [Oxford: Blackwell, 2000], p. 186).

25. Barth, *Ethics,* p. 16.

26. Wittgenstein, *Culture and Value,* p. 33e.

27. By autobiography, I do not mean an individual's story, but the faith of the church "in the history, action and suffering of the community. . . . The service of genuine confession [Barth's word for 'witness,' as I use it] will always in some sense be a participation in the service of the community, and thus not a separate undertaking of the individual" (Karl Barth, *Church Dogmatics,* trans. G. W. Bromiley et al. [Edinburgh: T. & T. Clark, 1956-1975], III/4, p. 83 [hereafter *CD*]).

*   *   *

The redemption of vision is a continual process of enhancing a community's ability not to foreclose on surprises. Its refusal to accept as final and definitive God's disclosure in any form not only affirms its belief that it must be open to further disclosures; the refusal itself is also its simultaneous act of opening itself to God. Open eyes anticipate seeing more. In *The Life of Moses*, Gregory of Nyssa commended this way of seeing. He knew that the divine nature could not be adequately described by concepts, even the most exalted ones, and that descriptions that absolutize divine concepts erect idols. For Gregory, Moses' leading of Israel into the unknown and unpredictable wilderness models Christian discipleship. "Moses himself watched the cloud, and he taught the people to keep it in sight."[28] When the cloud of the Lord led them into the barren desert, God met their needs. When the cloud stopped, the Israelites remained where they were and continued to feed on God's provision and enjoy his protection and comfort. Gregory depicts Moses as a fellow follower of the cloud rather than the leader of the Israelites, because Moses' leading clearly depended on his own ability to see clearly. Gregory also thought it significant that God leads by a cloud: inscrutable, intangible, and ungraspable. A cloud has no essence and lacks definite edges, which Gregory says resembles what can justifiably be said of God, who is also "enclosed by no boundary," and "[i]t is not in the nature of what is unenclosed to be grasped" (II.236, 238). Unbounded and adrift, the image of a cloud thus furnishes the enigmatic medieval tract *The Cloud of Unknowing* with the ultimate object of mystical contemplation. There is no beneath nor behind the cloud of God's leading, where one discovers a greater degree of solidity, rationale, or explanation. The attention it demands of the one who sees it only takes the form of following — not understanding, not knowing. There is no disclosing of essences, identities, or even words that, if beheld, would on their own tempt holders to take their eyes off the cloud.

God's presence to Israel as a cloud in the desert suggests to Gregory, for a people who had not yet received Law, an unmediated existence. Their following was direct; their living was day-to-day and ad hoc. Even their arrival at the solid mountain of Sinai was quickly controverted when the

---

28. *Gregory of Nyssa: The Life of Moses*, ed. and trans. Abraham Malherbe and Everett Ferguson, Classics of Western Spirituality (New York: Paulist, 1978), I.31 (hereafter, volume and page references to this work appear in parentheses in the text).

mountain disappeared in a surrounding cloud. "A fire shining out of the darkness presented a fearful sight to those who saw it. It hovered all around the sides of the mountain so that everything which one could see smouldered with the smoke from the surrounding fire" (I.43). Nevertheless, the unmediated glory of God proved too much for the Israelites, who could not look upon it and instead requested that Moses mediate the Law to them. They were overwhelmed by the undistilled uncertainty that comes with standing before a rootless and live presence.

In contrast to the rest of the Israelites, whose fear and doubt kept them from being drawn toward what they could not see and so refused to believe, Moses further typifies for Gregory an appropriate mode of seeing God in his approach through the darkness on Sinai. He moved past what is visible, becoming himself invisible to the people watching him, where, "while not being seen, he was in the company of the Invisible." By believing that God was present at the top of the mountain, he followed in total self-surrender to where his understanding could not reach. And while it is here that Moses received the Lord's teaching and the uncontained splendor of God came more fully into view, Gregory describes words that remain more mystical than didactic. They were

> about the divine nature, inasmuch as it transcends all cognitive thought and representation and cannot be likened to anything which is known. He was commanded to heed none of those things comprehended by the notions with regard to the divine nor to liken the transcendent nature to any of the things known by comprehension. Rather, he should believe that the Divine exists, and he should not examine it with respect to quality, quantity, origin, and mode of being, since it is unattainable. (I.46)

God's nature was not to be robbed of its transcendence through comparison to anything else that is knowable. What it is possible to know about God is itself active, present, and living — just as God is. But that knowledge fully negates itself and converts completely into falsehood when it is held on to as a possession by the brute faculties of comprehension. The fact that postmodern philosophy has discovered a parallel way of affirming a dialectic between knowing and unknowing does not necessarily render it theological, though it surely attests to philosophy's yearning for its true theological home. Christian thought may make use of philosophy's distrust of fixed essences as it attempts to come to terms with the uncapturable nature of God's self-disclosure, and of our knowledge of anything whatsoever, so long as our knowing anything that exists is tied to the reality of its analogical existence through God's being. A vision attuned to this kind of knowing and unknowing, seeing and unseeing, will display what John Milbank calls a belief in "unexpected emergence."[29]

Gregory sees in Moses the key traits of Christ's disciples. A disciple's following is endless but is nonetheless directed toward its beatific goal. Each step in God's direction only increases the desire to see him, but each step is also paradoxically nothing less than how God is seen: "To follow God wherever he might lead is to behold God" (II.252). This is a beholding beyond sense perception, though it is a practical activity in which even what is seen does not satisfy but makes the follower want to follow on (II.239). Even sight has an initial capacity for what it regards as fullness, an expectation that what it is seeing is now once and for all. But such seeing is, for the disciple, repeatedly exceeded by the vision of God each time that capacity is reached. There is no final seeing. Even the beatific vision is not something you walk away from once you have laid eyes on it. The prior assumption that we know what it will be like to see God is akin to the idolatry that presumes to know what God looks like, though the latter is perhaps more insidious for how it controls the pursuit of God by anticipating a terminus to the desire for a face-to-face encounter. If it has been established that the desire for an encounter with God will take a particular form, that form cannot be one of following, since following plainly does not admit of the kind of initial assessment necessary for desire to predict its own satisfaction. Consequently, God "would not have shown himself to his servant if the sight were such as to bring the desire of the beholder to an end, since the true sight of God consists in this, that the one who looks up to God never ceases in that desire" (II.233).[30]

For Gregory, the appetite for seeing God cannot be separated from the love of God himself. Intrinsic to love is its perpetuity of desire, its continual desire for more. Love for objects is forever being met and then ex-

29. John Milbank, "'Postmodern Critical Augustinianism': A Short Summa in Forty-two Responses to Unasked Questions," *Modern Theology* 7, no. 3 (April 1991): 225-37 (esp. p. 227).

30. Iris Murdoch depicts the so-called Kantian man of reason as overtaken by freedom of choice. When confronting Christ, "we must turn back to the pattern of rationality in our own bosoms and decide whether or not we approve of the man we see" (Murdoch, *The Sovereignty of Good* [London: Routledge, 2002], pp. 29-30). This differs markedly from Augustine, for whom "[t]he gaze of the soul is Reason" and that gaze is perfected by "love — which is the soul's longing to see and to enjoy [what one sees]" (Augustine, *The Soliloquies of St. Augustine*, trans. Rose Elizabeth Cleveland [Boston: Little, Brown, 1910], I.13; pp. 22-23).

ceeded. But its exceeding and deferral do not yield dissatisfaction, because what satisfies the lover is nothing other than the continually renewed process of meeting and exceeding desires. This satisfaction *is* the love, the openness of the appetite to being reawakened to greater fullness than it had seen or received before. Love is therefore *alive* and fundamentally animated with motion and stirring to be fulfilled — in anticipation of being *unfulfilled again.* (Hunger is an obvious example, sex even more so.) Since the appetite is never satiated but is continually taken up again and pushed forward through the exercise of the love of God — namely, following him — then to follow God is to behold him (and is not simply the way to get to the place where he will be beheld). "This truly is the vision of God," according to Gregory: "never to be satisfied in the desire to see him. But one must always, by looking at what he can see, rekindle his desire to see more. Thus, no limit would interrupt growth in the ascent to God, since no limit to the Good can be found nor is the increasing of desire for the Good brought to an end because it is satisfied" (II.239).

It is crucial that the manner of beholding God is in respect of his freedom. He will not be possessed even by (perhaps especially by) his followers, lest their love degenerate into idolatry, which is a form of self-love that submits to self-deception. It is a knowing that is not limited to what we want to believe nor prejudiced toward our comfort. Nietzsche knew that this kind of understanding opposes our drive to see things in light of our own fantasies for them:

> People who understand a thing to its very depths seldom remain faithful to it forever. For they have brought these depths into clear daylight; and what is in the depths is not usually pleasant to see.[31]

The live God commands a love antithetical to idols. Gregory adduces that this is why Moses is given to see God's backside, for "he who follows sees the back" (II.251). The one who sees God's face is facing him and so cannot help but be at variance with him, at odds with his way. The one who faces his guide faces the opposite direction and "good does not look good in the face, but follows it" (II.253). Since God is life, his guidance leads to life; facing the opposite direction, and so seeing God's face, leads to death (II.254).

The New Testament shows that Gregory's reflections on Moses are well-suited for thinking about Christian discipleship, as was his intention

31. Friedrich Nietzsche, *Human, All Too Human,* in *The Portable Nietzsche,* ed. and trans. Walter Kaufmann (London: Viking Penguin, 1968), sec. 489.

after all. Seeing in John's Gospel, for instance, is not everyday observing, or merely opening one's eyes, but beholding, receiving, knowing, attending, and believing. John the Baptist did not simply bear witness to the facts of events that he observed, such as that the Spirit descended on Jesus like a dove. Rather, his seeing such things was entailed in his seeing that Jesus is the Son of God. This made him a characteristic New Testament witness as both a witness to fact and a witness to truth.[32] The Spirit of Truth can likewise only be received by those who know and see him (John 14:17).

Moreover, the theme of following behind Christ is prominent in Mark's Gospel.[33] Peter is rebuked at Caesarea Philippi because he was on the wrong side of Jesus, who turned to see that the other disciples were still behind him and said, "Get behind me, Satan! For you are not on the side of God, but of men" (Mark 8:33). Peter opposed Jesus (Satan means "opponent") by facing the opposite way and blocking Jesus' free progression to the cross. To be on the side of God is to be behind him "on the road" — in Peter's case, the road to Jerusalem, to the cross. This is the turning indicated by the word *repentance*. Significantly, this episode immediately follows Peter's famous confession that Jesus is the Christ. Though Peter gives the right answer, Barth thinks it is wrong to call this a confession, since to confess is to bear witness in a sphere of false faith. The more genuine setting for Peter's confession, then, would have been in the courtyard of the high priest (Mark 14:66-72). Even so, we may assume that Peter's failure to testify in the courtyard was linked to his failure to follow on the road. After Pentecost, Peter's confession before the high priest was his true confession (Acts 4:8-12 and 5:29-32), as Barth observes.[34]

Similarly, when the crowds run ahead of the boat containing Jesus and the disciples and "got there ahead of them," Jesus has compassion for them as "sheep without a shepherd" (Mark 6:33-34). He subsequently leads them as a shepherd leads herds to green pastures. In one case, Jesus instructs his disciples to go ahead of him in a boat, but their way is difficult because the wind is blowing in the opposite direction (Mark 6:45-52). Jesus walks onto the water intending to "pass by them," an action that clearly recalls Moses' own theophany. This would have made them followers again, but instead they feared that he was a ghost and so Jesus entered the boat

32. Barth, *CD* IV/3.2, pp. 611-12.

33. Christopher Burdon identifies twenty occasions in which people are either identified as following behind Jesus or being called to do so. Burdon, *Stumbling on God: Faith and Vision through Mark's Gospel* (Grand Rapids: Eerdmans, 1990), p. 47.

34. Barth, *CD* III/4, p. 85.

saying, "It is I" (Mark 6:50; cf. God's revelation to Moses in Exod. 3:14). They did not understand, and their hearts were hardened. Jesus ended up in the boat because they missed the point about his identity. Even though the oppositional wind stopped, it was not countered by the disciples' own change of direction, because they were too afraid to let Jesus lead.

The disciple turns in order to respond to Jesus' initiative to lead. As early as the third century, if not before, Christians began to face east in worship, not as a posture of following, but of anticipating. Like the rising sun, Christ will return from the east at the Last Judgment. This reflects a difference with Jewish practice, in which prayers are directed toward Jerusalem.[35] However, this practice may be in some tension with the implication from Mark's Gospel that the disciple should face where Jesus is going rather than where he has been. Since Jesus was facing Jerusalem before the cross and was facing outward from Jerusalem to the rest of the world after the resurrection, Christian practice would have been more in keeping with the Markan tradition had it sought postures ordered to Christ's mission rather than his return. To repent is to turn from opposing Christ toward his mission. After all, the lamp that burns in anticipation of the bridegroom's arrival does not just light the east; it lights the whole world before dawn.

In contrast to following Christ, Mark's Gospel displays how possessing and holding onto him is the idolatry Gregory equated with the application of a comprehensible and final image of the divine. Mark's word for this is "seeking." Even though it is commonly thought salutary and commendable to seek God, Christopher Burdon notes how seeking is quite negatively depicted in the second Gospel.[36] Those who seek Jesus are the family he dismisses, crowds that interrupt his praying, and Pharisees who seek a sign in order to test him (Mark 3:32; 1:35-38; 8:11-13). After Jesus' arrival in Jerusalem, he is repeatedly sought by people who will later bear false witness (e.g., the scribes in Mark 14:1).

Whereas true disciples come to Jesus with Peter's query, "Lord, to whom shall we go? You have the words of eternal life" (John 6:68), seekers refuse to trust Jesus' guidance, and they come to him for disreputable reasons. They have determined ahead of time what they are searching for in

---

35. Howard Clarke, *The Gospel of Matthew and Its Readers: A Historical Introduction to the First Gospel* (Bloomington: Indiana University Press, 2003), p. 189.

36. Burdon, *Stumbling on God*, pp. 47-48. "Seek and you shall find" and "Seek first the kingdom" are in Matthew, not Mark.

Jesus and expect him to produce: signs, confessions, explanations. But these kinds of seekers stumble and fall: their coming to Jesus is always met with disappointment, because he does not provide them with what they demand. No signs will be given, no confessions made, no explanations offered. Jesus instead withdraws, in marked refusal to indulge their ultimatums, a signal that issues anew the call to follow even — and especially — for those whose predetermined expectations always keep them from doing so. In the language of desire, the seeker has a satiable desire that is preset according to its object and, once it has obtained the object, cannot be enlarged. Jesus' seekers are thus his enemies precisely because they seek him, and by seeking him, attempt to control him. Counterpoising desires may easily reside within the same person, and Mark makes clear that followers can readily become seekers, as in the case of the women who are told at the empty tomb: "You seek Jesus of Nazareth, who was crucified. He has risen, he is not here . . . he is going before you to Galilee; there you will see him" (Mark 16:6-7). Mark's message at the conclusion of his Gospel speaks a severe obstacle to anyone looking for evidence of the risen Christ without the will to face the challenges that it presents if it is true: if you seek him at the tomb, you do not believe that he is risen and you will not see him; if you believe, you will follow him and you will see him by your following. Gregory is important for our understanding of how *following* is itself already *seeing*.

Loving the truth begins with beholding Christ and following him. It is more than contemplating; it is actively engaging in a way of life called discipleship. Discipleship names the temporally extended process of following in order to behold and beholding in order to follow. The movement is from ever-changing desire to desire, delight to delight, and glory to glory, as Gregory says.[37] The beholder is made more and more spacious, growing larger in virtue and accommodating ever-greater levels of desire appropriate to Christ's surprises. The fact that Jesus cannot perfectly be beheld is not a problem peculiar to those generations of Christians who came after the first cohort of eyewitnesses, since, even for those who walked with Jesus in the Galilean hills, the temptation was constantly threatening that they would stop following and start seeking to grasp and control. The so-called problem has less to do with human limitation or the skeptical constraints that birthed modern epistemology. It has more to do

37. See Jean Daniélou and Herbert Musurillo, *From Glory to Glory: Texts from Gregory of Nyssa's Mystical Writings* (London: John Murray, 1961).

with the fact that we try to see a moving, complex object.[38] Nevertheless, the disciple strives to see Jesus by following him and, in doing so, develops the skills and habits of vision appropriate to followers of Jesus on the way. This is not a settled certainty easily grasped, but an active, embodied competence for seeing a free God who always goes before and ahead, elusive of our attempts to constrain him.

This was the experience of the disciples in the Emmaus story in Luke 24. They did not believe the testimony of the women who came from the tomb, thinking that they had been told "an idle tale." And without seeing him for who he is, namely, the risen Christ (because "their eyes were kept from recognizing him"), they were joined by Jesus "on the road." Jesus counters their lament — "we had hoped that he was the one to redeem Israel" — with rebuke, not because they were wrong to look for the kingdom, but because they failed to see that the suffering of the Messiah marks the kingdom's very arrival. They were kept from recognizing Jesus as the Christ on the road because they had failed to see Jesus as the Christ on the cross, and the cross as the height of his glorification.[39] Even when they had reached their destination, "he appeared to be going further." He was going ahead, just as Mark shows Jesus going before the disciples into Galilee. Before the cross, the road of discipleship led to Jerusalem; now the road leads away from Jerusalem — beyond Emmaus and to Galilee. These roads only "lead" to these places because these places are where Jesus takes them. But the disciples "constrained him, saying, 'Stay with us.'" Were these disciples

---

38. Barth sought to avoid theological systematicity for this reason. He thought the term "systematic theology" was a paradox: "A 'system' is an edifice of thought, constructed on certain fundamental conceptions which are selected in accordance with a certain philosophy by a method which corresponds to these conceptions. Theology cannot be carried on in confinement or under the pressure of such a construction" (Barth, *Dogmatics in Outline,* trans. G. T. Thomson [London: SCM, 1968], p. 5). Therefore, theology must be humble when it "acknowledges that *its* decisive word is not *the* decisive word. By this repetition [saying again its word and thus acknowledging its nonfinality] it shows that precisely at this decisive point all theology is not a masterwork but at very best an associate work, so that there can be no question of a dogmatic system that is in itself an adequate presentation of this lofty subject" (Barth, *Ethics,* p. 18). Stanley Hauerwas follows Barth in extolling humility as "that virtue most required if we are truthfully to tell one another what we know but do not understand" (Hauerwas, "For Dappled Things," in *Sanctify Them in the Truth: Holiness Exemplified* [Nashville: Abingdon, 1998], pp. 230-31).

39. John Howard Yoder, *The Politics of Jesus,* 2nd ed. (Grand Rapids: Eerdmans, 2000), p. 51. Here I can only gesture toward the idea that seeing Jesus clearly is to see Jesus as at once crucified and glorified, though I have developed this theme more fully in *To Share in the Body: A Theology of Martyrdom for Today's Church* (Grand Rapids: Brazos, 2008).

"seekers" in Mark's negative and disreputable sense? Was their invitation a move to tame the wildness of a God who intended to journey ahead? Perhaps Jesus consented to stay with them only when they still did not know who he was, because to know him as resurrected is to know that he cannot be constrained. After all, Jesus does not actually stay with them: "And their eyes were opened and they recognized him; and he vanished out of their sight." In fact, the disciples crucially recognize Jesus in the breaking of the bread, specifically signaling how the disappearance of Jesus is both a presence and an absence — understood eucharistically. In Luke's language, Jesus indeed stayed with them just as he is present in and (sacramentally) as the church. Reformation-era debates aside, the point is not that some will insist on Christ's presence really being an absence. It is that as his departure coincided with the disciples' vision being illuminated in the breaking of the bread, Christ's body is now available in a way that cannot be constrained. This means the Eucharist *must* be a mystery. As soon as they received their sight, Jesus disappeared from it because the sight of disciples is not for grasping.

No one has ever seen God, but Christians follow Jesus in order to see him and see him in order to follow him. Christian discipleship is a way of life that opens itself to the surprises of resurrection and lordship, and this cannot be separated from the following that discipleship is. The following of Christian witness is a practice that issues in training vision for not seeking its object (in Mark's negative sense), that is, for not attempting to master its freedom for contingency. In its seeing and knowing, it submits to the self-discipline required to receive what is simultaneously given and wrested from control according to the manner of gift that it receives. The following two chapters approach reasons why Christianity's peculiar ways of seeing and knowing are not only contested but also sustained only with great difficulty against the dominant background of modern habits.

CHAPTER 2

Borrowed Splendor

There is a reason that modern habits of seeing and knowing evolved in the ways that they did. Clear sight, after all, is not a given; it must be sought. It is possible to identify a general drift in the West's history that, in its seeking clarity of sight and ultimately of reason, places in the foreground how two kinds of problems became primary. One problem is epistemological and the other one is moral.

On the epistemological side is the problem of mediated thought and vision. Surely, one way to characterize all philosophy since Plato is as the attempt to see clearly, to see things for what they really are by the natural light of the sun, as opposed to by the artificial light of human ignorance. In the various idioms, this has been articulated as illumination, enlightenment, critique, and unmasking: whether what we see adequately reflects reality, whether it is limited or exhaustive. A singular accomplishment of postmodern thought that stretches back to Hegel recognizes the mediated character of all thought. Sight is also mediated by structures that determine what is worth seeing and not passed over, what relates one thing to another as the same, similar, or different, and what counts as a particular as opposed to an instance of a universal. The epistemological problem places the images in light of which we see in the foreground.

On the other side is the moral problem of self-deception, actually wanting to see falsely. Not only is sight mediated, but it is further complicated by an ignoble will to believe illusions. In order to see the truth, one must want to know and believe it; one must not only be capable of self-criticism but also possess the will to engage in it. Overcoming self-deception, being able to stand and face the uncertainty of a contingent world, refusing the comfort of fantasy and willful ignorance — these all require discipline and the therapy that any unafraid ethics names.

The modern strategy was generally to address both the epistemological and moral problems at the same time. Rather than overcoming self-deception, the tendency has been to give in to it fearlessly, erecting fantasies about having vanquished fantasy. Michel Foucault taught that the modern legacy of enlightenment displays a number of tensions that it is able to maintain only with great effort. It champions "a reason whose autonomy of structures carries with itself the history of dogmatisms and despotisms — a reason which, consequently, has the effect of emancipation only on the condition that it succeeds in freeing itself from itself."[1] Modernity trades in one or more sophisticated illusions designed to convince those who place their faith in them that in doing so they have prevailed over illusion itself and kept at bay superstition, wishful thinking, and flights of fancy. In its quest for certainty, it denies the uncertain and contingent character of things and underwrites these fantasies with epistemology. This device works on the principle that fantasies that are explained epistemologically cease to be fantasies since they instead now carry the authority of theory, custom, and accepted practice. Under such conditions, discovering and exposing the fantasies of self-deception become much more difficult. Once one assumes that the world displays uniformity and regularity rather than contingency and ambiguity, there is no longer reason to question whether seeing the world this way might be a sublime act of willful deception.[2] However, when it is more than just a philosophy, and it includes making contact with the natural and social world, the modern tendency produces disastrous results, as the next chapter illustrates.

Nevertheless, it is too simplistic to oppose modernity's conflation of both problems via a resignation to skepticism. Such moves inevitably either contradict themselves or make themselves irrelevant. They contradict themselves where they offer their own metaphysical accounts of contingency in the form of tragic randomness, while purporting to have abjured all metaphysical accounts. Alternatively, versions of skeptical resignation make themselves irrelevant when they confine themselves to proffering

1. Michel Foucault, introduction in Georges Canguilhem, *On the Normal and the Pathological*, trans. Carolyn R. Fawcett (Boston: D. Reidel, 1978), p. xii.

2. Foucault goes on to say that the Enlightenment's rationality "makes universal claims while developing in contingency" (*On the Normal*, p. xii). Stephen Toulmin, *Cosmopolis: The Hidden Agenda of Modernity* (Chicago: University of Chicago Press, 1990) is a notable effort to expose this.

overly formal recommendations for seeing clearly, ironically sharing in modernity's proclivity for making universal claims at the expense of attending to particulars. Either way, the skeptic has difficulty ascribing any purpose to vision. He struggles to say why it might be important since he relies on the unspoken conviction that he already knows what is out there to be seen. He wants to be open to contingency, but leaves little room for it.

My aim in this chapter is to describe this modern crisis, which was best diagnosed by Nietzsche, and discern how it presses Christian theology to clarify what it means to see like a witness of the resurrected Christ. Plato wondered about the qualities that make for a competent witness. But unlike Plato, and against modern objectivity and skeptical formality, I will not only be concerned with seeing in general, but with the moral skills that accompany a competent Christian witness as one who can see the risen Christ. Answering this will take us into chapter 3. Seeing like a witness is not a skill cultivated only for the sake of seeing more clearly, but it is a transitive activity that is *determined by its object*. It matters what is being seen. The Christian's goal is not simply to achieve a more objective vision generally; rather, such seeing is a skill that comes to be perfected because it is specifically needed in the course of discerning the movements of the risen Christ in the world. The witness's ability to see the works of God in Christ is the outcome of a way of life that requires that kind of vision. Like John the Baptist, the witness says, "Look, here is the Lamb of God!" (John 1:36).

Moreover, the seeing involved in Christian witness is a vision that, in its very exercise, displays an openness to the contingent nature of reality. Unlike failed modern attempts to see clearly by objective means, seeing like a witness involves the refusal to overcome contingency through mastery. This is brought about by a competence made possible by an imagination that is sufficiently captured by the inconclusiveness of the canons of knowledge conceived thus far. To put it positively, this competence is conditioned by a desire that simultaneously grants freedom to what is being seen. The redemption of vision depends on skills of practical knowledge for *beholding* (rather than merely seeing). One beholds when one's seeing is attended by love of the object. All right seeing is beatific.

The intellectual history of the West, however, has often sought right seeing by other means. What is enlightenment? is a question that gets asked in many different ways, from within a variety of intellectual agendas, and elicits a diversity of responses. For the purposes of this study, I ask the question again. However, I direct it not primarily toward a specific thinker of the Enlightenment movement that culminated in the eighteenth century, such as Descartes, Kant, de Condorcet, Voltaire, Locke, or Bacon, but rather in a more general way toward the great inheritance of the scientific mode of knowledge and inquiry that sought with such determination to be free from the mists of the medieval mind and, as the Enlightenment would pejoratively label its predecessor in European thought, the age of faith.[3]

What are the marks of enlightenment? The first mark is freedom, or liberty. Not only are these the political watchwords of modernity, but their status as such owes specifically to the newly conceived kind of freedom that the Enlightenment countenanced. If the medieval mind was shackled to superstitious dogma that bound the intellect to unquestionable commitments, then the Enlightenment declared and enacted a strident revaluation of inherited knowledge all the way back to its every foundation and source. Enlightenment is in this precisely linguistic sense *radical,* since it strives to dig its way back to the roots. And this is an expression of its status as confident claimant to freedom from the very things into which it is inquiring. (In fact, in a very real sense, enlightenment freedom is only acquired while it is expressing itself by demonstrating a profound indifference to an intellectual tradition's sacred cows.) Nothing is sacred to the enlightened mind. It is eminently self-confident and self-assured. It permits itself to give itself fully to a questioning that goes all the way down, because what is at the bottom, when most scrutinized, will either crumble, yielding inquiry yet further down, or be more solid for it.

All of this is in service to liberation from those things that others are afraid to touch because of their prejudice. But why are they fearful and prejudiced? Their reason is hampered by a doubt that suspects that panic might well set in if what is widely held to be the case cannot, in fact, withstand investigation. One of the Enlightenment's most enduring legacies is its politics: the reason is that the kind of freedom it promises is the inverse of a political fearfulness. Have the social and political arrangements of a people been purchased at too great a discount? Have they too easily accorded with the interests of rulers and elites? If so, then it is not immediately clear that all people will actually *want* to be free. Enlightenment requires great courage, Kant famously argued. But once it has begun, those who resist it can no longer plead ignorance, but only cowardice. Their yearning is no longer for

---

3. I will use "the Enlightenment" (capitalized) to refer to the period in history in which the movement flourished, from the mid-seventeenth to the late eighteenth century; "enlightenment" will refer to the style of thinking that this period produced and that is still with us in many forms.

what they still believe to be true, but for what they find themselves now refusing to believe to be false because they cannot imagine life in the truth. Kant described the fetters from which enlightenment emerges as *self-incurred* for exactly this reason: "It is so convenient to be immature!"[4] To be free takes great courage, enacted against the self's unbelievably strong will toward convenience and falsehood, which Kant sought to expose as being merely other names for political, religious, and intellectual servitude.

Instead, Kant counseled that the only thing that is needed is freedom to use one's own reason and understanding in public on all matters of conscience, but particularly on religious matters.[5] Clergy may be duty-bound to preach orthodox doctrines when performing their clerical duties; but in their capacity as scholars, they may speak with the public voice of reason alone, unconstrained by outside guidance. And the topics to which enlightened reason is to devote itself are, by Kant's reckoning, no one's intellectual property, meaning that subjecting them to reason is an activity that is eminently public — widely and generally available. Reason is a democratizing quality because it is available for use by everyone, regardless of rank and status. Tolerant princes knew this, and Kant thereby considered them enlightened. But reason can only democratize a people who are prepared to use it. Therefore, the more those whose allegiances are to reason alone — to questioning and arguing against the things that others have an interest in leaving alone — the more their enactment of reason's own freedom will become realized as a civic freedom. Political tyranny of all kinds is premised on the ability of rulers to generate an obliging public.

The second mark is distance. Enlightenment seeks to be rid of the entanglements of commitment, interest, and obligation, since one who is overcommitted to something will be too close to it, thus revealing the fact in refusing to subject that thing to the demands of reason. It is in this sense (as I will go on to discuss at greater length below) that enlightenment most obviously strives to perfect its vision. The clearest seeing will always be the most objective seeing; the greater the distance, the more perfect the clarity. As a consequence, enlightenment privileges thought that is conceived as an activity that is abstract from the objects of its thinking. It will become bound up with the objects of thought only as long as is needed to observe it — while remaining unaffected by it.

---

4. Immanuel Kant, "What Is Enlightenment?" in *Kant's Political Writings,* ed. H. S. Reiss (Cambridge: Cambridge University Press, 2003), p. 54.

5. Kant, "What Is Enlightenment?" pp. 54-55.

One difficulty that arises early on with this kind of distance-making has to do with the self. Who exactly is the thinking self who owes nothing to what she thinks about? Does it matter who the reasoner is? Can such a self subject one's own history to inquiry? The answer enlightenment gives is clearly yes. And implied in this is a robust denial that thinking and reasoning themselves have a history. If they did, they would not be able to devote their energies to making their own history an object of inquiry without in some catastrophic sense failing in the project from the very beginning. In other words, it is crucial that the distance enlightenment strives to achieve begins with the very grounds of its own tools. Reason itself can only be democratizing and leveling if it really is no respecter of the various and divergent histories and social statuses that characterize actual collections of people. All that is required is the will to inject the required distance between oneself as inquirer and the objects and effects of the inquiry. Enlightened science merely seeks to say what is the case. Whichever heavenly bodies, for example, revolve around whichever other heavenly bodies is only ever, for reason, a matter of what is real. The scientist must let the chips fall where they may and be thoroughly unconcerned with the impact of his investigations on whatever else people have already committed themselves to believe.

Third, enlightenment is characterized by its will. It does not merely strive for objectivity; objectivity serves a further purpose that makes plain its deepest, if sometimes hidden, desires. It attempts, through what it objectively knows, to gain mastery and control over what is unknown. This is most evident in what becomes of nature. With greater distance comes greater estrangement, though it is in the service of power and dominion. Horkheimer and Adorno adduce that enlightenment is related to things in exactly the same way as a dictator is related to human subjects: both associate their knowing them with how much they can manipulate, destroy, and remake them.[6] Its own preservation of distance, its own skill in achieving detachment, is put to use, not only in not being controlled by its objects, but precisely in itself exercising control over them. For example, Horkheimer and Adorno cite Francis Bacon, who claimed that "the sovereignty of man lieth hid in knowledge" (p. 1). No longer must sovereignty be given over merely to those whose claim to political power grants them obvious exercise of it. Instead, the knowledge available to reason is something that "kings

6. Max Horkheimer and Theodore W. Adorno, *Dialectic of Enlightenment*, ed. Gunzelin Schmid Noerr, trans. Edmund Jephcott (Stanford: Stanford University Press, 2002), p. 6 (hereafter, page references to this work appear in parentheses in the text).

with their treasure cannot buy, nor with their force command; their spials and intelligencers can give no news of them, their seamen and discoverers cannot sail where they grow" (p. 1). The mastery that enlightenment entails is enjoyed especially by those who, up until now, had been mastered by others. Their newfound freedom *is* their exercise of sovereignty in knowing.

However, enlightened reason cannot be quite as self-aware as all of this implies. If its project is premised on liberty and the discovery that power suffuses all relationships in which the knowing capacity is overcommitted to one thing or another, then enlightenment must necessarily disguise its own use of power. Its ability to control depends on its convincingly denying that it is doing so. Still, as a mark of enlightenment, this might actually seem benign enough. After all, the will to know is a strong will that enlightenment claims to foster for noble reasons. The world is very often inscrutable and certainly confusing to the casual observer. It lends itself to all manner of superstition in efforts to explain some things and how their causes relate to those of other things. Invoking the gods to explain the weather is unenlightened, but not because it seeks to explain the weather. What is unenlightened is allowing one's clinging to what is not subject to rational scrutiny (the gods) to outpace what is (the weather). Nevertheless, even the will to know is insufficient on its own to drive away the previous ways of knowing. One clings to the weather gods for fear that without them things would be meaningless, not for fear of rational explanations. What enlightenment promises, then, is not simply knowledge, but power. It advances a program whereby you may discover not only how things work but how to control how they work and even to harness their work for yourself.

The fourth mark is abstraction and totality. Horkheimer and Adorno call abstraction "the instrument of enlightenment" (p. 9). With it, the objects of inquiry are most readily dominated and efficiently mastered. Abstraction is both the intention and outcome of distance. As a tactic of perception, abstraction thus sees only unity and sameness among similar but slightly different things. No two things are alike; yet enlightenment excels at categories. It places things side by side and very often perceives that they are equivalent. Moreover, abstraction corresponds to the method of investigation. In order for the scientific modus to proceed steadily, it must do so with regularity, confident that the experiments conducted one day will be repeatable and thus yield the same results the next day. Therefore, enlightenment prizes ideal things. One can only know what something is by fitting it into a larger, totalizing class or taxonomy.

Its authority rests in its having this kind of knowledge of things. Hork-heimer and Adorno refer to the "authority of universal concepts" (p. 3). The unenlightened may know particular things, but enlightenment has true understanding because it can see how particulars fit into wholes. It catches up those things that lie outside the standard accounts by seeing only what is most essential to a thing; things may be more similar than different if you look at what they are essentially.

But what is essential and what is not? This is a problem for enlighten-ment. After all, any distinction between what is essential and what is not essential cannot be subject to scrutiny in the same way that these qualities are on their own. Instead, the modus risks circularity: what is essential to a thing is known by knowing what kind of thing it is. Of course, this only verifies what was already known or asserted on other grounds. In practice, what is essential is known by repeatable experiments on like things. Pre-dictable and consistent results confirm that the objects of the experiments were alike after all: they all share the same essential qualities. This entails no small measure of violence as it "amputates the incommensurable" (p. 9). Individual qualities do not merely vanish under the unity of con-cepts that subsumes them. Rather, the exercise of power over individual qualities, in the service of thinking and seeing them together as a single thing, brings them into actual conformity.

The fifth and final mark of the Enlightenment is certainty. It not only asks how this or that is really knowable, but also (and much more subver-sively) asks whether it is something that is worth finding out about in the first place. In other words, the totality of concepts, in extending to the an-swers that result from inquiry, actually arises from the *form* and *method* of inquiry. The questions one asks are themselves the first things that deter-mine the answers. Seldom are the questions turned back on themselves and subjected to the same rigor and scrutiny that they exert on other things.

Yet it is difficult to see how this could be avoided. Enlightenment cannot give an account of why some questions matter more than others do. For example, it cannot very well claim that its tools are well-suited to a particular kind of inquiry and ill-suited to another. That kind of admis-sion would only fall back into resembling the arbitrary ways of proceeding from which it aims to escape. After all, for enlightenment, knowledge is better than belief: knowledge derives from science, and belief is the stuff of faith. What is known is certain and will not change (repeatability has en-sured that). Belief is delayed, consumed, assailed in the welter, tossed about, hunkered down; it prays that the peace will last, that the storm will calm, that the Lord will deliver, that the gods will relent.

A primary good of enlightenment involves a great irony. On the one hand, enlightenment scrupulously pursues a new level of certainty through advancing thought beyond the past's fetters to greater knowledge. On the other hand, the goods implicit in such knowledge will involve reaching the end of inquiry (or at least of particular inquiries). The repeatable experiment comes to an end, the results are filed, and they are compiled into tidy categories and encyclopedias, as Alasdair MacIntyre shows with the ninth edition of the *Encyclopedia Britannica.*[7] This trait of the Enlightenment is usually obscured by its talk of progress and its refusal to be under oath to uphold the dogmas of previous generations. But progress also countenances its own goals, suggesting that its undogmatic decrees will likewise eventually run out as the goals are met. The irony is that it must continue to talk as though there is always more progress to be achieved, that its goals must be kept more ill-defined and less certain than the knowledge that converges on them. Therefore, questions about what things *are* will always be easier to answer than questions about what things are *for.* And answering the former questions will depend on successfully isolating them from the latter.

This means that the new way of life made possible by distance and abstraction is, as a further irony, a repose in freedom, but freedom of a particular kind. It is characterized most saliently by nonentanglement. Such a life is ideally less and less subject to forces that it cannot control as there are fewer and fewer things that can genuinely be said to lie beyond what can be anticipated, based on how things have gone so far. Certainty of the past means mastery of the future. But what kind of life lives into a mastered future? Repeatability and conformity, it turns out, cut both ways. The observer is alienated from the observed and is easily made redundant and superfluous, subsumed into the totality of other observers. Life is a casualty of enlightenment, as Nietzsche would so forcefully show.

*   *   *

I expand on and illustrate this account of enlightenment in the next chapter. For now, I focus in a more limited way on what may have been enlightenment's most salutary impulse (if sincere), even though it has since

---

7. Alasdair MacIntyre, *Three Rival Versions of Moral Enquiry: Encyclopedia, Genealogy, and Tradition* (Notre Dame, IN: University of Notre Dame Press, 1990), chap. 1.

proven disastrously ill-equipped to address it: the drive to overcome false-hood and to see clearly. I have already alluded to some of the tensions within the Enlightenment itself that make it eminently vulnerable to self-deception and to insulating and disguising vast areas of inquiry from its modus, particularly as those inquiries are self-directed ones. The many failures of the Enlightenment are by now well known. Its failure to make good on its central promises, I argue, was kept from view for so long be-cause of its ample capacity to deceive itself. So it will be important to in-quire further into some features of falsehood, particularly those that are not obviously categorized as lying. This will aid us in grasping the force of Nietzsche's judgment on the modern tendency toward believing fantasies either by ignoring the moral significance of vision or by subordinating vi-sion to the purportedly more exact science of knowing.

Consider the falsehood displayed in the following anecdote.

> In World War II, Herman Göring was told that an Allied fighter had been shot down over a German city, the first that had ever been seen that far behind the Axis lines. This meant the Allies had developed a long-range fighter that could escort bombers over Germany. Göring, a pilot himself, "knew" such a development was impossible. His reply: "I officially assert that American fighter planes did not reach Aachen . . . . I herewith give you an official order that they weren't there."[8]

Göring may have been a fool, but he was not technically a liar. When talk-ing about telling the truth, it is common to assume that the liar *knows* the truth (or thinks that he does) and desires to deceive his hearer. One may choose to lie, but will not generally choose to be deceived. On this account, the moral difficulty does not begin with the knowing, but with the telling. Augustine thought that someone who is misled on account of believing a liar is certainly at a disadvantage, but is nevertheless still morally more praiseworthy than the one who does the misleading.[9] If the one who is misled goes on to speak what he has heard from the liar, who can blame him? People innocently pass on misinformation all the time. We are in-clined not to hold responsible someone who tells an untruth out of igno-rance, and we indicate this by not calling his words a lie.

8. Daniel Goleman, *Vital Lies, Simple Truths: The Psychology of Self-Deception* (Lon-don: Bloomsbury, 1997), p. 18.

9. Augustine, *On Christian Teaching* (Oxford: Oxford University Press, 1997), I.87, p. 27.

Yet what about those who *do* want to believe what is false? What about Göring's foolishness? It was not that Göring did not know the truth; instead, he positively refused to consider that it might be true. We might say he did not *see* the truth. Even though it may not be right to call him a liar, there is still a kind of falsehood at work here. Falsehood obtains even in a sphere far below that of speaking.[10] I will consider the deceit of *telling* (that is, of lying) in part III, following two prior occasions for deceit: seeing falsely (the present part) and failing to come forward (part II).

Seeing truthfully involves overcoming self-deception, which is the most basic form of falsehood. The Enlightenment both preached this gospel and was its most remarkable victim. How we think about telling the truth may even be itself based on a lie, since we can tend toward deceit on account of wanting to think that we are honest people.[11] We think we basically tell the truth most of the time, with a few exceptions that we can justify on grounds that it is either harmless or for some positive good. We think we might become slightly better at telling the truth provided we supply the necessary effort; it is really rather straightforward and uncomplicated. But what if these are just more lies we tell ourselves? What if we are not basically truthful, but basically deceitful? We choose friends who tell us what we want to hear and reinforce our prejudices rather than challenge them; we have difficulty discerning the truth in what others say; we zealously want to know the truth when it benefits us. We want the politicians we loathe to get caught in lies about things of which we disapprove. We do not want the truth; we want the truth to *be* something particular, namely, grounds for blame and an ally in our case against scoundrels. It is difficult to regard the truth for its own sake when we cannot even tell the truth to ourselves about our ability to tell the truth.[12]

Nietzsche understood better than most that the human proclivity to falsehood cannot simply be reduced to lying. There is a deception that occurs even before speaking, a counterfeit inclination that implicates the agent's desire and distorts her vision. Nietzsche endeavored to unmask how the drive toward objectivity invites its own dubious underestimation of human limitation and the world's contingency. Because he knew that

---

10. Dietrich Bonhoeffer, "What Is Meant by 'Telling the Truth'?" in *Ethics*, trans. Neville Horton Smith (London: Touchstone, 1995), p. 364.

11. Stanley Hauerwas and David B. Burrell, "Self-Deception and Autobiography: Reflections on Speer's *Inside the Third Reich*" in Hauerwas, *Truthfulness and Tragedy* (Notre Dame, IN: University of Notre Dame Press, 1977), p. 87.

12. L. Gregory Jones, "Truth and Lies," *The Christian Century*, March 11, 1998.

willful ignorance is not called a lie in the technical sense of intentional deception, Nietzsche famously referred to it as lying in the "extramoral" or "nonmoral" sense. It is a form of deceit that less readily submits to moralizing. He observes that the human capacity for knowledge lends itself to arrogance and overestimation. Because of vanity and every form of self-love, we establish a particular useful relationship with our knowledge that really amounts to affectation.

> [D]eception, flattery, lying and cheating, talking behind the back, posing, living in borrowed splendor, being masked, the disguise of convention, acting a role before others and before oneself — in short, the constant fluttering around the single flame of vanity is so much the rule and the law that almost nothing is more incomprehensible than how an honest and pure urge for truth could make its appearance among men.[13]

Our deceit is as much about what we want others to believe as it is about what we want to believe ourselves (and we will very often find ways of believing only what we want to). Nietzsche argues that what we call true is really an artifice, an invented collection of agreed-upon metaphors and figures, the abuse and disguise of which is sanctioned socially.

The world we call true or real is thus just the interplay of the images that we, having forgotten that we invented them and agreed to use them, wrongly take to be definitive. When those things we designate as true serve our interests, bring us comfort, and wall off those things that do not, then it is easy to ignore the fact that we invented them and continue to instrumentalize them; indeed, we must find ways to ignore these things.

> It is even a difficult thing for [someone] to admit to himself that the insect or the bird perceives an entirely different world from the one that man does, and that the question of which of these perceptions of the world is the more correct one is quite meaningless, for this would have to have been decided previously in accordance with the criterion of the *correct perception,* which means, in accordance with a criterion which is *not available.*[14]

13. Friedrich Nietzsche, "From 'On Truth and Lie in an Extra-Moral Sense,'" in *The Portable Nietzsche,* ed. and trans. Walter Kaufmann (London: Viking Penguin, 1968), p. 43. The full text of this well-known essay appears in *Philosophy and Truth: Selections from Nietzsche's Notebooks of the Early 1870's,* ed. and trans. D. Breazeale (Amherst, NY: Humanity Books, 1999).

14. This quotation is taken from the Breazeale translation, p. 86.

If we forgot that our perception of the world depends on a linguistic, social convention, then Nietzsche is reminding us. But he is also issuing a warning that we cannot have it any other way.[15] The will to forget is the necessary flip side of the will to know. We cannot do away with language in order to get at the real world: this metaphysical opposition between reality and appearance is another sense of what he means by extramoral lying.[16] And we cannot appeal to something else in order to mediate between different ways of seeing the world — again, another sense of lying.[17] The drive to mediate between different perceptions is a form of human arrogance with which Nietzsche begins. It presumes to be able to know more than is possible, where what can be known is subject not only to human limitations but to the fact that any mediating criteria would only suffer from the same problem of linguistic determination.[18]

There are two things happening here: first, the human drive toward unmediated knowledge; second, the tendency toward self-deception. Nietzsche connects the two: our striving after unmediated knowledge is, at root, a way of deceiving ourselves into thinking that we are not limited. Not wanting to believe that our view of the world is contingent, we try to view the world in ways that overcome the contingency of other things by imagining them to be more uniform than they really are — smoother, less varied, and differentiated. This mastery, so well developed by the Enlightenment, has its roots in vanity and arrogance. Mastery occurs via our drive

15. Aquinas argued that a lie told out of ignorance is not a mortal sin. One example he gives is of a person who forgets his doubt about uncertain evidence and wrongly becomes certain of it on account of the frailty of human memory (*ST*, II-II.70.4). This is clearly similar to Nietzsche's accusation that we forget the indeterminacy of language, though his indictment is "extramoral" since it goes all the way down.

16. Nietzsche clarified this point later in his writings. "The antithesis of the apparent world and the true world is reduced to the antithesis 'world' and 'nothing'" (*The Will to Power*, trans. Walter Kaufmann and R. J. Hollingdale, ed. Walter Kaufmann [New York: Vintage, 1968], sec. 567). He seems to have maintained some such antithesis in this early essay, even though all language, since metaphorical, could not overcome it. Nietzsche never changed his mind concerning language, only regarding the possibility of uninterpreted facts (language aside).

17. Paul Griffiths notes that this essay by Nietzsche makes reference to at least three senses of truth, which he calls conventional, nonmetaphorical, and artistic (Griffiths, *Lying: An Augustinian Theology of Duplicity* [Grand Rapids: Brazos, 2004], p. 214).

18. By calling linguistic determination a "problem," I am only representing the style of reasoning Nietzsche was opposing. Linguistic determination, if true, is neither rational nor irrational, as Wittgenstein said: "It is there — like our life" (Wittgenstein, *On Certainty*, trans. Denis Paul and G. E. M. Anscombe [New York: Harper and Row, 1969], sec. 559).

to bring unity out of diversity and to tame the unfamiliar through incorporation into familiar categories and concepts. In the process, we reduce differences and overcome the individuality of objects. This is particularly evident in how we see ourselves since, as Nietzsche argues, most of us are not bold enough to tell brazen lies, especially those lies that, in their telling, would compel us to be honest with ourselves about the difference between what is true and false. Instead, we satisfy our desire to think of ourselves as good people with lies such as "I am a good person." So long as such lies keep us from telling more open lies — having repressed the distinction between truth and falsehood — "good people" is precisely what we would seem to be. Nietzsche teaches that this makes it almost impossible to face the truth about ourselves.[19]

To be clear, Nietzsche is not so much diagnosing a human impulse toward omniscience as he is the Enlightenment's myth of objectivity. Trying to see objectively means attempting to limit the factors that govern our ways of knowing. But Nietzsche thinks this actually has the opposite effect as a strategy, because there are things excluded by a so-called objective perception, and they are made all the more difficult to see by such methods. In order to see contingent things (things that could be otherwise, things that might just as easily not be there and *should* not be there if what is there is thought to be governed by necessity), we will have to admit that our seeing of them is likewise contingent.[20] Wittgenstein argued that if a blind man asked whether you have two hands, you would not be able to know just by looking. The reason is that if you doubt having two hands, then you should also doubt your eyes.[21] If we know anything by seeing, it is because we trust our sight; but if *everything* we know is by seeing, we cannot know whether our sight should be trusted. Still, *admitting* contingent vision is not the same as *having* contingent vision. Our desire for clear vision, like our desire for things, is bound up with what it is to see things. Nietzsche aids the project of surpassing assumptions that "seeing the

19. Friedrich Nietzsche, *On the Genealogy of Morality,* trans. Carol Diethe (Cambridge: Cambridge University Press, 1994), 3rd essay, sec. 19, p. 108.

20. Elsewhere, Nietzsche warns against the use of concepts like "knowledge as such" since "here we are asked to think an eye which cannot be thought at all, an eye turned in no direction at all, an eye where the active and interpretative powers are to be suppressed, absent, but through which seeing still becomes a seeing-something, so it is an absurdity and non-concept of eye that is demanded. There is *only* a perspective seeing, *only* a perspective knowing" (Nietzsche, *On the Genealogy of Morality,* 3rd essay, sec. 12, p. 92).

21. Wittgenstein, *On Certainty,* sec. 125; cf. sec. 413.

truth" or "seeing what is the case" is a purely *epistemological matter*. Iris Murdoch's claim that we desire in accordance with what we see could easily be reversed: we see what we desire.[22] Gregory of Nyssa understood this.

Indeed, the Hebrew prophets understood right seeing to be a *moral* matter rooted in the desire not to be told fantasies. Isaiah's prophecy was contested by the people because they did not desire the truth:

> For they are a rebellious people,
>   lying sons,
> sons who will not hear
>   the instruction of the Lord;
> who say to the seers, "See not";
>   and to the prophets,
>   "Prophesy not to us what is right;
>   speak to us smooth things,
>   prophesy illusions,
>   leave the way, turn aside from the path,
>   let us hear no more of the Holy One of Israel."
>
> (Isa. 30:9-11)

The "smooth things" are precisely those things that underwrite the world of deception that Israel wanted to maintain. Willful self-deception is located in the desire to hear smooth things when it is rough things that are true and real.[23] If overcoming the narcissism by which a people prefer deception to the truth requires the reorientation of their desire, the manner of reorienting is decidedly practical:

> And your ears shall hear a word behind you, saying,
> "This is the way, walk in it,"
> when you turn to the right
>   or when you turn to the left.
>
> (Isa. 30:21)

---

22. Iris Murdoch, "The Idea of Perfection," in *The Sovereignty of Good* (New York: Routledge, 2002), p. 39.

23. Wittgenstein asked, "Is my understanding only blindness to my own lack of understanding? It often seems so to me" (*On Certainty*, sec. 418). See Miroslav Volf, *Exclusion and Embrace: A Theological Exploration of Identity, Otherness, and Reconciliation* (Nashville: Abingdon, 1996), p. 236, where he relates Isaiah and the people's call for "smooth things" to political domination.

Here I think we find the biblical alternative to what modern philosophy often misled us into thinking was a puzzle of knowing and of reason rather than a moral failing. Scripture counsels discipleship, a new way of walking that both depends on and cultivates a new way of seeing, since seeing "rough things" is necessary for a people who love to walk this way. Moreover, for Christian ethics to serve a people "on the way," it will take appropriate account of the roughness of the road and find ways to keep from despising it. It will investigate how repentance (starting to walk a different direction) and faith (taking steps) make possible life on that road. It will retemporalize the life of knowing. Any postmodern awareness of the earlier preferences for smooth things will be most genuine — and certainly closer to the kind of life that Christianity counsels — when it commends a positive way of life that knows nothing of the desperation that otherwise sets in among those who long for the former illusions and their sham securities. "It is not that the pure ice beneath our feet has yielded to rough ground; the ground was rough all along."[24]

Moral observation is an indispensable part of this task, despite its relative neglect by moral philosophers until recently.[25] It is still common for moral philosophy to pay inordinate attention to making judgments and to overlook the conditions that make certain kinds of judgments more or less likely. Traditional ethical theories such as deontology, consequentialism, and situation ethics elevate the individual and the determinativeness of tough (often contrived) decisions that correspond to the choice of the individual moral agent. They offer a general framework for guiding those choices — duty, utility, greater good, love. These theoretical construals elevate abstract universals by making primary the ways that they function as foundations for rational decision-making and ethical action. Similarly, they subordinate particular everyday practices by making the latter attendant products of a prior ethically reflective process.

These ethical theories surely fall under Nietzsche's criticism. Their concern to identify which perception of the world is the right one is a project he claims is quite meaningless given criteriological decisions made previously, that is, prior to any ethical involvement. But there is no such "prior

24. Terry Eagleton, *After Theory* (New York: Basic Books, 2003), p. 58.

25. Jeffrey Stout laments the scant treatment within ethical theory as to how moral observation as a habit is developed by moral communities (Stout, *Democracy and Tradition* [Princeton, NJ: Princeton University Press, 2003], p. 221). Stout's objection obviously owes a great deal to the retrieval of virtue ethics in recent years, despite his criticism of some of its most celebrated practitioners, notably Alasdair MacIntyre and Stanley Hauerwas.

to," because all involvement in anything is already ethical and invested with notions of value being shaped by linguistic commitments.[26] "We do not see what it is that we do not see." "Every event is from its inception a moral event."[27] Although Nietzsche did not write these two sentences, they are thoroughly Nietzschean and represent precise points on which it has now become impossible to ignore him. Moral observation attempts to see clearly, though not by striving for unmediated objectivity. It contradicts the modern tendency to subordinate vision to epistemology, seeing to knowing. It takes seriously Nietzschean insights without sharing his pessimism regarding a solution. (Nietzsche is devastating only to ethical theories that prize the objectivity of normative ethical judgments. When Alasdair MacIntyre, in *After Virtue,* asked, "Nietzsche or Aristotle?" he was alert to this choice. The ability to keep from answering this ominous question with "Nietzsche" will partly depend on the role that moral observation plays.)

Admitting that how we see the world is already moral and linguistic does not attempt to ignore or bypass Nietzsche, but specifically rises to his challenge. Foundational ethical theories located the problem of truth-telling and lying first in the will, because they assumed that anything prior to the exercise of the individual, unconditioned will lies outside the moral sphere. This led Nietzsche to speak of them in the "extramoral sense." His use of that locution was no doubt meant to confirm his point, though perhaps it is easier to see a century later: that what is moral is already embedded in how we talk about morality given the set of conceptual possibilities available to us even when we did not choose them. In other words, what Nietzsche called the "extramoral sense" we might simply call the "moral sense."

26. I do not agree with Terry Eagleton that this puts Nietzsche at odds with Wittgenstein. Eagleton thinks that Wittgenstein is at variance with recent inheritors of Nietzsche, such as Stanley Fish and Jacques Derrida, who believe that interpretation "goes all the way down," since Wittgenstein held that you only get interpretation insofar as there is doubt over meaning. Eagleton writes: "It does not make sense to talk in a Nietzschean fashion of a perception as an interpretation when there could be no reasonable doubt about what it is we are seeing or smelling" (Eagleton, "Mystic Mechanic," *Times Literary Supplement,* April 29, 2005, p. 10). This confuses Nietzsche's point because, for him, the reason we do not doubt our perception is that we engage in self-deception. It becomes "interpretation" only when we remember that we speak in metaphors, not before. I admit that I do not know what this says about Derrida and Fish, if anything.

27. Goleman, *Vital Lies, Simple Truths,* p. 12. Sarah Kofman, *Nietzsche and Metaphor,* trans. Duncan Large (London: Athlone, 1993), p. 34.

Rising to this challenge, the discourse of moral observation articulates judgments made at the level of observation, not after it. What subsequent reflection concealed by its single-minded focus on action and a deferral of reasoning was that its interpretations were always "from above" and at a remove from vision. In contrast, the judgments of moral observation are *noninferential* judgments, not detached from observation as theories and norms applied to brute facts.[28] A craftsman knows good craftsmanship when he sees it, not because he infers from a first principle (an aesthetic norm) and applies it to this object, but because of the skills that were formed in his training as a craftsman according to the communally shared goods of the guild. His judgments are teleologically ordered and exercised at the level of observation. This has more in common with Aristotle than Nietzsche, because the latter thought that this kind of craftsman (shaped by skills but not possessing aesthetic norms) is a contradiction and lacks authority.[29] On the other hand, it is Aristotelian to recognize that craftsmen and craftsmanship exist first as practices and, so long as they can be practiced, being linguistically governed, they also make use of grammar that is particular to (but not prior to) that practice. This is Mac-

---

28. According to Alexander Nehamas, Nietzsche changed his mind over his lifetime regarding whether or not there were such things as uninterpreted facts. In his early essay that I have been discussing here, Nietzsche seems to have followed Kant and Schopenhauer in implying the existence of such facts, even though they could not be grasped by reason or language. In his first published book, *The Birth of Tragedy,* he discusses music (intoxicated by the Wagner cause) as a way more closely to approach the nature of reality. But by the time of his last works, including the unpublished *Nachlass,* Nietzsche had distanced himself from these influences and contradicts his earlier perspective: "[F]acts are precisely what there is not, only interpretations" (*The Will to Power,* sec. 481). See Alexander Nehamas, *Nietzsche: Life as Literature* (London: Harvard University Press, 1985), chap. 2.

29. Nietzsche often uses the image of the artist. Even though he affirms the artist's truth, he nevertheless thinks they were liars (but the *best* liars). As Richard Rorty says, "Only poets, Nietzsche suspected, can truly appreciate contingency" (Rorty, *Contingency, Irony, and Solidarity* [Cambridge: Cambridge University Press, 1989], p. 28). However, such appreciation surely comes at a cost since, as Rorty goes on to note, following Harold Bloom, it is poets who have the greatest fear of death. Their creativity is a function of staving off the destruction death entails. I take this to mean that both the appreciation of contingency and its mastery can follow from the fear of death. Murdoch (as I will discuss below), despite her Platonism, shares with Rorty a tragic notion of contingency as just "one damn thing after another." While Christian thought does not deny contingency, it denies that it is ultimately — both on the basis of God's non-necessary creation and on the freedom of Jesus Christ — that which calls forth an eye commensurate with that freedom, or so I argue in this section.

Intyre's defense of Aristotle over against Nietzsche: linguistic mediation only constitutes a problem in the absence of practices.

Nevertheless, this endorsement of practice still does not go far enough in view of Nietzsche's indictment of self-deception. "They [we, vain people] are deeply immersed in illusions and dream images; their eye glides only over the surface of things and sees 'forms.'"[30] Part of the reason for the success of the ethical theories mentioned above (deontology and so on) is that they are easily used in eliminating contingency, speaking to us smooth things about rough realities. This is why they routinely evoke contrived, too-simple scenarios: "What would you do if . . . ?" Not only has ethical theory wanted to believe that our choices are free and that we can be objective, but the theories to which we appeal in support of those conclusions comfort us that we are nevertheless right to believe this.

Attentive to this problem, we will take special care not to elevate the notions of practice, skill, habit, virtue, and so on to abstraction in service to mastering contingency, making things smoother than they really are. To put it simply, nothing can be said about a practice that is more true than its exercise, and likewise, everything that is said about it risks distortion. "Philosophical theory is itself a practice," says Gilles Deleuze. "It is no more abstract than its object."[31] Putting the matter oppositely, though in the same spirit, we might say that to invoke the notion of practice against Nietzsche is not in itself to invoke a practice but a notion, which is not the same thing. If "practice" names the point of dissent between Aristotle and Nietzsche — which, with MacIntyre, I think it does — we must go deeper in order to show that this is the case. We will need to look at particular practices. This reminder cautions us against assuming that the idea of practice, on its own, is an adequate response to Nietzsche apart from the actual practices in which differentia matters. It is one thing to identify those practices that respect contingency and aid in noticing the detail of particulars; it is quite another to describe those practices using language that similarly respects the contingency of those practices. Both skills of description are necessary.

30. Nietzsche, "From 'On Truth and Lie in an Extra-Moral Sense,'" in *The Portable Nietzsche*, p. 43.

31. Gilles Deleuze, *Cinema 2: The Time-Image*, trans. Hugh Tomlinson and Robert Galeta (London: Athlone, 1989), p. 280.

CHAPTER 3

Seeing Contingency

One does not see a tree, one imagines it lazily
without looking at the original details.

Sarah Kofman, *Nietzsche and Metaphor*

I have been making a case for thinking about bearing witness in terms of
its being a practice of respecting contingency. In contrast to the kinds of
discourses prized by the dispassionate modern mind, witness devotes itself
to a wholly different kind of rigor and undertakes a divergent association
with what is real. It does not give general accounts of axiomatic truths,
since such truths (if they indeed are truths) require only reason and no testimony. Attentive to particulars, witness will not police its speech when it
cannot make sense of what it sees using reason alone. Nor does it smooth
over the rough road of the unforeseen and unpredictable, because these
are precisely the things that make it necessary to have witnesses in the first
place. Witness reaches for whatever it can in the effort to be true to things
that may be either clear or opaque, but especially the latter, things that in
their tangled relationships with immense variety in life and the world do
not yield easily to explanation. Agony, beauty, and love constantly exceed
attempts to explain them; they require witnesses whose testimonies strive
for truthful narration. The same is true of aspects of living that we more
readily think of as straightforwardly factual.

In her essay "Lying in Politics," Hannah Arendt makes clear that the
contingent nature of facts makes testimony the necessary mode of their
transmission. "Factual truths are never compellingly true. . . . Facts need

testimony to be remembered and trustworthy witnesses to be established in order to find a secure dwelling place in the domain of human affairs."[1] It is not enough that facts be true for anyone to consider them important, since it is just as easy to ignore true things as false things. (Perhaps it is even easier to ignore true things, since what is false has generally been crafted to be more appealing.) And since facts are *contingent,* as Arendt observes, they cannot be demonstrated to be the case. It is easy to invent and report false facts because they may be just as plausible as what is true, sometimes much more so. Distinguishing them takes people — witnesses — who devote themselves to remembering and passing on what was real, particularly when what is real is difficult to believe.

It seems to me that when it comes to the substance of what Christians proclaim, this requirement of witnesses particularly holds. Christianity is only able to identify God through events, by what God *does.* God is not first a being whose self-disclosure is of the divine being as such, but is only ever approached by acts within history. The Lord is the one who delivered Israel from the bonds of slavery, out of the hands of the Egyptians, in order to create for himself a people devoted to his promises. The Lord is identified by and in the life and death of Jesus Christ, in the one Jesus called the Father, in the one the Father called the Son, and in the one the Father and Son call the Holy Spirit. God is whoever brought Jesus Christ out of the grave and sent his Spirit to the church to create and empower it to work in the world. It is impossible to identify God apart from God's story, and stories need storytellers, whose role is that of witness.

Facts *need* testimony. God *needs* witnesses. The truth about God cannot be deduced from logic; "Jesus is Lord" does not follow from anything else; "Jesus is risen" cannot be known in any way other than through trusting those who declare it. Nor does the uniqueness of Jesus allow for the construction of a theory that will do the work of his witnesses. Christians cannot say of Jesus, "We know what this is because we have seen one of these before; this is what is known as a 'Christ.'" Peter's confession that Jesus is the Christ (Mark 8:29), though true, just as surely was quickly shown to give Peter all the wrong ideas about what a Christ is and does. As Aquinas liked to point out, God is not a genus.[2] Jesus is a "one-off." Where Christianity has made Jesus into an example of something else, an instance of a larger set

---

1. Hannah Arendt, "Lying in Politics," in *Crises of the Republic* (New York: Harcourt Brace, 1972), p. 6.
2. *Summa Contra Gentiles,* I.25.

of noble ideas and sentiments, it has subordinated everything about him. The more Christians rely on argument and explanation rather than testimony, the more Jesus' uniqueness risks being compromised.

At the same time, articulating how bearing witness respects contingency likewise involves respecting the contingent nature of the practice that bearing witness itself names. I will return to that theme in part III, where I will show how, despite Arendt's insights, giving testimony cannot finally be necessary in a strong sense, that is, it cannot itself be non-contingent. There is no prior space carved out for the delivery of the witness's testimony. For the purposes of the present chapter, however, witness serves an antitheoretical function in a more straightforward sense. Here witness indicates not only that one cannot give a theory of Jesus, but one also cannot even give a theory of contingency.[3] Any would-be theory of contingency, any way of coming to terms with those things that might be otherwise than they are, depends on mastering and taming contingency, since clearly any contingency that is theory-described can no longer really be said to be contingent. The introduction of meta-level explanation still converts rough things into smooth things. This chapter expands on that idea. In particular, it takes its cues from Nietzsche in order to show how assumptions of objectivity in modernity contributed to a way of seeing that weakened desire for truth, and how this has been exemplified in areas such as modern agricultural practices and literature.

The social scientists Pierre Bourdieu, James Scott, and Michel De Certeau, as well as the novelist and philosopher Iris Murdoch, make clear how the attempt to master contingency in the service of achieving greater objectivity truly has characterized modern methods. Their appeal is for renewed approaches to "looking into dragons, not domesticating or abominating them, nor drowning them in vats of theory."[4] The living things breathe and move, expand and exert themselves, transgress boundaries. The thinkers I treat in this chapter illustrate how the desire for "smooth things" that accompanies attempts to understand in a particular way — especially in its most candidly modern form — generates difficulties in a

---

3. Thomas Aquinas did not have a proper doctrine of God for this reason. David Burrell describes the approach of Aquinas as therapy rather than theory (*Aquinas: God and Action* [Notre Dame, IN: University of Notre Dame Press, 1979], p. 15). Likewise, Christology does not strive to be a theory of Jesus, but a mode of chastening speech about him. Nevertheless, explaining too much is still a temptation inherent in every Christology.

4. Clifford Geertz, "Anti-relativism," *American Anthropologist* 86 (1984): 275.

number of areas that exemplify the point, particularly in state planning and literature.

The cultural ethos of modernity, with its attempts at unmediated objectivity, fostered a particular way of seeing. As Nietzsche knew, it was an ethos that wrongly absolutized the metaphorical play of language by elevating the world it produced to a normative status by, again, forgetting — by, in turn, denying — that that status was arrived at linguistically in the first place. Models and concepts came to overdetermine the perception of particulars. Furthermore, this way of seeing yielded to the rise of one of modernity's leading characters: the expert.[5] An expert derives his or her expertise from a field of knowledge canonized in the institutions of modernity. In being institutionalized, experts are bureaucratized, surrounded by versions of that exalted knowledge that derive from and reinforce each other. Therefore, the expert is a bureaucrat to the extent that he or she has special knowledge of how the institutions work. What is easily hidden from view is that the expert's knowledge is of a particular socially and culturally sanctioned type, though it claims universality inasmuch as its institutions purport to serve universal ends.

Consider how this is displayed by governments. In a fascinating study, James Scott observes that a tendency to smooth over contingency is characteristic of the large-scale planning in which governments typically engage. Allegedly carrying out the noble task of bringing technological progress to all of its citizens, states have often adopted social-engineering strategies that simplify the view of actual social life in order to make it conform in theory to the limitations of the technology they are using.[6] Scott notes that "the lack of context and particularity is not an oversight; it is the necessary first premise of any large-scale planning exercise" (p. 326). The rise of the modern character of the expert is explained and illustrated by the expert's role in the state's supporting institutions. If states cultivate a field of knowledge commensurate with the limitations of its vision, which, in turn, corresponds to the limitations of the nature of the progress it is institutionalizing, the resulting field of knowledge cannot escape enforcing and preserving its own narrowness. As the field of knowledge establishes

---

5. Alasdair MacIntyre, *After Virtue,* 2nd ed. (Notre Dame, IN: University of Notre Dame Press, 1984), pp. 73-78.

6. James C. Scott, *Seeing like a State: How Certain Schemes to Improve the Human Condition Have Failed* (New Haven: Yale University Press, 1998), p. 35 (hereafter, page references to this work appear in parentheses in the text and notes).

itself as such, the expert emerges as both its exemplar and guarantor. Scott discusses this by using the example of forestry.

Forests are places of great variety of activity. Animals of various species make their homes among the diversity of trees, bushes, and plants in innumerable nests and burrows. Fruits, nuts, wild mushrooms, and seeds are gathered by humans and other animals for food. The human uses of the forest's trees are just as numerous: they use the sap for syrup and resin; they use the bark for medicine; they use the leaves to feed cattle, or they apply them to wounds; they use reeds and straw for thatch; walnut and oak for furniture, joinery, flooring, and paneling; firs and cedars for railroads, scaffolding, fence rails, and stiles of doors. Not all forests, of course, exhibit all these activities, nor do they lend themselves to all of these uses. This may perhaps lead one to wonder what exactly makes "forest" a helpful concept. What is the single thing it designates? What is its essence? Scott raises these kinds of questions when he contrasts the diverse particulars of actual forests with how the invention of scientific forestry in the late eighteenth century structured itself as a discipline by seeing these actual forests in decisive ways. As the title of Scott's book puts it, this is "seeing like a state."

The state in what Scott calls the high-modernist tradition employs a vision that is ideally suited to discovering unity: "[T]here is only one thing going on" (p. 347). A forest may only be a locus for the commercial growth of lumber that provides a certain quantifiable utility for construction, an acreage that is mappable onto an agricultural schema, and so on. To know it for one of these purposes is to see it solely in that purpose's light. "Certain forms of knowledge and control require a narrowing of vision" (p. 11). This tunnel vision benefits the expertise gained with regard to the object in focus. The object is simplified and measured, manipulated in calculations, mapped, and schematized. In the course of study, it is normed and generates ideas like the "average tree." This is not a real tree, but it is a concept meant to represent all actual trees, if only in theory and for the purposes of testing and more easily producing statistics. Forests become protolumberyards with available quantities such as average board feet per tree or average tree yield per cord of firewood. The vocabulary also changes. It becomes specialized and more economic/scientific, often marked by a move from collections of singular nouns to singular collective nouns: cows become cattle, trees become timber, plants become a crop.

Semantic and pictorial schemes of representation first rely on people seeing resemblances between different objects that nevertheless can serve the same purpose as each other when reified or purified. No two trees are the same until their resemblance is construed under conditions that isolate their similarities for one purpose and their differences minimized by how that purpose circumscribes the frontier of attributable similitude. Michel Foucault notes that the kind of resemblance so prized by science in this period is really a myth that trades on our inclination toward idolatry. These idols "make us believe that things resemble what we have learned and the theories we have formed for ourselves."[7] The real world — if I am permitted to use such a term here without qualification — is much more irregular than the order we tend to see in it.

At this point, someone will surely object that this ordering and representing is not all so bad. How else are you going to study something you do not know? Scott himself admits that one probably always needs to engage in a certain level of abstraction if the goal is to analyze something (p. 13). The level and type of analysis will obviously determine the kind of model — the kind of simplification — that one uses. Even so, the dangers are twofold.

First, this way of seeing is made to accord with theoretical models arrived at ahead of the actual encounter with the object. The entire process can be self-fulfilling as the work of abstraction is driven by what the analyst hopes to find; thus his modus makes it much more likely to find it. Pierre Bourdieu refers to this seeing as "objectivist." An objectivist treats what he observes as objects but cannot avoid distorting them, because in order to make sense of them, he must catalogue and schematize the objects according to rules and norms that are foreign to what he is describing. The excesses of structuralism traded description for prescription of practices as necessary within those structures that modestly purported only to explain what was happening. Bourdieu illustrates the problematic using what has become a common anthropological motif: gift exchange. In particular, an objectivist methodology tends to ignore the consideration of time. Based on observations of how one family reciprocated with another, descriptions of the rules followed in gift exchange transmuted, in the hands of the objectivists, into sets of predictive conditions by which probability was converted to certainty.[8] It was precisely the *un*certainty of gift exchange that was left out. And it is the temporal element between one gift and the next

---

7. Michel Foucault, *The Order of Things: An Archaeology of the Human Sciences,* trans. Alan Sheridan (London: Routledge, 2002), p. 57.

8. Pierre Bourdieu, *Outline of a Theory of Practice,* trans. Richard Nice (Cambridge: Cambridge University Press, 1977), p. 9.

(if there is a next one) that constitutes the real insight into what it is like to participate in an exchange. Even though an objectivist's system might still be able to accommodate this temporal aspect, so long as the objectivist describes the practice primarily in terms of *rules* (even if they are temporal ones), a model subordinates actual encounters.

The irregularity of the world, like the uncertainty and unpredictability of how people exchange gifts with each other, resists the techniques used for seeing in the world the "smooth things" of objectivists. Reality is always pressing to break free and show its roughness. The factors that are the first to go are the most contingent, such as time. These are factors that are in practice only approached with a great deal of complexity. But they are also readily evacuated by rules that reduce those practices to theory. What is neglected or simply rendered unnecessary is the know-how and skill that a practitioner must have in order to "play the game" well, those qualities that only an insider to that culture would possess, enabling her to respond appropriately to a gift in a wide variety of situations. The actual practitioner is a craftsman who has learned to trust herself to improvise based on skills. But these are left out of the objectivist's calculus insofar as that calculus is a search for principles and rules that govern action.[9] The difference between acting according to rules and acting according to disposition is very often characterized temporally. Even in the presence of principles and rules, once the practice is retemporalized, decisions about whether to follow them, how to follow them, and so on are all matters of learned skill, negotiation, and know-how. To see temporally structured practices clearly, we must preserve the contingency of time.[10] As is the case with all contingent things, the ability to apprehend the importance of tempo requires surmounting the detachment inherent in the vision of the high-modernist, objectivist tradition.

9. Paul Feyerabend argues similarly with regard to the physical sciences: "A theory of science that devises standards and structural elements for *all* scientific activities and authorizes them by reference to 'Reason' or 'Rationality' may impress outsiders — but it is much too crude an instrument for the people on the spot, that is, for scientists facing some concrete research problem" (Feyerabend, *Against Method,* 3rd ed. [London: Verso, 1993], p. 1).

10. Bourdieu, *Outline of a Theory of Practice,* p. 8. The appeal to rules overly formalizes action, as Scott suggests: "Formal order . . . is always and to some considerable degree parasitic on informal processes, which the formal scheme does not recognize, without which it could not exist, and which it alone cannot create or maintain" (p. 310). As James McClendon helpfully puts it, "The shortcut to principles never turns out to be short" (McClendon, *Witness: Systematic Theology* [Nashville: Abingdon, 2000], 3:366).

Second, the real idolatry of objectivist vision arises when, combined with power, a way of seeing becomes indistinguishable from a way of making and remaking. In a different example, Scott argues not only that cadastral maps fail accurately to represent all of what is there in reality, but that this failure is actually its very purpose. By representing only one thing (such as land plots for taxation), they are enlisted in a mechanism of control that is simultaneously enforced by and serves to legitimate the use of state power. The tax system is not just shown on a map, but is precisely created by such maps (Scott, p. 3). Social space and nature are reconfigured by mechanisms that claim only to be representing what is already configured in a certain way. One technique for doing this is to use traditional language in referring to new and often imaginary entities. Consider the contemporary abstract meanings of "market" and "futures." Time is structured in a similar way: the "fiscal year" is the creation of bookkeeping and has nothing to do with the movement of heavenly bodies.

To be sure, there is a prima facie attempt at honest representation in high-modernism's almost obsessive drive toward precision and careful categorization. The first stages in the rise of scientific forestry involved the meticulous counting of trees in wild forests according to size and within a designated plot; the counts were empirically corroborated by yield volumes of wood from sample trees. But categorizing trees into size classes with a focus only on commercial timber production indicates how even precision can be a way of accurately recording some things while totally ignoring others. Restricting the field of vision was the only way to achieve the economic/scientific ends of the emerging industry, "the only way in which the whole forest could be taken in by a single optic" (p. 15).

The crucial move is the next one: the *creation* of forests that made it easier to count trees in the future, to manipulate and control the accounting and managing of the timber industry through the actual manipulation and control of the forests themselves. Description gives way to prediction and anticipation; modes of assessing probability are driven by the need for certainty. Just as Nietzsche described the creation of metaphorical language as an instinctive artistic impulse to create self-images or idols in order to gain mastery over the world, forest creation serves a similar means of control. The planting was done in neat rows and was carried out at the same time so that each mature tree would be the same size. They would also be the same kinds of trees on the same-size space in which the undergrowth was cleared. This further aids the processes of felling and collecting the trees for lumber, because orderly growing means orderly collection, requiring much less skill on the part of those who work the plantations. What began as an attempt to categorize reality turned into attempts to make reality correspond to the simplest possible categories. Charles Taylor discusses how French gardens under Louis XIV, such as those at Versailles, displayed a similar ordering through symmetry and balance. In reaction, the eighteenth-century *jardin anglais* relinquished this ordering to show nature as unforced and was intended to cultivate romantic sentiments.[11] Taylor's account differs from Scott's, however, since Taylor sees the order of French gardens as intending partly to *reflect* an order that was thought to be already present in nature and in which human reason participates. "Our being rational is identified with our being attuned with the order of things, potentially capable of seeing and loving it" (Scott, p. 300). This was part of the heritage of the Enlightenment and incorporates Platonic aspects, finding beauty in order. In contrast, the *jardin anglais* was not primarily meant to be disordered but evocative of awe, which indicates a turn toward the self that Taylor identifies as a noteworthy characteristic of modernity. Below I gesture toward Christian seeing that is equally unrestricted by ordering nature according to reason and looking in awe at chance.

What can be said about the corresponding way of seeing entailed by the practices of scientific forestry? Quite literally, the forest could now be, as Scott says, "synoptically surveyed by the chief forester" (p. 18). This is a woodland counterpart to Bentham's "panopticon," the enabler of the great Enlightenment dream of a God's-eye view. To see one tree is to see them all. But if there is also a lurking disquiet and anxiety, not to mention a very real failure and inadequacy, it is because this way of knowing has only been perfected in fantasy. It expresses the limits of Enlightenment epistemology: the all-knowing subject is shown to be a fraud, a power-wielding fashioner of objects according to very specific knowledges. The panopticon affords a visibility that is, after all, a trap.[12] This type of forester was an expert, though not by way of possessing an expertise of real forests. He was only an expert of scientific forests with the codes, discourses, and methods that go into managing and administrating them. He could precisely and cost-effectively determine needed amounts of fertilizer and predict other expenses, because he was master of a system that minimized extraneous factors.

11. Charles Taylor, *Sources of the Self: The Making of the Modern Identity* (Cambridge, MA: Harvard University Press, 1989), pp. 296-302.

12. Michel Foucault, *Discipline and Punish: The Birth of the Prison,* trans. Alan Sheridan (New York: Vintage, 1995), pp. 195-228.

The problem, as Scott points out, is that even these carefully engineered forests could not be kept entirely from turning into real forests; contingency could not be kept at bay. Factors thought to have been surmounted kept reappearing, setting the experts at a disadvantage insofar as these factors were not permitted to enter into the proficiencies for the limited range of techniques thought necessary for modern forestry's controlled environment. After the first generation of growth, some scientific forests (the first of which were in Germany) began to suffer negative or even disastrous effects. "A new term, *Waldsterben* (forest death), entered the German vocabulary to describe the worst cases. An exceptionally complex process involving soil building, nutrient uptake, and symbiotic relations among fungi, insects, mammals, and flora — which were, and still are, not entirely understood — was apparently disrupted, with serious consequences. Most of these consequences can be traced to the radical simplicity of the scientific forest" (p. 18). Moreover, the relative success of the first generation was largely the result of old-growth remnants remaining in the soil. By neglecting what is now much better understood in forestry and agriculture generally, the experiments of the first scientific forests largely failed. Soil and species diversity were later mimicked and artificially introduced in order to achieve the right balances. The new forests became exercises in virtual ecologies and imitations of old-growth, prescientific forests.

It is important not to miss the obvious point: in dealing with historical attempts to address the *uses* of forests, we are talking about what is essentially the work of an abstraction enacted by civilization. This is a civilization that does not live in the forests themselves, but instead treats them as resources that benefit ways of living that have been staked out somewhere else. In his book *Forests: The Shadow of Civilization,* Robert Pogue Harrison argues that "a historical age reveals something essential about its ideology, its institutions and law, or its cultural temperament, in the manifold ways in which forests are regarded in that age."[13] Harrison relates a fascinating history of civilization as the progressive overcoming of forests in which civilization functions as a geographic description of life in a clearing. Accordingly, civilization has always had a forest-edge that represents wildness and chaos and thus continually haunts the civilized world by being everything to which societies established themselves as alterna-

13. Robert Pogue Harrison, *Forests: The Shadow of Civilization* (Chicago: University of Chicago Press, 1992), p. 115.

tives. The edges are, for Harrison, places that hold promise for people who have forgotten that they live in a clearing that was made possible by overcoming forests. Some will find ways of living at the edge, "where history meets the earth." Harrison refers to these edge places as *provinces.* "The provincial dweller knows that if you pull a rock from out of the ground and turn it upside down, you are likely to find on its underside a covert world of soil, roots, worms, and insects. A nonprovincial dweller either never suspects or else tends to forget such a thing, for the stones that make up his city have already been abstracted from the ground, wiped clean, and made to order. A province, in other words, is a place where stones have two sides."[14] Harrison's worries are similar to Scott's. Both fear that a world of one-sided stones is not the real world, but one that is estranged from reality and easily known and understood for being wiped clean.[15]

The failures of high-modernist objectivity were many. The attempt to take in a practice or object all at once is a move that inevitably requires maintaining a great distance between the observer and what is observed. As a result, it fails to account for contingent factors like time and variety: to see one tree is decidedly *not* to see them all. Overcoming the limitations of this vision often leads to the disastrous manufacture of false versions of reality. All the while, the tenor of the observation is not generous, but is a kind of Stoic *apatheia* that converts into a predatory gaze. It privileges the remove of the observer by legitimating the object's interpretation on the sole basis that it has been understood.

An extended metaphor like this lends itself irresistibly to clichés: the uniformity of scientific forestry techniques rejected diversity in favor of efficiency and, with all of its eggs in one basket, was dangerously vulnerable to all the attendant risks. Scott, too, cannot help but conclude that, for the lumber industry, "the consequences of not seeing the forest for the trees sooner or later became glaring" (p. 21). Nevertheless, forestry is more than an extended metaphor for the pitfalls inherent in any seeing activity, the principal one being Christian witness. As I suggested at the beginning of

14. Harrison, *Forests,* p. 246.

15. Some human populations have always existed in forests, though their doing so is seen as uncivilized by the civilized. Civilization thus obviously involves more than clearing forests; it also means clearing human populations. In her essay "Listening to Grasshoppers: Genocide, Denial, and Celebration," Arundhati Roy notes the nearly organic relationship between "progress" and genocide (Roy, *Field Notes on Democracy: Listening to Grasshoppers* [Chicago: Haymarket, 2009], chap. 9). This is a reminder of the haunting violence encoded in stones "wiped clean."

this section, witness can too easily adopt the modern penchant for assuredly grasping the object of sight in disregard of particulars and even its proclivity for making idols in order to see them comfortably — trading discovery for self-fascination, but still claiming, "We are discoverers!" But if witness is a skill, then the benefits of its proficient exercise will no doubt also issue in seeing all particulars as contingent creations, even the trees of forests. I will explain what I mean by this more fully below.

The main problem illustrated in the above account is that of teleology. Scientific forestry failed to account for the complexities of forests in answering the question "What are forests for?" It is only in light of what something is for that one is able to describe what is going on. By answering that forests are for timber, state interests unduly limited what could be said and done about what is happening in and with them. The care of forests was then restricted to realms that could not recognize any other ends. Certainly forests are for timber. But they are also for thousands of other things, not the least of which is glorifying God.[16] Not to see those other things is a failure of an imagination that is too constrained to look for what it wants to know, to see what it already knows only too well. At its worst, a failed imagination actually supplies the object of its sight by creating it where it did not exist before.

Nevertheless, merely knowing what forests are for is still not enough. Or, rather, knowing is not just a matter of having a *notion,* since any such notions, if they are to have any meaning at all, need to derive from how they are used in a way of life, that is, in everyday practices that require certain manners of knowing and thus are in need of certain kinds of notions. In its detachment, modern objectivity unsuitably and ironically set itself at odds with the nature of actual objects and practices as they exist and are lived in real time. As such, modernity's seers could not help but work within overly theoretical frameworks, removed from the practices that would, in a very different circumstance, have given rise to those frameworks. Scientific forestry is not first an ideology, but a practice (however limited) that corresponds to a particular way of buying, selling, and pro-

---

16. Gregory A. Barton describes how, even though Kant and Hume (in different ways) precipitated doubt about the order and purpose of the natural world, teleology was not altogether removed from consideration. Instead, former notions of stewardship were replaced by newer notions of progress (Barton, *Empire Forestry and the Origins of Environmentalism* [Cambridge: Cambridge University Press, 2002], chap. 2); see also Michael Northcott, *The Environment and Christian Ethics* (Cambridge: Cambridge University Press, 1996), p. 47. The monotonous idea that forests are "for timber" owes to this shift.

ducing followed by corresponding ways of planting, growing, and harvesting. The way that scientific forestry interacted with the land (how it planted and so on) emerged largely from market-determined geographical factors, reflecting a separation from particular plots of land that characterized earlier techniques. Such separation comes at a great cost.

Scientific ways of seeing are pervasive and involve more than attempts to smooth over the roughness of only the natural world. Their limitations can also be shown within the sphere of everyday human living. As I have already noted, the objectivity of scientific ways of seeing yielded maps that claimed to represent configurations of space on account of a more nearly panoptical vision. Michel de Certeau discusses a similar account in how people give verbal descriptions of how their homes and neighborhoods are spatially configured.[17] He contrasts two types of description: the tour-type and the map-type. The tour-type walks you through the house: you turn right past the kitchen and there's the living room. The map-type looks down on the house from above: the living room is next to the kitchen. In describing the layouts of their houses, residents in New York City overwhelmingly used the tour-type of description. This is description that arises from everyday practices of living in the homes and apartments that they are describing, as opposed to the kinds of descriptions that, say, an architect may give of the same spaces. However, like the emergence of scientific forestry, the scientific descriptions of space followed the map-type.

As de Certeau notes, before the modern era, maps were simultaneously suited to — and the products of — particular kinds of activities. A map designed to help pilgrims find a shrine, for example, was also produced by pilgrims. Therefore, even though they were maps, we might just as well think of them as pictorial *itineraries,* that is, tour-type descriptions. Little pictures of sailing ships in the ocean parts of maps and other such symbols both identified what a feature was *for* and how it came to be included on the map, functioning as a kind of tribute to those who first walked or sailed this itinerary. However, according to de Certeau, the modern era saw a change in this. The depictions of maps were slowly separated from the practices that produced them, making them autonomous:

17. Michel de Certeau, *The Practice of Everyday Life,* trans. Steven Rendall (Berkeley: University of California Press, 1984), pp. 118-22. My reading of de Certeau has been enriched by Peter McCray Candler, *Theology, Rhetoric, Manuduction: Or Reading Scripture Together on the Path to God* (Grand Rapids: Eerdmans, 2006).

"[I]f one takes the 'map' in its current geographical form, we can see that in the course of the period marked by the birth of modern scientific discourse (i.e., from the fifteenth to the seventeenth century) the map has slowly disengaged itself from the itineraries that were the condition of its possibility."[18]

There are still maps, of course, but their purpose changes; the itineraries disappear, but the maps remain. This does not mean that tour-type descriptions are no longer given (since New Yorkers mostly continue to describe their homes this way), but that such descriptions no longer have spatial legitimacy in discourses increasingly dominated by scientific modes of perceiving and construing what is perceived. The conventional ways of speaking became more and more alienated from "proper" kinds of discourse, the latter no longer typified by actions like walking through doorways, eating in this room, and sleeping in that room, but by more specialized practices of urban planning and architecture.[19] The language is suited to the aims of experts, whose expert knowledge is increasingly isolated from the knowledge that is required to negotiate living with these objects as everyday realities. The everyday practices are much closer to the contingent realities of space because they do not rely on the givenness of predefined spaces, but only on the continually cultivated practices that give them shape. "[T]he geometrical space of a map, an imaginary representation of all theoretically possible roads and routes, is opposed to the network of beaten tracks, of paths made ever more practicable by constant use."[20]

This description of urban spaces is similar to the above analysis of forests. Both point to how contingency becomes tamed by modes of control that entail corresponding ways of seeing (or passing over) particulars. They are absorbed into esoteric and technical descriptions that also legitimate the kind of seeing on which they depend. Scientific forestry is an apt cognate discipline to the human sciences as the latter came to be modeled on developments in the natural sciences in the modern era. The expertise of the scientific forester and the architect is reflected in the modern bureaucratic manager, whose authority derives from his ability to negotiate

18. De Certeau, *The Practice of Everyday Life,* p. 120.

19. I believe that Nietzsche would have argued for the legitimacy of itineraries, since he claimed that "only thoughts reached by walking have value" (Nietzsche, *Twilight of the Idols or, How One Philosophizes with a Hammer,* in *The Portable Nietzsche,* ed. and trans. Walter Kaufmann [London: Viking Penguin, 1968], sec. 34, p. 471).

20. Bourdieu, *Outline of a Theory of Practice,* pp. 37-38.

and control complex factors in social reality. The modes of this control are expressed as knowledge of a quasi-scientific, technical kind that purports to have at its disposal a neutral body of given social facts. But, as MacIntyre argues, the kind of expertise possessed by the manager is only a "moral fiction" because the kind of knowledge on which it depends is a self-serving fantasy; it simply does not exist.[21] Therefore, when such experts make their claims to authority, they are self-referentially leaning on an ability to organize the very social facts that belong among the creations that they have themselves produced. Like the scientific forester who expertly manages artificial forests, the modern bureaucratic manager has recourse to the same fiction of neutrality that nevertheless disguises the mechanisms of construction. Occurrences on the world political and economic scales are likewise bureaucratic when, for example, the authority that the West exercises over developing nations comes in the form, not only of alleviating troubles, but of having created them to begin with. "Expert" alleviation summarily fits the profile of earlier forms of "development."[22]

*   *   *

Up to this point, we have looked at some instances of how modernity fostered a way of seeing that masters contingency by excluding particulars and edging out practices that require and cultivate those skills that correspond to alternative visions. We must now begin to ask how this narrow vision might be overcome. Can knowledge escape the institutionalization that supervenes on it? Can knowledge be plastic? It is important for us, in answering these and related questions, to take care not to be tempted by the myth of objectivity, which, at least in part, produced the problem in the first place. The role the agent plays already largely determines the way he will observe: "The administrators' forest cannot be the naturalists' forest" (Scott, p. 22). The expert is more likely to see things in terms of his field of expertise than is either an expert in another field or a nonexpert. Whether this is a liability or an asset depends on what is observed, since expertise-as-such does not necessarily ensure or imperil more adequate perception. The point is not to do away with expertise, but to expand what it entails.

Charles Pinches suggests that the *naturalist* possesses precisely this

21. MacIntyre, *After Virtue*, p. 75.
22. Feyerabend, *Against Method*, p. 3.

kind of expanded expertise as one whose knowledge enables greater perception rather than interfering with it.[23] The naturalist uses skills for the classification and individuation of trees, enabling her to see patterns and meanings where the nonnaturalist might simply see an uninteresting grouping. The naturalist does not impose a foreign system but has knowledge that helps in the discovery of what is truly there. Seeing-the-world-as-it-really-is does not mean possessing the right universals, but possessing the right skills. The purposive ends of the naturalist's profession are bound up with its very practice, while at the same time furnishing the practice with its *telos*. Because there is no general expertise that will always prove beneficial to observation, the observer may be either helped or hindered by the naturalist's expertise. After all, scientific foresters were experts within a certain kind of discourse. The reason there is no general expertise is simply that there is no general object of study. The naturalist's practice is more clear-sighted because beholding objects is a constitutive aspect of its exercise. "Skill" is no more a coherent description of a universal quality than "beholding" is a formal technique exercised in isolation from its object. As I will show, this was Iris Murdoch's reason for suggesting how another nonuniversal (love) makes room for contingency.

Within moral philosophy, Murdoch's work is a notable attempt to overcome the myth of objectivity by shifting the nature of observation away from a disinterested gaze to an interested act of beholding and attending in love. Pinches follows Murdoch in considering vision to be an important and timely concept in challenging the ascendancy of humanistic claims about the resoluteness of autonomous human actions as self-creations.[24] When the substance of ethics is organized around an obsession with individual human acts (and thus with decisions, usually in the form of difficult dilemmas), it opens itself up to being problematized in several ways. One way, as Murdoch claims, follows from discerning that every act is performed within an already moral world. Descriptions of moral acts depend on broader descriptions of the world within which such acts

23. Charles R. Pinches, *Theology and Action: After Theory in Christian Ethics* (Grand Rapids: Eerdmans, 2002), p. 7. Pinches calls the naturalist a "forester," but I do not want to confuse Pinches's forester with Scott's scientific forester, so I will use the term "naturalist."

24. This may be more Pinches than Murdoch, since he also follows the early work of Stanley Hauerwas. See esp. "The Significance of Vision: Toward an Aesthethic Ethic," in *Vision and Virtue: Essays in Christian Ethical Reflection* (Notre Dame, IN: University of Notre Dame Press, 1981). Both Pinches and Hauerwas follow Iris Murdoch's critique of Stuart Hampshire.

are intelligible. Without such descriptions of the world, it is impossible for us to know, for example, where a particular act begins and ends. We need to know these things in order to speak of an act as in any sense discrete. How else can we justify universalizing some things and not others? What makes the idea of love more universal than the idea of loving one's enemies? Why is the idea of enemy more universal than the idea of those who harbor a particular kind of grievance or a desire to do a particular kind of harm? Only a moral world that is described in one way rather than another permits moral acts to be described in one way rather than the other.

Consider the significance of distinguishing between sins of omission and sins of commission. Aquinas taught that this well-known distinction is between two categories of the same sin. Not doing something may be just as significant morally as doing something, because, by not doing something one should have done, one is not simply doing nothing, but is crucially doing something else. Thus we may pose the question of why one was doing the other thing, the thing being done that took the place of what should have been done. In other words, our moral world is not only indicated by what we do and fail to do, but also by what we consider as possible actions and — by extension — nonactions, and what exceeds the limits of possible action. Such a world is not simply given; instead, it is the complex intersection of a panoply of these interinterpretive acts. The thing not done was left undone because the moral agent was too busy already doing something else and, depending on what these things are, the agent may be said to be purblind to the real world.[25] Seeing the world clearly means apprehending the moral significance of reality. Changing the subject from free actions within a morally neutral world to the vision necessary to see the real world also changes the ensuing debate. It rightly places in the foreground perception as a moral matter that precedes whatever decisions get made within that world. Moral observation attempts to put the matter this way without implying a separation between will and action. The first ethical question, as H. Richard Niebuhr notes, is not "What should I do?" but "What is going on?"[26] Adequate description depends on adequate perception.

The historical shift at the end of the eighteenth century from tradi-

25. Pinches gives the example of a man who nonchalantly steps over a dead body. The man sees enough to know to step over it, but fails to see it as any different from a rock or a log (Pinches, *Theology and Action*, pp. 167-69).

26. H. Richard Niebuhr, *The Responsible Self: An Essay in Christian Moral Philosophy* (Louisville: Westminster John Knox, 1999), p. 63.

tional foresting methods to scientific forestry is only one instance of wider cultural and intellectual shifts in modernity. Murdoch points out that a similar change was occurring in literature. Influenced by Romanticism and what Murdoch describes as Kant's theory of art, eighteenth-century prose writers generally thought about their role in terms of dispensing information and didactic instruction. Characters in novels were secondary to general ideas about human nature and morality, and thus were made to exemplify these relatively simple and unitary ideas. Apart from making for flat characters and moralistic (and therefore unrealistic) storytelling, this tendency says a good deal about how these writers saw the world. Murdoch refers to these writers (and we may assume, not just writers of literature, but their philosophical analogues) as Symbolists. Even though they were captivated by the senses, and the sense of sight in particular, the Symbolists wanted to see very precise things. Murdoch describes how they wanted to see only "small, clean, resonant, and self-contained things of which the image or symbol was the type."[27] These are just another version of Isaiah's "smooth things" and Harrison's one-sided stones that have been wiped clean: a view of reality purified and purged of its contingency through the imposition of order and corroborated by a particular, prior aesthetic approach.

Ironically, as Murdoch argues, the Symbolists were driven to their love of small dry things by their understanding of freedom.[28] Recalling how Kant conceived of enlightenment, they saw the ordering of reality as the work of reason in which reason and freedom are in perfect harmony; freedom, in fact, simply *is* the freedom of reason itself. As such, what was really going on was that the contingent represented the ultimate threat to a human freedom understood as independent choice. Consequently, in the name of freedom, anything exceeding reason's capacity must be tamed and brought to order. The fear of contingency transmutes to the celebration of necessity, which it is reason's task to elaborate. Necessary truths of reason are the most beautiful things. Murdoch notes that fearing contingency was only a symptom of a greater fear of reality:

> What is feared is history, real beings, and real change. Whatever is contingent, messy, boundless, infinitely particular, and endlessly still to be

---

27. Iris Murdoch, "The Sublime and the Beautiful Revisited," in *Existentialists and Mystics: Writings on Philosophy and Literature* (New York: Penguin, 1999), p. 273.

28. Murdoch quotes T. E. Hulme: "We must find beauty in small dry things" (Murdoch, *Existentialists and Mystics*, p. 273).

explained; what is desired is the timeless non-discursive whole which has its significance completely contained in itself. . . . The Symbolists desired an art which would have satisfied Plato.[29]

Though they are difficult to write, the best novels display a variety of different people.[30] Murdoch faults writers in the eighteenth century and again in the twentieth with succumbing to the constant temptation to make their characters into puppets, not really allowing them to be themselves, to live their own lives apart from being instrumentalized in one way or another. Puppet characters tend to be one-dimensional or are in some other way made to play too determinedly a part in a didactic story. But real life is not that way: real people are not reducible to types, and lives are not lived in order to make a point.[31]

While it is common to hear such protestations in literary circles, Murdoch suspects we were not merely let down by overweening writers and the poverty of the philosophical concepts on which they drew. Instead, she sees the problem as a spiritual and moral failure. The fear of contingency that produces bad art appeals to our desire to be consoled by myth and fantasy. This is a sentiment Nietzsche shared. Murdoch comments: "The modern writer . . . attempts to console us by myths or by stories. On

29. Murdoch, *Existentialists and Mystics*, p. 274. See also Iris Murdoch, *Metaphysics as a Guide to Morals* (New York: Penguin, 1994), chap. 1. Murdoch concludes the latter book with a self-critical reflection that perhaps her Platonism, too, is in danger of being a fantasy generated by her own need to be reassured by smooth things, and thus discovering a pattern in Plato's texts that is not really there (p. 510).

30. Murdoch is decidedly Wittgensteinian in her approach to novels. For example, Terry Eagleton speaks of how Wittgenstein's *Philosophical Investigations* accomplishes this: it "seeks to return us to the rough ground of our ambiguous, fuzzy-edged practices. It is this nose for the density and irregularity of things, their distinctive, untotalizable tones and textures, that links Wittgenstein's thought to the great European tradition of realist fiction . . . . [Wittgenstein's was a] generous-hearted refusal to regard the unfinished, rough-hewn, or approximate as conceptual flaws" (Eagleton, "Mystic Mechanic," *Times Literary Supplement*, April 29, 2005, p. 10).

31. In her novels, the contemporary writer Anne Tyler is remarkably successful in portraying contingent characters. For example, Barnaby Gaitlin in *A Patchwork Planet* (New York: Ballantine, 1998) disappointingly fails to appreciate and maintain small triumphs but cannot be reduced to either hero or antihero — and is all the more believable because of it. If Tyler's world is "patchwork" in its contingency, it surely reflects what Nancy Cartwright suggests regarding the limitations of science: "The laws that describe this world are a patchwork, not a pyramid" (Cartwright, *The Dappled World: A Study of the Boundaries of Science* [Cambridge: Cambridge University Press, 1999], p. 1).

the whole: his truth is sincerity and his imagination is fantasy."[32] Forms and symbols (the stuff of grander myths) convince us that life is not merely all about chance, that we are not forsaken in midair, that randomness is not actually the heart of things. Like Nietzsche, Murdoch thinks that overcoming these fantasies is a matter of summoning an exceptional courage that is able to face the fact that life is indeed all about chance and lacks a *telos*. In contrast to the Enlightenment, true freedom is freedom for contingency that releases objects to an infinite number of chance encounters and occurrences.

Christian thought has something to say about this courage, though it seems clear that it cannot finally share Murdoch's and Nietzsche's metaphysics. Instead, Christianity understands contingency as gift and part of God's nonnecessary creation. The Christian *telos* is not just another totalizing, consoling myth (as Murdoch thinks), but issues in a hope in the constant presence of God to creation that will not leave it fated to pointless existence.[33] Murdoch misses the point when she accuses Christianity of romanticizing death: she thinks the consolation of purgatory and the positive role of suffering are attempts to resolve the otherwise tragic contingency that death denotes.[34] Her error, however, is not so much that she gets Christianity wrong, but that she misconceives contingency itself. For her, contingency is a tragic feature of existence. So long as contingency is not thought of as a function of *creation,* death is and should be unbearably tragic, merely exposing, as it does, that existence is gloriously free from having any point whatsoever. Not only may Christian thought be free from romanticizing death in the way Murdoch thinks, but it may refuse to share her own ironic romanticization of contingency in the name of the givenness of tragedy (which, we may add, paradoxically supposes its own doctrine of creation).

Still, Murdoch is right to challenge as false those notions of freedom that require codifying reality in consoling myth. Because the desire for

32. Murdoch, "Against Dryness," in *Existentialists and Mystics*, p. 292.

33. These statements might seem in tension with what I have said above about our inability to give a theory of contingency. However, the point is not that we cannot say *anything* about contingency but rather that what we say about it must not become a theory about how contingency is really necessary. Linking contingency with creation is thus crucial, since creation is by grace, that is, neither random nor predictable. Murdoch complained that Christianity destroys the contingent through totalizing metaphysical theories (Murdoch, *Metaphysics as a Guide to Morals,* esp. p. 196).

34. Murdoch, *The Sovereignty of Good* (London: Routledge, 2002), p. 80.

consolation is a moral problem, the solution is also moral, though it is not immediately related to choice as it is for Kant and the Symbolists. She points out how the virtues function on a level prior to any choice, reason, or action, since they are first concerned with right seeing, that is, moral observation. Seeing other people as they actually exist, apprehending contingent particulars, is the purpose of virtue.[35] The virtues are necessary to be freed from neurotic self-possession, according to which one attempts to render the world intelligible in consoling terms.

It is appropriate to ask which virtues Murdoch has in mind and how they are acquired if we are not to be left with an overly abstract or purely methodological account. Nietzsche thought the courage necessary to overcome the "cult of the untrue" is suicidal since we would find the sheer extent of our delusion unbearable. Instead, we too easily think the fact that we have come to terms with a few details about ourselves — made possible by what we have allowed ourselves to see reflected back to us in a world of our own making — somehow makes us courageous. In reality, though, it only reinforces what it pretends to unmask.[36] Perhaps Murdoch suspected as much when, in another essay, she invokes the moral imagination to indicate how we can overcome fantasy: "I can only choose within the world I can *see,* in the moral sense of 'see' which implies that clear vision is a result of moral imagination and moral effort."[37] The imagination is directed to the object of perception: attention as opposed to mere looking. Attention is a special kind of looking that involves moral effort and discipline for seeing what is really there. In this, Murdoch distances herself from modern assumptions about the neutrality of perception. This is made plain in an example that runs throughout her essay "The Idea of Perfection." Murdoch asks readers to consider a woman who disapproves of her daughter-in-law, thinking her to be undignified and crass at times. As a description, this is clearly a judgment on the part of the mother-in-law, even though she never speaks about it or consciously lets it affect her behavior.

35. Murdoch, "The Sublime," p. 284.

36. Friedrich Nietzsche, *The Gay Science,* trans. Josefine Nauckhoff (Cambridge: Cambridge University Press, 2001), sec. 107. But elsewhere Nietzsche is more genuine about the need for virtue, since he took the fact that seeing is a moral matter as an indication that clear sight requires the virtue of courage. "How much truth can a spirit *bear,* how much truth can a spirit *dare?* that became for me more and more the real measure of value. Error (belief in the ideal) is not blindness, error is cowardice" (Nietzsche, *Ecce Homo,* trans. R. J. Hollingdale [London: Penguin, 1992], p. 4).

37. Murdoch, "The Idea of Perfection," in *The Sovereignty of Good,* pp. 35-36.

But Murdoch emphasizes that the woman fails to discern reality because she lacks love and justice toward her daughter-in-law. Just opening her eyes is not a moral move sufficient to keep fantasy at bay, since looking must be accompanied by virtues such as honesty and patience.

Murdoch's explanation helps us to see why states (in their perception of the natural world) and institutions (in their perception of human community) give distorted accounts of reality that lead to failures like forest death. So long as the moral dimension and its concomitant virtues are absent from seeing and the techniques that support vision, perception is alienated from the object of sight. This yields a distorted picture. The naturalist, with a naturalist's mind, performs a moral endeavor and is engaged in a moral practice in her respect for forests. Her respect issues in the patience and humility necessary for seeing forests as they really are — full of variety and contingency. Though Murdoch is surely more interested in human individuals than trees, the point is the same: the best observer is not disinterested, objective, and neutral, but practically involved, prejudiced, and inclined in love toward what is being observed.[38] This point must not be construed as a general statement about subjectivity, as though somehow merely having a subjective (partial) standpoint makes one a competent seer. Any subjectivity will be conditioned by the object; therefore, it matters what the object is.

All of this, admittedly, sounds paradoxical. On the one hand, Murdoch wants us to live like good writers, who let other characters be themselves, respect the freedom of others, and do not try to overcome and master the contingency of reality. On the other hand, she does not conclude that we therefore need to be more objective, more removed from others in order to give them room to exercise their freedom. She actually wants us to be *more* involved, not less. Of course, this is not a paradox at all, except according to the canons of modernity, which did the opposite of what Murdoch thinks we should. They claim neutrality and distance but, in fact, disguise their involvement and still impose their own order. Modernity accomplishes this by appealing to freedom, not freedom of the object, as Murdoch wants to recover, but freedom of the agent. The agent and object coinhere in the involvement of the one with the other in practical reason,

38. Samuel Byrskog's study of witnesses in ancient and biblical traditions indicates the same point, namely, that the best eyewitness is not a dispassionate observer but a participant in what is being reported (Byrskog, *Story as History — History as Story: The Gospel Tradition in the Context of Ancient Oral History* [Tübingen: Mohr Siebeck, 2000], esp. chap. 4).

which, as Charles Taylor notes, was given over to *procedural* rather than substantive articulation in the thought world of modernity. By contrast, for the ancients — and for Aristotle in particular — practical reason was *substantive*. The use of reason issued in perceiving a certain amount of order already present in nature and in actions that follow from that perception.[39] This is equivalent to Murdoch's dictum about acting only in a world one can see. However, modernity made practical reason bear the burden of needing to justify actions by converting what was substantive into what is procedural. It became more important to be able to justify the primacy of individual choice than to enable the means by which reason gives rise to one form of action rather than another. However, the procedural account of practical reason accomplishes this at the expense of practical engagement with real life. "We gain knowledge, but only to lose the world."[40]

Like the engagement that practical reasoning denotes, Murdoch's move toward emphasizing love might similarly seem to imperil attempts at objectivity. Modernity's ideal observer was not only practically detached from its object, but also possessed an unemotive aloofness devoted to the principle that love is blind. Even Nietzsche, who otherwise wastes no sentimentality over exposing the myth of objectivity, nevertheless takes love to be positively deceptive, remarking that love is "the state in which man sees things most decidedly as they are not. The power of illusion is at its peak here."[41] Nietzsche clearly worries that love accompanies self-deception. But here we become aware of the temptation to turn love into a technique for achieving clear sight when love (as we have said regarding practice, virtue, and later, as I will suggest, regarding story) functions as a secondary category that does not tell us much apart from considering its object. Put

39. Taylor, *Sources of the Self,* p. 86.

40. Cary Wolfe, "Exposures," in *Philosophy and Animal Life,* ed. Stanley Cavell et al. (New York: Columbia University Press, 2008), p. 5. I am grateful to Jonathan Tran for alerting me to Wolfe's essay. Modernity's procedural reason scrutinized instrumentality using mathematical probability and deduction, a practical form of Cartesian rational disengagement — a kind of scientific contemplation at odds with earlier ascetic and scientific practice. See also Taylor, *Sources of the Self,* p. 243. Bourdieu is among those involved in the social scientific recovery of a substantive practical reason: "It is possible to abandon the sovereign point of view from which objectivist idealism orders the world, without being forced to relinquish the 'active aspect' of apprehension of the world by reducing cognition to a mere recording: it suffices to situate oneself *within* 'real activity as such,' i.e., in the practical relation to the world" (Bourdieu, *Outline of a Theory of Practice,* p. 96). The "active aspect of apprehension" is a substantive practical reason.

41. Friedrich Nietzsche, *The Antichrist,* in *The Portable Nietzsche,* sec. 23, p. 591.

simply, love is an abstraction that cannot possibly curb self-deception on its own, since we would need to know what and who is loved.

This is the argument Martha Nussbaum makes in her article "Love's Knowledge," where she argues that even though love can expose self-deception and serve truth, it may in other cases simply underwrite falsehood.[42] Wanting to know the difference leads to the question: Where is the criterion of truth? But even in asking this question, Nussbaum is aware that the demand for such a criterion can also itself be a ruse of self-deception that epistemology alone is ill-equipped on its own to surmount. The problem manifests itself when love functions as a philosophical principle abstracted from its actual exercise. Against this, Nussbaum explains how the telling of a love story overcomes the philosophical limitations. "We suggested that theories about love, especially philosophical theories, fall short of what we discovered in the story because they are too simple. They want to find just one thing that love is in the soul, just one thing that knowledge is, *instead of looking to see what is there.* The story could show us a complexity, a many-sidedness, a temporally evolving plurality that was not present in the explicit theories."[43]

Nussbaum does not argue that philosophy is useless compared to what literature is capable of doing. She acknowledges that philosophy is often the discipline that should be credited with initiating the inspection in the first place, when it asks the fundamental questions and says, "Look and see." Nevertheless, for the same reason that Murdoch spent much more of her time writing novels than philosophy, Nussbaum recognizes that it is in literature's performances that philosophy's warnings against cataleptic certainty and invitations to observe complexity hold the most promise. At the same time, the answer is not to be found in a genre alone, because "no form of discourse is cataleptic. None contains in its very style and methods a sure and certain criterion of truth. None is incapable of being used for self-deceptive ends."[44] Nussbaum's conclusion — that both philosophy and literature can be used for either truth or falsity — resembles her comments about how love can similarly be used. So long as love constitutes a kind of genre or technique, it also risks the abstraction of disciplines that are articulated according to ends removed from their actual exercise. What

---

42. Martha C. Nussbaum, "Love's Knowledge," in *Love's Knowledge: Essays on Philosophy and Literature* (Oxford: Oxford University Press, 1990), p. 261.

43. Nussbaum, "Love's Knowledge," p. 283 (emphasis added).

44. Nussbaum, "Love's Knowledge," p. 284.

Nussbaum advocates is attentive and loving conversation between literature and philosophy, that is, an exercise of both disciplines that always tries to exceed the ways either of them has so far been construed and defined. Love is the *way* the conversation transcends each party in recognition that no matter which word each makes regarding the simplicity of love ("it is one thing"), it is not final. In the language used above, nothing we can say about love can ever be a truer description than its exercise.

However, insofar as love functions for Murdoch as the key to granting contingency its freedom, it is likely that she has not started back far enough. We can agree with Murdoch that we can only choose within a world we can see, and that what we see is the outcome of morality, and so what we see is simultaneously a moral world. Nevertheless, the morality that conditions how we see is still one step removed from the activities and practices that give rise to moral concepts.[45] The way a naturalist sees forests is not a first principle, but results from engaging in specific activities with forests as naturalists practice them. Every way of seeing can be pushed back still to the practices that engender it. So, while Murdoch offers a rich ground for a virtue-based metaethics, she cannot point to any antecedent practices.[46] She needs to speak of the Good metaphysically as

45. Karl Barth similarly complains that Kant's categorical imperative is not actually an imperative itself since it does not do what, say, a prophet does, namely, set aside the general formula and declare what should be done in this specific situation or on this particular question. As it stands, Kant's formula is a version of what Barth called "general ethics": "at best an insight *about* it. This is something quite different" (Barth, *Ethics,* trans. G. W. Bromiley [Edinburgh: T. & T. Clark, 1992], p. 78); cf. *CD* II/2, p. 518. On Barth's critique of Kant, see particularly Nigel Biggar, *The Hastening That Waits: Karl Barth's Ethics* (Oxford: Clarendon, 1993), p. 17. David Clough successfully shows that it is wrong to take the negative side of Barth's dialectic to reflect an ultimate indeterminacy of a "contentless ethic," as some have supposed. Those who do so miss the way that Christian activity is tied to a concrete encounter with God, in which a subsequent ethic may lack a rational foundation but does not lack content as a result. Such thinking is still Kantian (Clough, *Ethics in Crisis: Interpreting Barth's Ethics* [Aldershot, UK: Ashgate, 2005], pp. 38-41).

46. Stanley Hauerwas often appends to Murdoch's dictum: ". . . and we can only see a world we can speak," raising the Wittgensteinian element beyond the level of Murdoch's own account. See, e.g., Hauerwas, *The Peaceable Kingdom: A Primer in Christian Ethics* (Notre Dame, IN: University of Notre Dame Press, 1983), p. 117. I think this is surely right, but it should not mislead us to assume that language itself (in the form of description) is prior to seeing in a way that is separable from the practices that give rise to that language. As Wittgenstein liked to show, the language of chess ("you cannot castle while in check") is prior to the possibilities allowed for by that language; but it is also unimaginable that you would have chess language apart from chess. I am sure I learned this from Hauerwas.

that in light of which we see correctly. But this may only be a desperate move to rescue her account of love from its lack of a *telos:* If life is contingent, what is it contingent on? The Good is metaphysical but not teleological, making her account tragic. Murdoch's evacuated Good does not admit of true transcendence because she cannot imagine how, as a metaphysical idea, it might simultaneously uphold the particularity of things while also challenging a metaphysical doctrine that leaves them unresolved and ambiguous. Her mistaken refusal to think of her "Good" as God is merely a function of not being able to imagine this.[47]

Nietzsche had a similarly tragic — though increasingly nonmetaphysical — account: in an early work he describes tragedy as the contrast between the world of essences and the world of appearances where the essence of nature is purposeless. Ironically, tragedy both exposes as a lie the myth that culture is the only reality, while also bringing "metaphysical comfort" that allows us to celebrate the purposelessness of life.[48]

It is useful to distinguish acts from practices. What Pinches calls an act and Murdoch calls a choice are both subsequent to an already moral world. Therefore, right seeing of that world is crucial for right acting and right choosing. Therefore, a practice is what one is engaged in that enables and activates a certain kind of vision. Good practices yield clear-sightedness (particularly of contingency, as I argue) and bad practices yield fantasy (and master contingency, which in reality proves impossible except as a construction that anticipates idolatry). Nevertheless, too strong a separation between love and action erects a false choice. Murdoch explicitly chose the mother-in-law example to demonstrate that "whatever is in question as *happening* happens entirely in M's [the mother-in-law's] mind."[49] In this, Murdoch is right to challenge those moral philosophers who located morality exclusively in the domain of acts, ignoring intention and emotion.

Even so, by implying that seeing clearly results from an internal choice to love, she seems to leave little room for the routine practices that are both involved in shaping vision and embody the transformations of love beyond simply a change of attitude. In contrast, and to anticipate the

47. "[A]ll truth is indeed contingent, on God. . . . It opens us up to the sheer profundity and inexhaustibility of things" (Colin Gunton and Robert W. Jenson, "The *Logos Ensarkos* and Reason," in *Reason and the Reasons of Faith,* ed. Paul J. Griffiths and Reinhard Hütter (New York: T. & T. Clark, 2005), p. 85.

48. Friedrich Nietzsche, *The Birth of Tragedy,* trans. Ronald Speirs (Cambridge: Cambridge University Press, 1999), secs. 7-8.

49. Murdoch, "Perfection," p. 17.

argument of the next section, consider Karl Barth's claim that only the one who does the Word of God hears the Word of God, being taken hold of *in the very act of doing.*[50] Like the true seer, the true hearer is engaged in a form of life that makes clear apprehension more likely. This allows us to approach more closely than does Murdoch the crucial questions: What are love's practices? What is its form of life? What are vision's practices and the corresponding objects of clear vision? I addressed these questions partially in the first chapter. Here we may return to the forest and imagine it according to Christian seeing.

*　　*　　*

God is more complex even than forests. Nevertheless, the love of forests is associated with the love of God in this way: Augustine knew that nothing could be loved properly apart from the love of God, since loving God reorders all other loves. For example, the Christian love of neighbor derives from first loving God and is exercised for the sake of loving God, meaning that there is no conflict between the love of God and neighbor: "[E]very human being *qua* human being, should be loved on God's account; and God should be loved for himself."[51] Thomas Aquinas followed Augustine in arguing that the knowledge of God's creatures in love and love of God are in a kind of circular relationship to each other.[52] God is known first through his creation, since human knowledge is limited by the finitude appropriate to creatures. But at the same time, love of God precedes love of other things and flows to them from our love of God. As other things are known in the light of charity, they will be known more perfectly for what they truly are. If creation is, as Christians believe, the work of love (both as an act in the past and as the continual presence of God upholding what he created), then love discloses the real by illuminating the true nature of things. This is not because they are being apprehended as things-in-themselves, but as things-in-God, which is to say that they belong to God and are steadfastly sustained by God's spiritual closeness and creative activity.[53] The proper love of forests, as of all God's

50. Barth, *Ethics,* p. 15.

51. Augustine, *On Christian Teaching,* trans. R. P. Green (Oxford: Oxford University Press, 1997), p. 21 (I:59).

52. Aquinas, *ST,* II-II.27.4.

53. Of course, this contrasts strongly with Murdoch, not only in her atheism, but in her regard for the sheer *whatness* of the world that she took to be the reason for loving things as they are, namely, that they exhibit a randomness that is inscribed into the very universe. As a

creatures, depends on first loving God. This love is constantly exceeding it-self because "the more we love God the better our love is."[54]

In a christological key, the one who sees clearly loves the truth. This is first the case because Jesus, the truth par excellence, discloses himself to those who love him.[55] That the truth is known by love does not imply that we come to love what we already believe in, but that *our knowledge is only constituted as knowledge as it is loved for being true.* A scientific forester who sees only one thing in a forest is not only seeing wrongly because he is seeing without love. He is also loving the wrong thing. He does not desire the truth about the forest (which in reality is only ever a kind of forest-in-God) but wants the forest to be something it is not, because of a disordered love for control, mastery, and a refusal to acknowledge trees as created gifts. "It is easy to live in a world where pieces of wood are just pieces of wood. But to live in such a way is not to live in the world 'as it is.' For to live in the world 'as it is' is to be the kind of people who can see that everything has been created to glorify its creator."[56] This is a realism without empiri-cism: what is real is what is created and sustained in love.[57] Seeing the

---

consequence, any wonder at the world is nontransformative. This is how Peter Ochs reads Wittgenstein and William James, in contrast to Charles Peirce, who he suggests offers a differ-ent kind of wonder — one that is nontragic because it is a wonder that transforms communi-ties through horror and gratitude mediated by love of God. Ochs contrasts this to "wonder-as-such" (in his review of Stanley Hauerwas's *With the Grain of the Universe,* in *Modern Theol-ogy* 19, no. 1 [January 2003]: 77-88). It is hard to know if this is a fair reading of Wittgenstein, but it would not be surprising if Murdoch read him this way. By suggesting, in this section, that Wendell Berry's recommendation of gratitude in the face of contingency is not "wonder-as-such," I see him in line with Wittgenstein — against Murdoch. After all, there are many languages, and we should not be surprised that Berry and Murdoch speak differently. McClendon rightly notes that, even if Wittgenstein was a Christian, he did not produce a Christian philosophy, nor could he have on his own grounds, since a life is not reducible to a philosophy. Murdoch knew this, too, but she lived a different life. See McClendon, *Witness,* chap. 6.

54. Aquinas, *ST,* II-II.27.6.

55. Bruce Marshall concludes as much in *Trinity and Truth* (Cambridge: Cambridge University Press, 2000), p. 181: "The gospel of Jesus Christ, it seems, proclaims a truth which cannot be known unless it is also loved (see 2 Thess. 2:16)." Similarly, Aquinas describes the order of things in that "God is knowable and lovable for Himself, since He is essentially truth and goodness itself, whereby other things are known and loved" (*ST,* II-II.27.4).

56. Stanley Hauerwas and Philip D. Kenneson, "The Church and/as God's Non-Violent Imagination," *Pro Ecclesia* 1, no. 1 (Fall 1992): 76-88 (esp. p. 83).

57. Wittgenstein thought that achieving a realism without empiricism was the "hard-est thing" in philosophy. *Remarks on the Foundations of Mathematics,* rev. ed., ed. G. H. von

world without God is not seeing the world as it really is, the way that it unfolds before the neutral observer who is armed with a sincere determination to use empirical capacities of reason, balance, and evenhandedness,
doggedly scattering all prejudice and dispatching every possible attachment. In a monumental irony to the spirit of the modern age, such an observer, in removing herself from every possible attachment, forsakes the
purpose and goal of everything and so cannot help but arrive at attenuated
and limited knowledge. Trees defined by the practices of agribusiness are
decontextualized from the nurturing of life necessary for people who can
see that if the world belongs to God, life is a mystery that is always insufficiently represented when isolated from practices of care. A naturalist who
loves forests knows he is *part of* the nature he observes and he can never
claim empirical detachment.[58]

Staying with bucolic themes for the moment, consider Wendell
Berry's critique of the seeing involved in economic practices determined by
consumption and dominated by images drawn from the marketplace. He
suggests two alternative cultures or economies of seeing the world: industrial and agrarian. An industrial culture that focuses on production
unsurprisingly thrives on consumption, which in turn requires the shaping
of desires according to anticipation and short memories. Consumers will of
economic necessity run up against — constantly and quickly — dissatisfaction with what they consume: the things that previously delighted them
and the delight itself must quickly fade. "We buy new stuff on the promise

Wright, R. Rhees, and G. E. M. Anscombe, trans. G. E. M. Anscombe (Cambridge, MA: MIT
Press, 1983), sec. VI:23. Sabina Lovibond comments on Wittgenstein this way: "The difficulty
is presumably this: we wish to purge our critical concepts (such as 'truth', 'rationality', 'validity') of the absolutist or transcendent connotations attaching to them in the context of a
foundationalist epistemology; but we do not wish, in the process, to find ourselves abolish-
ing those concepts altogether. What is difficult is to pursue the twofold aim of showing, on
one hand, that it does not make sense to look for a source of authority external to human
practice which would *certify* as true (e.g.) those propositions that we *call* true; while, on the
other hand, resisting the proffered alternative to our former, metaphysically contaminated
use of those concepts — an alternative which would consist simply in jettisoning the concepts in question and replacing them by others" (Lovibond, *Realism and Imagination in Ethics* [Oxford: Basil Blackwell, 1983], p. 45).

58. Wendell Berry points out how our language about nature reveals what we think
about our relationship to it. He critiques how the word "environment" is often used like the
word "surroundings" — "a place that one is *in* but not *of*" (Berry, *Life Is a Miracle* [Washing-
ton, DC: Counterpoint, 2000], p. 25). Berry's criticism illustrates how you cannot be both an
objective observer and a conservationist.

of satisfaction because we have forgot the promised satisfaction for which we bought our old stuff."[59] What we anticipate satisfaction in is not the "stuff," but in consuming, purchasing, and acquiring. This makes industrialism first an economy and only secondarily a culture; in other words, it is premised primarily on exchange rather than use. By contrast, agrarianism is only economic on the household and local scale, and because it is directly tied to the land from which it arises, it is first a culture that is lived and only secondarily generalizable as an idea. To illustrate this contrast, Berry discusses the ways of seeing a horse that Allen Tate describes:

> This modern mind sees only half of the horse — that half which may become a dynamo, or an automobile, or any other horsepowered machine. If this mind had much respect for the full-dimensioned, grass-eating horse, it would never have invented the engine which represents only half of him. The religious mind, on the other hand, has this respect; it wants the whole horse, and it will be satisfied with nothing less.[60]

Though I am not sure what a "religious mind" is, we may surely agree that because the agrarian mind sees the whole horse, it therefore has something in common with the *Christian* mind. Seeing the whole horse is like seeing the whole forest rather than just one aspect limited by its functional use in another application and another economy.

The Christian mind displays love of the object. The exchange of love never diminishes love, risks poverty, or fears loss. Nor is the exchange of love at odds with its use, as is the case for the consumer of things. Rather, love is enriched and grown through exchange because its exchange *is* its use. It gives itself freely in the belief not only that there will be more, but under the conviction that the more will only ever come through the free gifts of love. Likewise, the respect Tate describes is the love of the object: this love enables seeing that is not prejudiced toward limitation. It does not stop short by policing and truncating its engagements in advance of them. Rather, the Christian mind exhibits a love for creation that is exercised and perfected by loving God, as I have argued. But this love is decidedly practical in the way that it grows on account of following Jesus in or-

59. Wendell Berry, "The Whole Horse," in *The Art of the Commonplace: The Agrarian Essays of Wendell Berry*, ed. Norman Wirzba (Washington, DC: Counterpoint, 2002), p. 237.

60. Quoted in Berry, "The Whole Horse," p. 236. Elsewhere, Berry comments that "if you think creatures are machines, you have no religion" (*Life Is a Miracle*, p. 51).

der to see him. This following is analogous to everyday practices like forestry and agriculture. Love is not just a technique that allows right vision to be separated from right action, because the practices that emerge from such vision are not merely consequent to it. Instead, they are partially determinative of what it means for sight to be undistorted by "industrial" instrumentalization.

> The agrarian mind begins with the love of fields and ramifies in good farming, good cooking, good eating, and gratitude to God. Exactly analogous to the agrarian mind is the sylvan mind that begins with the love of forests and ramifies in good forestry, good woodworking, good carpentry, etc., and gratitude to God. These two kinds of mind readily intersect and communicate; neither ever intersects or communicates with the industrial-economic mind. The industrial-economic mind begins with ingratitude, and ramifies in the destruction of farms and forests.[61]

We might, then, also say that the sylvan mind is quite opposed to the mind of the scientific forester.[62] Berry warns that the slogan "think globally, act locally" is a distortion since it is simply not possible to think globally: this is not first a statement about the human mind, but about the size of the earth.[63]

There is a difference between knowing something and "figuring it out." The former maintains a relationship of love and respect for the object, and the latter attempts to possess, manage, and own it. When Berry says that "life can only be known by being experienced," he is targeting reductive science (such as bioengineering) that tries to know life through

61. Berry, "The Whole Horse," p. 241.

62. Stephen Sillett of Humboldt State University is the kind of naturalist who exemplifies the sylvan mind. Sillett's work among the giant redwoods of Northern California is described in Richard Preston, "Climbing the Redwoods," *New Yorker*, February 14 and 21, 2005, pp. 212-25. Sillett is a botanist specializing in tree-climbing in order to study redwood canopies, sometimes over 300 feet above the ground. It has long been assumed that there was not much of interest up there; but Sillett and his colleagues have found numerous epiphytes (plants that grow on other plants), hanging gardens of ferns or "fern mats" which can weigh tons, and even unidentified species of earthworms. Even though Sillett is engaged in a scientific pursuit, his discoveries clearly owe to a way of attending to trees that is anything but scientific forestry as described here. Perhaps it is best described as *relational*: "[A tree is] a being. It's a person from a plant's point of view" (p. 224).

63. Wendell Berry, "The Futility of Global Thinking," in *Learning to Listen to the Land*, ed. Bill Willers (Washington, DC: Island Press, 1991), pp. 150-56.

prediction and control.[64] Instead, life is a beautiful mystery that calls for rejoicing, gratitude, and wonder, and it should not be surprising that figuring it out often means destroying it, which is an indication that, even if it has been figured out, it has actually not been understood at all.

The discussion in this section has turned on two complementary notions necessary for limiting the distortions of illusion: love and skill.[65] The two are not only complementary, but in fact require each other. A skill must be practiced in love of its object; otherwise, it risks overpowering the object's freedom. This often has disastrous consequences. "[T]he more [people] surround themselves with objectivity, the greater is the wrong they inflict upon others."[66] Conversely, love must be accompanied by skill; otherwise, it risks disengagement and self-love. Moral vision involves us in the pursuit of knowing the truth about ourselves and the world. Like any skill worth having or love worth pursing, such vision arises out of discipline and transformation, the shape of which is conditioned by its object. Yet moral vision is not only necessary for accepting the realities of a contingent world against the limits and self-deception complicit in the truncated pseudovision of objectivity. These lessons are also preeminently valuable for coming to terms with what it means to see like a witness of the resurrected Christ. Such witnesses do not suddenly see once and for all as they clamor out of a cave into the bright sun, but they continually train their sight by looking for the contingent Christ in the unexpected. They adjust their vision to a focus and clarity appropriate to the free and unconstrained motion of one whose living evokes relationships in constant need of being sustained. The constant motion that this implies and that is required of Christian discipleship consistently faces temptations to grind to a halt, to arrive too soon, and to make premature peace with the way things are by freezing a rushing river.

The contingent nature of things is not an expression of randomness

---

64. Berry, *Life Is a Miracle*, p. 8. Berry uses the example of cloning sheep: "Cloning . . . is not a way to improve sheep. [It is] only a pathetic attempt to make sheep predictable" (p. 7). I take Berry to be making a subtly different point from the "playing God" argument, though this is part of it. For Berry, the hubris is less about creating, and more about refusing to love creation. When God plays God, he does not just create, but he *tends* to his creation. Berry might well suggest that we should play God more, not less.

65. Scott uses the term *metis* to describe the practical knowledge he has in mind. I believe that "skill" works just as well, given how I have developed the theme here.

66. Karl Barth, *The Epistle to the Romans*, trans. Edwyn C. Hoskyns (Oxford: Oxford University Press), p. 479.

and chance that needs to be tamed and controlled; rather, it testifies to the creative activity of a God who cannot be grasped. In not grasping God, Christian witness can turn to God's creation dispossessed of a vision that seeks to control but that only re-creates reality as a self-image, an idol. The theological presumption of so many fundamentalisms is just as much a failure of discipleship as liberalism's disinterested observers. The former "seeks," and the latter stands at a distance. Both refuse to follow. In the distorted vision of an anemic discipleship, the current order of things unsurprisingly only looks like a version of what has already been grasped, where there can be nothing genuinely new or real, and the maintenance of stasis privileges the self-images of the powerful. In the following section I explore how a politics of witness confronts power in order to *come forward* and testify. After all, as Nietzsche knew, those whose steadfast fidelity to virtue compels them to want to know the truth will no doubt pay a price for it.

PART II

COMING FORWARD

And look! He is speaking with outspokenness [*parrhēsia*], and they are saying nothing to him!

Can it be that the rulers really do not know that this is the Christ?

John 7:26 (my translation)

In this world, history continues not because of what kings and presidents might do but because ravens keep alive a prophet starving in a desert (1 Kings 17) and because even as kings and presidents count their people and take their polls and plan for the future, the word of God comes into the wilderness (Luke 3).

David Toole, *Waiting for Godot in Sarajevo*

CHAPTER 4

Greek parrhēsia

Christianity does not countenance truth going unspoken in service of the comfort of those who "have" it. Instead, it enjoins witnesses to come forward with true testimony and face a confrontation with power. Michel Foucault understood how truth and power are associated: "The task of speaking the truth is an infinite labor: to respect it in its complexity is an obligation that no power can afford to shortchange, unless it would impose the silence of slavery."[1] As I indicated in the last section, theories have their limits, particularly as they threaten to obscure the uniqueness of Jesus that must be preserved if the witness is to see. If the truth refuses to be described by systems, then Christian theology has not always successfully resisted the lure of epistemological schemes designed to give the upper hand, particularly when it is assumed that knowing the truth is primarily adjudicated epistemologically. The Johannine language of being "of the truth" reflects the importance of wanting to hear the truth in order to listen to it. Some ways of life are more conducive to hearing the truth than are others because, for those living lies, the truth is unwelcome.[2] Acknowledging this gave rise to the importance of discipleship for Christian witness. At the least, systems of thought can distract from the question of the truth-teller's *character*. At its worst, they can positively function as a repression strategy — as attempts to restrict the way and extent to which the

---

1. Michel Foucault, *Foucault Live (Interviews, 1961-1984)*, ed. Sylvere Lotringer, trans. Lysa Hochroth and John Johnston (New York: Semiotext(e), 1989), p. 464.
2. Miroslav Volf, *Exclusion and Embrace: A Theological Exploration of Identity, Otherness, and Reconciliation* (Nashville: Abingdon, 1996), p. 269.

truth is allowed to be spoken. Knowing the truth is not simply a matter of what goes on in the mind, whether it either satisfies criteria for correspondence to reality or coherently arranges the objects of its knowledge. In addition to this is the question of one's character. "You must have an affinity with the truth."[3] Successful (i.e., faithful) witness rests on the formation of a character that desires the truth; and this formation is prior to what theories, systems, or mental structures can say about the truth and the mind's abilities to know. Therefore, this section picks up from the preceding one by exploring the relationship between the truth and those who tell the truth, between the testimony and the witness, and the skill and training that truth-telling requires.

This chapter, in particular, looks at what it means to be "of the truth" by engaging the later work of Michel Foucault, guided by the motif of the witness *coming forward,* by which I mean *overcoming obstacles of power,* in order to speak the truth. We will look in some detail at Foucault's discussion of *parrhēsia,* which, I argue, is the virtue of witness that lies behind the moment of coming forward and, for Christians, enables a witness that is simultaneously bold and patient. Foucault's work illuminates three themes in truth-telling that I will elaborate at some length. First, he explores *parrhēsia* as the nonepistemological character of truth-telling in classical Greek notions of the person of the truth-teller. Second, his work on discursive practices addresses the question of what the truth-teller has to say. Third, Foucault uses his well-known critiques of sovereign power and discourse in a consideration of the truth-teller as a protester against domination — and truth-telling as an act of resistance. In the following chapter I will turn to these themes in the New Testament, and finally to the work of John Howard Yoder, to extend some of Foucault's insights into a theological register.

The second moment of witness — the action of coming forward — involves overcoming obstructions of power, threats that silence and intimidate. In response to an onus of legal obligation incumbent on the executors of justice, measures are often taken to protect the witnesses who come forward. If witnesses are abused through inappropriate questioning, others will be discouraged from coming forward to testify.[4] The fact that

---

3. Volf, *Exclusion and Embrace,* pp. 269-70. See also Miroslav Volf, "Johannine Dualism and Contemporary Pluralism," *Modern Theology* 21, no. 2 (April 2005): 195-96.

4. This is obviously true, but see Louise Ellison, *The Adversarial Process and the Vulnerable Witness* (Oxford: Oxford University Press, 2001), p. 112.

Christians are enjoined to witness despite the treatment they might receive suggests a relativizing of the sovereign and juridical powers (including the law courts and their claim to legitimacy) that might otherwise either ensure or disqualify the presentation of testimony. First — before I consider what is involved in speaking the truth to those in power — I will consider how power functions with respect to speaking the truth.

To begin with, we need to become clear on what truth has to do with power. Foucault addresses this question by way of discussing discourse and discursive practices. For Foucault, all discursive practices are intimately related to power, because they are the institutionalizing of sets of rules that delimit the boundaries of acceptable statements. A discursive practice is more general than a grammar that merely determines the linguistic *form* of statements, because a discursive practice accounts for why some statements rather than others count at all. Foucault's analyses of discursive practices such as torture and punishment, mental illness, and human sexuality are all attempts to give an account of why certain descriptions and not others have come to predominate them. One commentator describes how discursive practices work for Foucault: "The practice of discourse is a 'violence' done to things, not by virtue of men's ideas nor through the grammatical systems of language, but by a set of rules that determine what can be stated at a particular time and how these statements are related to others."[5] The aim of such practices is to master historical contingency and chance, recalling what has been said here in the previous chapter. In a pivotal essay, "The Order of Discourse," Foucault describes how his own work was in the process of attempting various ways of signaling this: "In every society the production of discourse is at once controlled, selected, organized and redistributed by a certain number of procedures whose role is to ward off its powers and dangers, to gain mastery over its chance events, to evade its ponderous, formidable materiality."[6] Foucault had attempted in earlier works to show that language underwent an important shift since the sixteenth century from transparent representation to a medium of knowledge.[7] Identifying that shift led him to see that discourse not only

5. James Bernauer, *Michel Foucault's Force of Flight: Toward an Ethics for Thought* (London: Humanities Press International, 1992), p. 107.

6. Michel Foucault, "The Order of Discourse," in *Untying the Text: A Post-Structuralist Reader,* ed. Robert Young (London: Routledge and Kegan Paul, 1981), p. 52. In this inaugural lecture at the Collège de France in 1970, Foucault experimentally set forth hypotheses for his later projects as a kind of prospectus.

7. This was the central shift highlighted in Michel Foucault, *The Order of Things: An*

represents boundaries and limits set elsewhere, but is partly constitutive of them. In some cases, discourse is paired with nondiscursive practices of control, such as prison systems. But this should not disguise the fact that discourse itself wields power. "[D]iscourse is not simply what translates struggles or systems of domination, but is the thing for which and by which there is struggle; discourse is the power which is to be seized."[8] Speech is not only produced within certain knowledge regimes but is permitted to be intelligible within the corresponding institutions of that regime. In short, power and knowledge are coupled in discourse.[9]

The will to truth — that is, the strong desire for the truth — cannot be separated from the institutions and methods of control that are erected by it. But this identification of truth with power cannot be perceived from *within* a particular discourse, because discourses are built precisely on the need to disguise it. Institutions and disciplines justify their existence using the forms of knowledge they consider true discourse. What is true and false cannot be seen for being arbitrary, institutional, and violent until the scale is liberated from the discourse that shapes true and false by setting it against another scale — by a genealogical history or a survey across discourses. The division between true and false is historically constituted.[10] As examples, Foucault notes how economic practices since the sixteenth century have relied on theories of wealth and production and also how penal systems and practices of discipline have been justified by theories of justice.

In order for a proposition to be true or false, it must meet the preliminary requirements of the system that upholds the criteria for judging the truth and falsity of propositions. Practices like buying and selling logically precede the accounts offered for being able to say whether those exchanges (or exchange in general) are true, since this could only mean something like "true to theory." The conceptual limitations of the theory provide the warrant for something to be true or false. Following Georges Canguilhem, Foucault teaches that the location of the proposition must be "in the true":

Archaeology of the Human Sciences, trans. Alan Sheridan (London: Routledge, 2002). Kant's move to ground experience in the human subject made him the first modern philosopher, according to Foucault, because he initiated a kind of critique that sought to assess the validity of representations themselves.

8. Foucault, "The Order of Discourse," pp. 52-53.
9. Michel Foucault, *The History of Sexuality 1: The Will to Knowledge,* trans. Robert Hurley (London: Penguin, 1978), p. 100.
10. Foucault, "The Order of Discourse," p. 54.

"[P]erhaps there are no errors in the strict sense, for error can only arise and be decided inside a definite practice."[11]

The task of discovering the thought and events that have been debarred from power structures begins in the refusal to accept the legitimacy of the exclusionary scheme. If the scheme names a kind of epistemology, it is not possible to see what that epistemology leaves out except by going outside of it.[12] The rub, though, is in how this is done. Foucault does not think this is simply a linguistic activity of broader incorporation for aberrant events since this would not directly challenge the power of discourse. Instead, he uses political imagery of conflict — war rather than language — reflecting investments of power rather than meaning.[13] Foucault sees power as more basic than meaning, and every encounter and event as an exchange of power. In short, truth is not hermeneutical but political. (This is partly because, for Foucault, all epistemology is finally politics, since it is constituted by contests over power.) "[T]ruth isn't outside power, or lacking in power . . . truth isn't the reward of free spirits, the child of protracted solitude, nor the privilege of those who have succeeded in liberating themselves. Truth is a thing of this world: it is produced only by virtue of multiple forms of constraint. And it includes regular effects of power."[14] Social power is exerted to control the dissemination of truth and its availability for consumption, meaning that it is consequently political and economic power. "'Truth' is linked in a circular relation with systems of power which produce and sustain it, and to effects of power which it induces and which extend it. A 'regime' of truth."[15]

The images of war and battle that Foucault uses to describe the struggle against the regimes of truth provides a language for confuting those regimes by surpassing them.[16] He does not think intellectuals should

---

11. Foucault, "The Order of Discourse," p. 60. One might think about the technical meaning that baseball gives to "error." Insofar as "practice" here also means "system," there is a parallel development in Anglo-American philosophy of science in Thomas Kuhn's work on paradigms and Imre Lakatos's research programs.

12. Richard Rorty sees Foucault's later distancing from the concept of archaeology to be a way of refusing epistemology altogether (Rorty, "Foucault and Epistemology," in *Foucault: A Critical Reader,* ed. David Couzens Hoy [Oxford: Blackwell, 1986]).

13. Michael Foucault, "Truth and Power," in *Power/Knowledge: Selected Interviews and Other Writings 1972-1977,* ed. Colin Gordon (Harlow, UK: Pearson Education, 1980), p. 114.

14. Foucault, "Truth and Power," p. 131.

15. Foucault, "Truth and Power," p. 133.

16. Though I will not argue it here, I suspect that Foucault's appeal to the linguistic domain of battle indicates how difficult it is to think about resisting power nonviolently. As I

primarily dismantle the reigning ideologies, but should instead imagine the "possibility of constituting a new politics of truth. The problem is not changing people's consciousness — or what's in their heads — but the political, economic, institutional regime of the production of truth."[17] Even resistance to power is part of the power relationship itself:

> Where there is power, there is resistance, and yet, or rather consequently, this resistance is never in a position of exteriority in relation to power. Should it be said that one is always inside power, there is no escaping it, there is no absolute outside where it is concerned, because one is subject to the law in any case? This would be to misunderstand the strictly relational character of power relationships. Their existence depends on a multiplicity of points of resistance: these play the role of adversary, target, support, or handle in power relations. These points of resistance are present everywhere in the power network. Hence there is no single locus of great Refusal, no soul of revolt, or pure law of the revolutionary. Instead there is a plurality of resistances, each of them a special case. But this does not mean that they are only a reaction or a rebound, forming with respect to the basic domination an underside that is in the end always passive, doomed to perpetual defeat. Resistances do not derive from a few heterogeneous principles; but neither are they a lure or a promise that is of necessity betrayed. They are the odd term in relations of power; they are inscribed in power as an irreducible opposite.[18]

Every power has corresponding resistances intrinsic to it. There is no liberating truth from power since "truth is already power," but only the hope of enervating the power truth holds in the operation and posturing of the political, economic, and social institutions that serve it and are served by it.[19] The hope for liberation can never be fully realized; it can only be instantiated in micropolitical acts of chipping away at the discourses and nondiscursive practices in particular concrete instances, one institution at a time as they presently exist. Foucault thinks that our imaginations are so constrained by the current system that we cannot even imagine an alterna-

---

will show below, resisting power nonviolently is precisely what seems to attend to Christian *parrhēsia*.

17. Foucault, "Truth and Power," p. 133.
18. Foucault, *The History of Sexuality 1*, pp. 96-97.
19. Foucault, "Truth and Power," p. 133.

tive to it without merely extending our own involvement in it.[20] The difficulty is not so much that we have a hard time imagining what another system would look like, but that we think that liberation from one system will take the form of *a system.* System-thinking is required to justify both the existing particular systems and the existence of systems as such. Liberation typically refuses the former but is unable to escape the latter.[21]

Chipping away at the pretensions of powerful discourse is Foucault's attempt to avoid counter-system-building. Knowledge regimes such as schools, businesses, armies, and cities rely on forms of institutionalized power that manage relationships with exterior threats and also control inputs and outputs from a clearly defined interior space. One army that opposes another still obeys the same strategic logic of controlled space. Max Weber was able to point to the way Marxist revolutionaries' use of the same theoretical forms as capitalism in the attempt to overcome capitalism could not help but devolve into Soviet repression.[22] Antirevolutions make any resulting morality nothing more than a continuation of the status quo that perpetuates only slightly modified versions of the conventions it purports to overthrow, thus further entrenching those conventions. This state of affairs entails its own "form of oppression, authoritarianism, or despotism, made all the more frightening by its ubiquity in every little description we apply, every little thing we do."[23] Genuine resistance cannot merely oppose specific institutions, but must oppose the ways the institutions maintain themselves. Resistance must oppose strategies without mirroring them; for this, resistance must take ad hoc, tactical forms. While a revolutionary army embodies strategic relationships institutionally, and is therefore never truly revolutionary, Foucault knew that, on the other hand, small acts of resistance crucially lack a centralized locus of control and cannot easily calculate how effec-

20. Michel Foucault, *Language, Counter-Memory, Practice* (Ithaca, NY: Cornell University Press, 1980), p. 230.

21. Foucault observed that the inability of contemporary liberation movements to develop a new ethic in the absence of principled religious convictions owes to the fact that the search for an ethic nevertheless still presupposes a reliance on these kinds of systemic principles. Foucault, "On the Genealogy of Ethics," in *Michel Foucault: Beyond Structuralism and Hermeneutics,* 2nd ed., ed. Hubert L. Dreyfus and Paul Rabinow (Chicago: University of Chicago Press, 1983), p. 231.

22. See David Harvey's summary of Weber in *The Condition of Postmodernity: An Enquiry into the Origins of Cultural Change* (Oxford: Blackwell, 1990), p. 45.

23. Charles R. Pinches, *Theology and Action: After Theory in Christian Ethics* (Grand Rapids: Eerdmans, 2002), pp. 202-3.

tive they will be. Yet, precisely because of this, the latter form of resistance may be the most effective after all.

It is interesting that one of the tactics of struggle Foucault was later to analyze is truth-telling. In light of what we have said about Foucault's identification of truth with power, it could be seen as ironic that he turns to a practice that is explicitly identified with truth. If truth can only be decided within a determinate practice, what could be gained by analyzing the practice of truth-telling? After all, if every practice tells its own truth, does not each practice of truth-telling merely repeat the prevailing dogma and hold all thought, speech, and action to it? Is it not the identification of power and truth in its purest form? Nevertheless, Foucault argues that truth-telling can be a form of radical protest, a direct challenge to the power that dominates. To see how, we turn now to his lectures on the practice of truth-telling.

It is significant that, in his reading of ancient texts, Foucault saw truth-telling as a practice. In earlier works, he tried to show that language is autonomous and constitutive of reality; but he later thought this to be a mistake, arguing that language is produced by social reality.[24] Discourse cannot be autonomous, since it is called on to take its determinate forms by the needs of social power and corresponding institutions and disciplines. *Discipline and Punish,* for example, was an attempt to show that it is not possible to analyze language on the one hand and social practices on the other, because, as one interpreter writes, "Discourse is now recognized to be a social practice itself."[25] What makes truth-telling noteworthy within Foucault's intellectual development is that it constitutes a practice that not only is explicitly in the form of discourse but is also a mode of protest within the power relationships that epistemology names.

In 1983, the year before his death, Foucault delivered a series of lectures at the University of California at Berkeley in which he developed a genealogy of truth-telling in ancient Greece.[26] These lectures, along with his 1984 course at the Collège de France, were part of a larger project on the history of truth. This project was never completed, though he had for years considered his many projects to be variations on this question. Foucault of-

24. The early works I refer to here are *The Order of Things* and *The Archaeology of Knowledge.* I am relying partly on the analysis of David Couzens Hoy in his introduction to *Foucault: A Critical Reader,* pp. 4-6.

25. Hoy, *Foucault: A Critical Reader,* p. 5.

26. These lectures were posthumously published from an audio transcript as Michel Foucault, *Fearless Speech,* ed. Joseph Pearson (Los Angeles: Semiotext[e], 2001).

ten referred to his work as being in the history of thought, something he took to be distinct from the history of ideas. The governing question for him, on a range of topics from sexuality to punishment to madness, was this: "How is it that thought, insofar as it has a relationship with the truth, can also have a history? . . . What I tried to do was a history of the relationships that thought maintains with the truth, the history of thought insofar as it is thought about the truth."[27] So it was probably inevitable that Foucault would finally turn to a history of truth itself. He wanted to show that the preoccupation with metaphysical notions of truth, as they came to be articulated in Platonic modes and subsequently in Western philosophy, resulted from historical contingencies.[28] It emerged out of a tradition, not of philosophical reflection on the nature of truth as such, but of producing and forming ways of *acting,* that is, of producing people who tell the truth. We will first consider Foucault's lectures on the practice of truth-telling before turning to the work of Yoder and how Christian witness might be considered as a mode of resistance that is first a practice of telling the truth.

Foucault was investigating the notion of *parrhēsia,* which may be translated as "frankness in speaking the truth." For the ancient Greeks, *parrhēsia* depended on three characteristics. First, it has something to say: the idle chatterer lacks an ability to discern when to speak and when to keep silent, but is inclined to babble, saying whatever comes to mind, often in the guise of frankness.[29] The trouble with chatter is that it is speech that is unqualified by aims at a truthful, purposeful activity. Instead, the chatterer has a "mouth like a running spring" or, from the literal Greek, has a tongue but not a door (p. 62).

Second, the *parrhēsiastēs* must believe what he says: he cannot, like the rhetorician, rely only on the persuasion of words to win over his audience. Not only must he have something to say; he must believe that it matters and believe that there are good reasons for speaking it rather than not. This is the *parrhēsia* of Socrates in Plato's *Apology,* claiming not to be wise nor to speak as the Sophist rhetoricians do, but only to speak the truth plainly.

27. Foucault, *Foucault Live,* p. 456.

28. Elsewhere, Foucault asks: "What philosophy has not tried to overturn Platonism?" (Foucault, "Theatrum Philosophicum," in *Language, Counter-Memory, Practice: Selected Essays and Interviews,* ed. Donald F. Bouchard [Ithaca, NY: Cornell University Press, 1977], p. 166).

29. Foucault, *Fearless Speech,* p. 63. Hereafter, page references to this work appear in parentheses in the text.

Third, there must be an element of risk. Flattery is distinguished from *parrhēsia* in its failure to recognize the danger that telling the truth may involve. Telling the truth is not always a parrhesiastic act, such as when a teacher teaches grammar to children. The reason that it is not parrhesiastic is that there is no risk (p. 16).[30] However, the paradigmatic instance for the *parrhēsiastēs* involves standing before a sovereign who has power over the *parrhēsiastēs* only because of his position as sovereign and not because of any possession of the truth. The *parrhēsiastēs* exposes the injustice, for example, of the tyrannical ruler at great personal risk.

Foucault again draws connections with Plato's *Apology* and also with Euripides' *Ion*. In the latter case, the courage of Ion's mother, Creusa, is summoned to speak the truth to the god Apollo, who had raped her years before. Creusa, having traveled with her son, Ion, to Delphi to seek the advice of Apollo, engages in an encounter with Apollo that reverses the established direction in which the truth normally flows. Apollo is unable to speak the truth, and thus he resorts to lies and other tricks. But Creusa, in speaking the truth to Apollo, uses *parrhēsia*, powerfully illustrating how it is a moral virtue rather than an institutionally guaranteed legal right. The question of whether Creusa might summon the ability to tell the truth drives the plot of the play in a way that is parallel to the question of King Oedipus's identity in the tragedy by Sophocles. For *Ion*, the hierarchy of humans and gods is already radically called into question by the ways the gods are seen manifestly behaving as though they were human. Nevertheless, the most dramatic revaluation of the hierarchy comes with unexpected, nonsovereign, and lower-ranking *parrhēsia* directed godward. The ability to tell the truth is not first a matter of creating forums in which citizens are free to speak it. It is rather a matter of a dogged will that the truth must be made known — in the face of injustice and tyranny.

Foucault claims that it is this virtue that founded Athenian democracy. It is from among the "powers of the weak" and the crucial practice of truth-telling that the Golden Age of the Greek polis emerged, quite irrespective of legal statuses and institutions.[31] We might say that *parrhēsia* originally exhibited an association of truth with justice *without* sovereignty, but that it was no less a political virtue and no less an exercise of authority as a result. The truthful speech is accompanied by the courage to

30. I am following the text of *Fearless Speech* in the convention of italicizing all forms of *parrhēsia* except the adjectival "parrhesiastic."

31. See Arpad Szakolczai, *The Genesis of Modernity* (London: Routledge, 2003), p. 179.

speak it in a setting of power differential from the weaker party; and it is the courage that qualifies the act as *parrhēsia.* In *Ion,* it is thought, Euripides presents the first and strongest meaning of *parrhēsia* as a political virtue through a myth of origins by which Athenian citizens were confronted with the true meaning of their most esteemed rights. But Euripides not only makes ideological use of the concept to show by way of founding myth that a venerable right in Athenian society really amounts to empty formalism where it is assumed that it can be secured at the level of institutions rather than through fostering the character of citizens who will display it. He also offers an explanation of the shift of the culture's religious center from Delphi to Athens. This is a move away from the oracles, whose truth-telling was sought by those who ventured outside of the city for a word of wisdom, and marks instead a secularized return to the city itself, which is able to produce the human will to say what one thinks. In not being able to tell the truth, Apollo disgraces and ultimately renders absurd and superfluous any privileged association with truth afforded him by his power. Therefore, democracy emerges out of the *parrhēsia* of ordinary humans and the irrelevance of the gods to the political project.

However, *Ion* makes the matter more complicated. Foucault highlights the way that Euripides does not simply praise Athenian democracy for depending on *parrhēsia.* Instead, the tragedian confronts his Athenian audience with the very real possibility that they may have already given up on the true nature of this essential virtue. Before Creusa confronts Apollo with the truth about the rape, the identity of Ion's mother is likewise hidden, something that is clearly beneficial to Apollo. But for Ion, it means that his status as a *parrhēsiastēs* was uncertain. He laments not knowing whether or not his mother is Athenian, hoping that she is, because otherwise he would not have the parrhesiastic rights of a citizen. In order for him to exercise his natural parrhesiastic virtue, he needs to find out the truth about his birth. Yet Ion's concern to be able to act as a *parrhēsiastēs* already discloses that he is one. He is the kind of person crucial to the proper functioning of a democracy, and the fact that his official status is uncertain — and is, as we come to find out, dependent on his mother's own *parrhēsia* — reveals how much Athens is at great risk of abandoning its original virtue. The question is resolved much more importantly by Creusa's parrhesiastic activity; the fact that she turns out also to be Athenian is clearly meant to be secondary. A mother and son united in a commitment boldly to speak the truth at great risk founds a polis in which the right to speak freely continually threatens to outpace the determination to do so. *Ion's* great irony is to show that Creusa's truth-telling leads to the revelation that her son is someone whose legal status in fact falls into precise step with his natural *parrhēsia,* rather than the reverse.

It is clear that *parrhēsia* shares very little with flattery. The latter is marked by a lack of courage and a concession to the power of the sovereign, preferring the gain flattery brings to the risk of danger that telling the truth brings. Foucault notes that Plutarch was particularly interested in how flattery functions with respect to self-love *(philautia),* and how the desire to deceive and flatter ourselves means that we need friends who will tell us the truth: "*We* are our own flatterers, and it is in order to disconnect this spontaneous relation we have to ourselves, to rid ourselves of our *philautia,* that we need a *parrhēsiastēs*" (p. 135). Plutarch worried that friends may speak with an air of frankness, pretending to tell us the truth, but only reinforce our need to be flattered since *philautia* can solicit its own version of flattery disguised as *parrhēsia.* In response, for Plutarch, and increasingly for Hellenistic culture generally, the question of how to recognize the true *parrhēsiastēs* became very important.

The identity of the authentic truth-teller is crucial for the founding vision *Ion* sets forth for Athenian democracy. Foucault notes that *parrhēsia* is always a commendable virtue in *Ion.* But in later works by Euripides (such as *Orestes,* written ten years later), one confronts a much less salutary sense. Democracy, it turns out, is particularly vulnerable to a particular crisis of truth: it depends on some people playing a parrhesiastic role, but its emphasis on equality also invites others who speak nonsense and ignorance, albeit with boldness. Democracy alone is too indiscriminate when it comes to the question of who the real truth-tellers are. Foucault cites Isocrates, who laments the way Athenian democracy had, in the name of freedom, come to drive away anyone who took a critical tone in the public assembly. They preferred to hear flatterers and could only accept criticism in the theater in the form of comedy. The flatterer is neither interested in the truth nor the good of the community; he is only concerned with his own pleasure, and he accomplishes it by voicing and reinforcing the majority opinion rather than speaking his mind. The formal, legal requirements for free speech may be in place democratically, but this is insufficient for ensuring that true and good *parrhēsia* succeeds in being displayed. The institutionally sanctioned possibility of *parrhēsia* not only does nothing to bring about its actual and helpful exercise; it also seems to have stimulated its exact opposite: flattering, untrue speech. Therefore, the moral question so crucial to securing political goods (i.e., who the true *parrhēsiastēs* is) is clearly not one that can be answered politically. How, then, can the moral question be answered?

One way to deal with this question is simply to substitute another one in its place. The story Foucault tells enables him to make sense of the shift away from moral and political questions about truth-telling and toward philosophical questions, such as "What is truth?" The latter is not concerned with the political and moral courage of speaking in the assembly but with access to the truth. The democratic impulse of equality can be detected here since those with the natural virtue of *parrhēsia* may now be passed over in favor of technologies aimed at artificially cultivating it more widely and especially among those who are not naturally inclined toward it.

As Foucault describes, the subordination of the *parrhēsiastēs* to the interlocutor with the attendant risks for the *parrhēsiastēs* remained one of the strongest criteria for identifying a real truth-teller; hence the endurance of the paradigm of the philosopher before the sovereign. Of course, democracy countenances a different notion of sovereignty than does monarchy, but the paradigm for *parrhēsia* is nevertheless strikingly relevant. In some of his late writings, Foucault discussed "governmentality" as a way of referring to how even modern democracies have yet to fully recognize ways of engendering nonlegal power that is not built on older and enduring forms of sovereignty. The lectures on *parrhēsia* show Foucault to be locating the problem in antiquity as well. Governmentality finds ways of mitigating the risks of truth under the shelter of a sovereignty that may take many forms. The sovereign, as the holder of power, is subordinate to no one, meaning that he does not take a risk. Consequently, kings cannot usually use *parrhēsia*. Kings may tell the truth, of course, but their position generally disqualifies them from the dangers inherent in truth-telling in its parrhesiastic mode, because in *parrhēsia* you prefer to risk death in order to tell the truth over living a tranquil and protected life in which the truth goes unspoken (p. 17). The risk is a result of the fact that the truth may be unwelcome to those who hear it, that is, to those to whom it is addressed. Therefore, it is said to serve a critical function. It is either an admonition or a confession: an admonition when it is critical of the interlocutor, a confession when it is critical of the speaker.

The risk that the *parrhēsiastēs* takes is a function of speaking outside the grammar of power in order to subvert it. By definition, the king stands within a power regime, since kingship itself is constituted by the same ordering of power that makes the king's speech true. This is why Foucault maintains the necessity of risk: the truth-teller declines the power that telling the truth might otherwise bring (if done in support of that same power), yet still tells the truth. The truth-teller is necessarily a protester. Also, as in the paradigmatic instance of the philosopher before the sovereign or the courageous human before the mischievous god, the *parrhēsiastēs* has less power than her interlocutor does (p. 18). *Parrhēsia* is criticism from below: it is not a teacher scolding a pupil, but a pupil criticizing a teacher, or a citizen speaking out against the government on a volatile issue such as national security.

We should not miss an obvious point here: asking the question about speaking the truth to power, or giving testimony before governors and kings, assumes that the truth is not being spoken from a position of power in the first place. As an alternative to governmentality, speaking the truth to power can only be done "from below." Recognizing and embracing this as a normative perspective has two consequences for political theory and moral reasoning, both having to do with sovereignty.[32] The first is refusing to let the sovereign codes and discourses of power set the terms for subsequent ethical debate; those terms privilege outcomes in favor of those who set them. The flatterer only speaks squarely within them. Refusing to do so involves the ability to imagine a debate beyond the present one and beginning to engage in it by criticizing the givens that structure the current debates, questioning the questions that are asked, and possibly even refusing to take part in an argument if the terms have already been so severely set in a particular direction. The second consequence of truth being spoken from below involves realizing that at this moment in history, the king is little more than a fantasy that, ironically (so long as the focus remains on sovereign power), can disguise the fact that power is actually dispersed and decentralized. As Gilles Deleuze observes, power is "exercised rather than possessed."[33] The political power wielded by states is not original to them, but states are only agents of acephalous power's organization and distribution. They constantly exercise power to position themselves as indispensable for social construction and the organization of political architecture. However, if Foucault is right about power, states are neither natural nor

32. "What we need . . . is a political philosophy that isn't erected around the problem of sovereignty, nor therefore around the problems of law and prohibition. We need to cut off the King's head: in political theory that has still to be done" (Foucault, "Truth and Power," p. 121; *History of Sexuality 1*, pp. 88-91).

33. Gilles Deleuze, *Foucault*, trans. Séan Hand (London: Athlone, 1988), p. 25. Here Deleuze discusses the way power differs from how Marxism understands it; nevertheless, Marxism is not the only ideology that has been captured by the image of the sovereign.

necessary. Neither are states the primary instantiation of "the political"; indeed, they are epiphenomena.[34]

It is clear why these observations are important for truth-tellers. The moral ability of the witness, or *parrhēsiastēs,* to speak the truth within the assembly or before the king coincides with acknowledging that the greatest ethical concern or grasp of authentic human goods does not lie with those who have the most power. When truth is in the hands of conquerors, it is inevitable that the truth will also be conquered. Unseating the centers of power as the loci of the most determinative exemplars of moral instantiation is a requisite measure for bearing true witness. Not only do the victors write the histories of wars fought and won; they also largely determine the parameters of the ethical debate.[35]

One thing is for sure: on this account truth-telling is marked by how it functions as a role carried out by a certain class of people with certain characteristics. It is not an isolated act. Foucault notes that the concept of *parrhēsia,* for the Greeks, became problematized in later iterations as writers began to ask questions about *who* could speak the truth and what qualities one needed to receive through education in order to grow up speaking the truth. But the Greek genealogy does not immediately problematize *parrhēsia* over questions familiar to modern epistemology, especially in the analytic mode. They simply did not concern themselves, in the notion of *parrhēsia,* with criteriological questions of deciding whether a particular statement is true or with our ability to know the truth (*Fearless Speech,* p. 170). The *parrhēsiastēs* does not doubt his own possession of the truth, a confidence at odds with Descartes, for example, whose legacy made the problem of certainty a problem (perhaps *the* problem) of modern epistemology, which relies on evidence to show how a belief might be true.

---

34. This only makes Foucault an anarchist if we assume that the only legitimate *archies* are states. I show below how Foucault has been misunderstood for this reason.

35. As I noted above, however, in unthinking the normativity of ethics for the powerful, we should not assume that the king is always clearly monarchical or even aristocratic. Foucault notes how, in the West, the "mythology of the sovereign" is no longer a reality that correctly identifies where power lies. "We all know about the great upheavals, the institutional changes which constitute a change of political regime, the way in which the delegation of power right to the top of the state system is modified. But in thinking of the mechanisms of power, I am thinking rather of its capillary form of existence, the point where power reaches into the very grain of individuals, touches their bodies and inserts itself into their very actions and attitudes, their discourses, learning processes and everyday lives" (Foucault, "Prison Talk," in *Power/Knowledge,* pp. 38-39). Power is not exclusively exercised from the top down, but is exercised from within the social body.

Parrhēsia does not evince this kind of separation of belief from truth. Instead, in a very strong claim, Foucault teaches that for Greek *parrhēsia*, "there is always an exact coincidence between belief and truth" (p. 14). Instead of being an epistemological matter rooted in skepticism, *parrhēsia* is a moral matter rooted in criticism: "In the Greek conception of *parrhēsia* . . . there does not seem to be a problem about the acquisition of the truth since such truth-having is guaranteed by the possession of certain *moral* qualities: when someone has certain moral qualities, then that is the proof that he has access to truth — and vice versa" (p. 15). *Parrhēsia* involves the morality of the agent for both knowing and telling the truth, and they cannot be separated in the way modern questions tempt us to do. The Greeks were interested to know whether someone was a truth-teller, not *how* the truth-teller could claim certainty for her beliefs.

It is easy to see why Foucault is attracted to this notion of the truth-teller. It clears the way for a principled apathy toward sovereignty when it comes to truth and thus funds truthful critique of political power. Likewise, the one who has this status irrespective of the *philosophical* authority that epistemology or the metaphysics of truth might grant is the one who can subvert the ascendancy of knowledge regimes. Reigning methods in discourses of truth do not necessarily lead to it; they exist (sovereignly) to *authorize* it. This is not to say that the power of the truth-teller is autonomous or can ever fully exist outside of the regimes to which it scrupulously attempts to owe nothing of its authority. Truth-telling is still a form of resistance, and thus still largely part of the system it challenges. But because, for Foucault, power is not observably centralized but is really dispersed throughout the whole of a social system, the expressions of power will be contingent (not perfectly unified), though they will reinforce each other. The truth-teller subverts the dominant seats of power. But he does not primarily accomplish this through superior knowledge over against his interlocutors (since superior knowledge is already the primary characteristic of the representatives of the knowledge regimes — its kings and related social institutions). Instead, the truth-teller subverts dominant power by defying the expectations that it calls forth in the restriction of speech and what is considered worth saying. The focus is not on what the truth-teller knows and how he knows it; these are questions for epistemology. Instead, the focus is on what kind of moral formation is required to produce people who will tell the truth even at great cost.

In the second century CE, Galen noted how renouncing flattery meant renouncing power: "When a man does not greet the powerful and wealthy by name, when he does not visit them, when he does not dine with them, when he lives a disciplined life, expect that man to speak the truth" (quoted by Foucault, p. 140). Galen's truth-teller is emblematic of the social critic Foucault wants to enable. More generally, Foucault points to the Cynics as offering a major alternative to Platonism.[36] The Cynic was known as a *parrhēsiastēs*, "a kind of prophet of truth-telling."[37] The focus was on deliberately living in such a way as to be freed and enabled to speak the truth. As a result, Cynic philosophy focused on living a true life rather than providing a theoretical scheme that first describes what makes that life true.[38]

✳　　✳　　✳

Before looking more carefully at what the above account of *parrhēsia* contributes to Christian witness and protest (in the next two chapters), we must consider some objections. Critics and criticisms of Foucault are legion. Here I will address some that cluster around a common set of concerns. It is not necessary to defend Foucault against his critics, but only to show how this account of *parrhēsia* is one of his ways of responding to them.[39] After *Discipline and Punish,* many thought that Foucault had painted himself into a corner by suggesting a genealogical method for criticism of present structures of power that simultaneously depends on notions of liberty, truth, and justice to which that very method does not entitle him.[40] One commentator summarizes this critique:

36. Thomas Flynn, "Foucault as Parrhesiast," in *The Final Foucault,* ed. James Bernauer and David Rasmussen (London: MIT, 1988), p. 111.

37. Flynn, "Foucault as Parrhesiast," p. 109.

38. Szakolczai also cites Foucault in a lecture: "[C]ynicism made out of life, of existence, of *bios,* an *aleaturgy,* a manifestation of truth" (Szakolczai, *Genesis of Modernity,* p. 205). In a suggestive observation that I cannot elaborate on here, Thomas Flynn points out that the irreducibility of cynical truth-telling practices is liturgical ("Foucault as Parrhesiast," p. 110).

39. Indeed, Edward Said warned that "we shouldn't indulge ourselves in the practice of saving Foucault from himself in order to make self-interested use of him" (Said, "Foucault and the Imagination of Power," in *Foucault: A Critical Reader,* p. 151).

40. With Foucault in mind, Bernard Williams makes a version of this critique by calling into question the possibility of the project of giving a history of truth: "One thing I shall not consider . . . is the history *of the concept of truth,* because I do not believe that there is any such history. The concept of truth itself . . . is not culturally various, but always and everywhere the same. We could not understand cultural variation itself without taking that role

He is clearly critical of the process of this social cancer [the forces of normalization and control], and calls his book a "history of the present" to admit frankly that the account is not a neutral, objective description, but is intended to subvert and disrupt the growth of this malignancy. Yet his critics believe that he fails insofar as he has no social alternatives to offer, and no moral or political standards on which to base his angry charge that modern society is becoming more and more like a prison, however progressive and benevolent it appears to those who have let themselves be successfully normalized.[41]

Foucault's lectures on *parrhēsia* were a way of addressing this problem. He concluded the lectures this way: "At issue for me was . . . the attempt to consider truth-telling as a specific activity, or as a role" (*Fearless Speech*, p. 169). Truth-telling is a discursive practice that is a mode of protest against the hegemony of power-knowledge and *its* corresponding discursive practices. Put simply, what Foucault provides is a demonstration that social critique is possible without appealing to transcendent metaphysical notions that his Nietzschean sensibilities will not allow. His is an anti-Enlightenment (and anti-Platonic) project, to be sure. But Foucault does not think that doing without a metaphysics of truth means that everything is up for grabs. "All those who say that for me the truth doesn't exist are simple-minded."[42] He wants to show that some forms of power or some modes of speech are better than others; telling the truth is better than telling lies.[43]

---

for granted" (Williams, *Truth and Truthfulness* [Princeton, NJ: Princeton University Press, 2002], p. 61). This claim strikes me as obviously untrue, and it is offered without anthropological or sociological support, assuming none is needed. Williams would have done better to show Foucault's flaws rather than dismiss him out of hand. And though Gillian Rose does not specifically mention Foucault, she is more coherent than Williams is when she writes, "Any account of 'freedom' and 'justice' is deemed to depend on the 'metaphysics' of truth. When 'metaphysics' is separated from ethics in this way [i.e., by disowning metaphysics for its totalitarian resonances in politics], the result will be unanticipated political paradoxes" (Rose, *Mourning Becomes the Law: Philosophy and Representation* [Cambridge: Cambridge University Press, 1996], p. 5). One such political paradox would presumably be the subsequent inability to have an ethics at all.

41. David Couzens Hoy, *Foucault: A Critical Reader*, p. 13. Foucault does not want to offer alternatives through genealogy, since "you can't find the solution of a problem in the solution of another problem raised at another moment by other people" (Dreyfus and Rabinow, *Michel Foucault: Beyond Structuralism and Hermeneutics*, p. 231).

42. Foucault, *Foucault Live*, p. 456.

43. Foucault admits that his "position leads not to apathy but to a hyper- and pessimistic activism" (*Michel Foucault: Beyond Structuralism and Hermeneutics*, p. 232). In an in-

Nevertheless, critics have serious doubts. For example, Michael Walzer and Charles Taylor think that Foucault should not be able to say many of the things he does, particularly when he prescribes a form of action or makes any value judgments at all. Walzer, in particular, worries that Foucault leaves no room for social criticism, since an account of dispersed power that issues in no more than local resistance unwittingly underwrites conservative politics.[44] Walzer argues — against Foucault — that an independent standpoint is needed to engage in social criticism. He also sees a contradiction between Foucault's anarchistic tendencies and his refusal to advocate social forms. On the one hand, political anarchy is inconsistent with Foucault's insistence that the self is always socially constructed. Wouldn't he instead need to advocate another society? But Foucault's refusal to offer a utopian, anarchistic vision is a result of the fact that he does not think any society can fully uncouple truth from power.[45] Walzer makes plain his own commitment to political liberalism when he notes that, for Foucault, thus to imagine society would require the latter to give a positive account of the state and the rule of law (if only in theory) — something Foucault spurns.[46] Since Walzer considers liberal politics to be the only legitimate politics, he can only see Foucault as either an anarchist or a nihilist. And since Foucault disabuses the prescient politics seemingly required by anarchy (which is to say, a determinate eschatology or notion of transcendence), he cannot escape the ignominy of Dionysus.[47] This trap is

teresting parallel, John Howard Yoder describes the biblically realistic approach to powers as "lording it over you" as "pessimistic empiricism" (Yoder, "The Christian Case for Democracy," in *The Priestly Kingdom: Social Ethics as Gospel* [Notre Dame, IN: University of Notre Dame Press, 1984], p. 170).

44. Michael Walzer, "The Politics of Michel Foucault," in *Foucault: A Critical Reader*, pp. 51-68.

45. In his unsympathetic but still helpful analysis, J. G. Merquior describes Foucault as a "neo-anarchist," with Foucault's refusal to describe a utopian, ideal society differentiating him from ordinary anarchists (Merquior, *Foucault* [London: Fontana, 1991], pp. 155-57). This refusal marked his disagreement with Noam Chomsky in a televised debate (Amsterdam, 1971) in which Foucault refused to uphold abstract notions like justice (see Merquior, pp. 148-49).

46. Elsewhere, Walzer writes that the state is "invisible," needing to be imagined and personified in order to be seen. Walzer, "On the Role of Symbolism in Political Thought," *Political Science Quarterly* 82, no. 2 (June 1967): 191-204. Though this resembles Foucault's claim about the state's epiphenomenality, its difference becomes apparent when Walzer specifies the nature of political symbolization, indicating that his imagination is far more constrained in favor of established forms of liberal state sovereignty.

47. See David Toole, *Waiting for Godot in Sarajevo: Theological Reflections on Nihilism,*

clearly a function of Walzer's inability to think beyond liberal politics and the constituent forms of social critique that liberalism tolerates.

One may respond to this critique by simply elaborating how it misses the mark. When Foucault speaks as a social critic, he uses temporal rather than spatial terms. Oddly enough, perhaps, he speaks *from the future:* "My hope is my books become true after they have been written — not before."[48] He does not claim to have a standpoint from which he can speak the truth: neither a present standpoint for a diachronic Hegelian critique of the past nor a social standpoint for a synchronic critique of other societies or aspects of his own, but an appeal to a possible future that may be opened up by what he says in the present. "I do not appeal to any 'we' — to any of those 'we's' whose consensus, whose values, whose traditions constitute the framework for a thought and define the conditions in which it can be validated. But the problem is, precisely, to decide if it is actually suitable to place oneself within a 'we' in order to assert the principles one recognizes and the values one accepts; or if it is not, rather, necessary to make the future formation of a 'we' possible, by elaborating the question."[49] Questions of social critique aside, it is not clear that Foucault should be able "to decide" to place himself within a "we." He is not doubting how much socialization influences rationality. His question has more to do with appeals for justification than with descriptions of identity. An ability to create a future "we" by asking the right question is not a way of escaping the role present social forms play in constituting who we are (this would only be a move for asserting autonomy). Instead, it is a way of naming historical descriptions as true without claiming an independent, privileged standpoint.

This is why Foucault often described his genealogical work as fictional. "I am well aware that I have never written anything but fictions."[50] "Fiction" does not mean "untrue" here, but something like "not yet true." The fiction does not just wait for a future politics to deem it as true, but is also instrumental in bringing about that future politics. Foucault continues: "It seems to me that the possibility exists for fiction to function in truth, for a fictional discourse to induce effects of truth, and for bringing it

Tragedy, and Apocalypse (Boulder, CO: Westview, 1998), p. 133. My debt to Toole's book is great, particularly in his careful analysis of Foucault's work.

48. Foucault, *Foucault Live*, p. 301.

49. Foucault, "Polemics, Politics, and Problematizations: An Interview," in *The Foucault Reader*, ed. Paul Rabinow (New York: Pantheon, 1984), p. 385.

50. Foucault, "The History of Sexuality" in *Power/Knowledge*, p. 193.

about that a true discourse engenders or 'manufactures' something that does not as yet exist, that is, 'fictions' it. One 'fictions' history on the basis of a political reality that makes it true, one 'fictions' a politics not yet in existence on the basis of a historical truth."[51] The manufacture of a future that makes the present true is the creation of what amounts to a fiction according to the present. Foucault is not exactly claiming to stand in the future, since he is refusing all privileged standpoints and this must include future ones. Instead, he redefines the role of the will to truth by simultaneously affirming that truth matters and also not allowing an appeal to the truth as truth to be a power move; hence the appeal to truth as fiction until it can be recognized as true. I will refer to this as Foucault's attempt to "unconquer" the truth. Unconquering points to tactics of "detaching the power of truth from the forms of hegemony, social, economic, and cultural, within which it operates at the present time."[52] It does not attempt to do without truth (since this may be just another strategy for conquering it); but it asks about the "possibility of constituting a new politics of truth," a possible future "we." Even asking about its possibility is the first step toward its realization.

All of this has appeared to be too much artistry and verbal contortionism for many critics. Charles Taylor, for example, suspects that Foucault cannot actually do without transcendent metaphysical concepts like liberty and truth.[53] As we have seen, for Foucault, truth is always subject to power, because each power regime has its own version of the truth, and there is no getting around the power in order to get at the truth. Truth is always enlisted for one or more version of power, often in the form of knowledge, and it is impossible to separate them from each other. Taylor asks what we are to make of a hermeneutic that takes power as its sole ubiquitous rubric. Foucault teaches that "power is everywhere, not because it embraces everything, but because it comes from everywhere."[54] Likewise, all manifestations of power are relative to the truths they endorse and sustain. But is not power itself, then, absolutized in a way that is inconsistent with how the hermeneutic of power is invoked, namely, as a way of exposing the extent of control? Does not power itself become the master principle? If so, is the critical function of Foucault's work actually a way of

51. Foucault, "The History of Sexuality," p. 193.

52. Foucault, "Truth and Power," p. 133.

53. Charles Taylor, "Foucault on Freedom and Truth," in *Foucault: A Critical Reader,* pp. 69-102.

54. Foucault, *History of Sexuality 1,* p. 93.

further ensuring that power always wins? If everything is power, then power is everything.

Foucault refuses to get himself involved in discussions of value, claiming that he is only engaged in a description of the history of ideas. But Taylor (like Walzer) thinks that Foucault is bluffing, since it is not really possible to stand nowhere, and those who claim to do so are always disguising or suppressing something.[55] On Taylor's critique, then, it seems that Foucault has no way to unconquer the truth, even though he may want to, and he has no way to articulate "wanting to" without contradiction. His claim that the truth is always relative to the forces that conquer it and so define its shape leaves him unable to say that anything is true, even the very critiques against power he wants to make.

By now we can see that, in his analysis of *parrhēsia,* Foucault should be understood as attempting to answer critics like Taylor and Walzer. *Parrhēsia* is a way of combining two aspects of Foucault's work generally. First, it is a modified return to his early work on discursive practices. Having moved from archaeology to genealogy and thus from a focus on words and language to disciplines within which discourses arise, Foucault finally turns to a practice that we would be tempted to call nondiscursive because of its determinate practical form — except for the fact that it is so obviously a kind of discourse.[56] Opposing discourse and practice where one proceeds from the other in different directions, depending on whether the analysis is archaeological or genealogical, actually breaks down in truth-telling. Foucault's work on prisons, for example, analyzes disciplinary practices (which are nondiscursive, taken alone) and corresponding discourses (which are clearly discursive). But with *parrhēsia,* the discourse is the practice and the practice is the discourse. The two meet here, just as the various histories of thought about truth were bound to culminate in a history of truth.

55. Other critics make this same point. "If Foucault did not want to accept the general outline of his society's views, he faced the awkward task of criticizing them while lacking any way at all of arguing that his own position was to be preferred to those he wanted to attack" (William Placher, *Unapologetic Theology: A Christian Voice in a Pluralistic Conversation* [Louisville: Westminster John Knox, 1989], p. 98). From the left, Terry Eagleton seems to agree, though he notes that "Foucault objects to particular regimes of power not on moral grounds — for where would such criteria spring from in his theory? — but simply on the grounds that they are regimes as such" (Eagleton, *The Illusions of Postmodernism* [Oxford: Blackwell, 1996], p. 31).

56. Foucault thought that what was missing in some of the archaeological works like *The Order of Things* was "the problem of the 'discursive regime,' of the effects of power peculiar to the play of statements" (Foucault, "Truth and Power," p. 113).

For our particular concerns, it is important to raise some questions about the nature of the *parrhēsiastēs*'s activity. Is it part of a discipline that has produced it as a form of discourse, or is it something else? Where does the *parrhēsiastēs* stand relative to the power of discourse regimes? Questions of this kind lead to the second aspect of Foucault's work that truth-telling illuminates, namely, that of the critique of power. He concludes the lectures by stating that one of their aims was "to construct a genealogy of the critical attitude in Western philosophy" (*Fearless Speech,* pp. 170-71). Criticism is shown to emerge from a practice that has its own discursive genealogy. But this was also a contingent development since it could well have developed quite differently. Foucault claims that *parrhēsia* preceded epistemological questions that later developed about what the truth is and how we can know it. These questions eventually emerged as theoretically detached from more concrete questions about how to recognize a person who tells the truth, the importance of having truth-tellers in the city, what moral qualities made someone a truth-teller, and so on. Questions about the truth of statements that appeal to the history of Greek philosophy should not be separated from questions about truth-telling. "There is no being behind the deed," as Nietzsche put it generally and normatively: "[T]he doing is everything."[57]

However, we know that eventually the questions about the truth-teller transmuted into questions about truth. This kind of genealogical discontinuity is what Foucault calls a "problematization," a way of describing the shift between moments in how a behavior or process is understood, but which also makes clear that such shifts are not inevitable from what has gone before (p. 171). Instead, a practice like *parrhēsia* becomes a problem when one seeks specific answers to those specific questions occasioned by the practice or behavior. Foucault can thus give a different account of truth than, say, Taylor thinks he requires. What is real for Foucault is not truth as such, but the answers specific individuals give in concrete situations to the questions that constituted the problematization.

> These answers are not collective ones from any sort of collective unconscious. And the fact that an answer is neither a representation nor an effect of a situation does not mean that it answers to nothing, that it is a pure dream, or an "anti-creation." A problematization is always a

---

57. Friedrich Nietzsche, *On the Genealogy of Morality,* trans. Carol Diethe (Cambridge: Cambridge University Press, 1994), 1st essay, sec. 13.

kind of creation; but a creation in the sense that, given a certain situation, you cannot infer that this kind of problematization will follow. Given a certain problematization, you can only understand why this kind of answer appears as a reply to some concrete and specific aspect of the world. There is the relation of thought and reality in the process of problematization. . . . And it is this kind of specific relation between truth and reality which I have tried to analyze in the various problematizations of *parrhesia.* (pp. 172-73)

My purpose here has not been to evaluate whether Foucault is successful in responding to his critics, but to examine what he hoped to accomplish in writing about *parrhēsia* and how he saw these lectures in the context of his larger project. Foucault's demonstration that the epistemological questions relating to truth follow from a problematization about truth-telling is meant to show that truth is not metaphysical. Instead, it arises from a "concrete and specific aspect of the world." What comes first, both logically and historically, is the activity and the person of the truth-teller.

CHAPTER 5

Christian parrhēsia

What can the preceding account of the truth-telling role contribute to understanding Christian witness? In particular, I want to ask whether the prophetic edge of Christian witness can be described as *parrhēsia*. It is worth recalling that the biblical language of witness does not simply refer to proclaiming the gospel; it belongs to a more specific set of images and motifs related to the law court. When a witness is called on to testify, she must consider whether she is prepared to confront those for whom the testimony will constitute an intense challenge and contradiction. It is not enough merely to have something to say, because if she does not have the will to come forward, the testimony will go unspoken. Furthermore, because the gospel is clearly not good news for everyone, the pressures not to come forward are genuine. The "world" before which Christian testimony is given is often a hostile and brutal antagonist. The news that the church bears is not embraced everywhere.

The Old Testament prophets spoke of Israel as God's witnesses to the nations (e.g., Isa. 43:12), as uniquely capable of a missionary task that declares to their neighbors the saving acts of the Lord. In the New Testament, Jesus acts as what Karl Barth called "the true witness," and the apostles bear witness to him. Both encounter the kind of resistance that the law court motif clearly intends to communicate. This chapter asks how we should characterize the ways that witness relates to power, to the good pressure to expand its encounter with the world using words, and to the forces that try to reduce it to silence.

In his essay "What Is Critique?" Foucault suggests that the tradition of criticism in the West emerged in response to the Christian obsession with governing. That obsession gave rise to this response: "Don't govern me like that!" And that became the defining element of critique, or "the art of not being governed quite so much."[1] Nevertheless, Foucault's focus in this essay and elsewhere is on how the confession of sin was a Christian practice through which the church wielded hegemonic power according to monastic ideals and Nietzsche's ascetic priests. For example, he narrates the transition of *parrhēsia* from being a political and public virtue to being a moral and private virtue. The Greek esteem for the courage to tell the truth *to other people* gave way to the Christian value of having the courage to tell the truth *to oneself*. The self was henceforth metaphorically put on trial in the juridical setting of the confessional, awaiting the punishment of penance. The confrontation of truth with power was no longer connected to the political courage of the citizen, that is, to political critique. It was now connected to the privacy of solitary self-examination. This might support Foucault's thesis that confession over time became depoliticized and that it even tamed potentially subversive activities by encouraging quietism. To Foucault, this is the meaning and function of *parrhēsia* in its normative Christian sense, something he narrates as an anticipation of Christendom, if not its principal feature.[2] In other words, for Foucault, *parrhēsia* lost its political edge in the hands of Christians. But it is necessary to question the story Foucault tells to back this up, because he almost entirely skips over a consideration of how *parrhēsia* functions in Christian Scripture, particularly in the New Testament: consequently, he does not adequately associate confession as a private act of worship with public resistance to political power and authority. It is possible to show how the New Testament use of *parrhēsia* involves such resistance, not only registering how Foucault is mistaken about confession, but, more important, indicating how a distinctly Christian form of *parrhēsia* bears on the confrontation between Christ's witnesses and power.

Others have critiqued Foucualt's research into the care of the self for starting too late with the second-century *Didache* rather than the New Testament.[3] As a result, these critics contend, he misunderstands how baptism

---

1. Michel Foucault, "What Is Critique?" in *The Politics of Truth* (Los Angeles: Semiotext(e), 1997), p. 29.

2. The only mention Foucault makes of the Christian obligation to bear witness is "to bear witness against *himself*" in the form of confessing faults and temptations. Foucault, "Sexuality and Solitude," *London Review of Books,* 21 May–3 June 1981, p. 5, quoted in Michel Foucault, *Fearless Speech,* ed. Joseph Pearson (Los Angeles: Semiotext[e], 2001), p. 139, n. 107.

3. Arpad Szakolczai, *The Genesis of Modernity* (London: Routledge, 2003), p. 163.

is connected with the power granted by the Holy Spirit as primarily expressed in speech, how such speech exhibits power for the Christian mission in opposition to unbelief, and how the rite of baptism is continuous with that power. It is likewise true of Foucault's neglect of the New Testament understanding of Christian *parrhēsia*: his neglect causes him inordinately to focus on *parrhēsia* as an apolitical quality that serves private confession rather than also serving the mission of the gospel to the nations, that is, of witness and proclamation. What Foucault misses is that what makes Christian *parrhēsia* distinctive is the role of the Holy Spirit in carrying out the church's mission. The moment of coming forward is the moment of the Holy Spirit's activity, the one who is promised to help with this task.[4] The Spirit is described as helping the witnesses in two ways, both of which encourage the witnesses to come forward by addressing the fears that may come with doing so. These two ways are by acting as a corroborative witness and by actually speaking on behalf of the witness. I will briefly survey these by proceeding in an exegetical mode. Because my purpose here is primarily constructive rather than polemical, I will not dwell narrowly on repairs to Foucault's project but on how its deficiencies invite opportunities for developing further a Christian account of witness as a form of resistance to power.

*　　*　　*

In the biblical thought-world, the Spirit of Truth functions as an additional witness to corroborate the truth of the testimony given. This corresponds to the fear of not having the testimony seconded and speaking something that, while true, is not likely to be accepted on its own. Deuteronomy 19:15 sets the requirement for two witnesses in order for a charge to be maintained; Jesus sends out disciples two by two in Luke 10; Revelation 11 depicts the two witnesses as two olive trees and two lampstands, symbols of the church's martyr-witness. In Acts, Peter alludes to the Holy Spirit's role as a second witness: "And we are witnesses to these things, and so is the Holy Spirit" (Acts 5:32). The Holy Spirit's corroborative witness functions in two ways: through signs and wonders that accompany the proclamation of the gospel, and the apostles' boldness *(parrhēsia)* in preaching it.

---

4. See Allison A. Trites, *The New Testament Concept of Witness* (Cambridge: Cambridge University Press, 1977), pp. 151-53.

First, as to signs and wonders, Augustine recognized the miraculous nature of the Spirit's corroboration to the testimony of witnesses:

> A few fishermen, uneducated in the liberal arts, completely uninstructed in the doctrines of their opponents, with no knowledge of grammar, not armed with dialectic, not adorned with rhetoric: these were the men whom Christ sent out with the nets of faith into the sea of this world. And this way He caught all those fish of every kind. . . . The world has believed a small number of obscure, insignificant, untutored men precisely because the divine nature of what they proclaim is all the more evident in the testimony of such lowly witnesses. For the eloquence which made what they said persuasive consisted of miraculous works, not words. Those who had not seen Christ's resurrection in the flesh, and His ascension into heaven in that flesh, believed the testimony of those who told what they had seen because they not only spoke of it, but wrought miraculous signs.[5]

Though Jesus' disciples did not use Sophist rhetoric, their testimonies were nonetheless made eloquent because of the supporting witness of the Spirit through signs. Their simple words were made believable because they were accompanied by convincing attestations. But Barth teaches that the miracles in the New Testament are part of Christ's work and not proofs of something else; rather, the proofs are part of the testimony. Making signs and wonders into evidence misconstrues part of the gospel by shoring up externalizing corroboration with what has not been given, namely, witnesses *outside* the church.[6] In other words, the signs of attestation are not external because the church is itself also a sign of attestation. That the Spirit creates the other signs is continuous with the sign the Spirit creates by creating the church.

Second, the gift of the Holy Spirit coincides with *parrhēsia* in giving witnesses boldness and courage to replace their fear. John's Gospel tells of Jesus himself speaking with *parrhēsia* in the presence of the authorities in Jerusalem and amid accusations that he is possessed because he is pleading his case for healing on the Sabbath (John 7:26). He speaks boldly and openly in response to being challenged by his relatives to show himself

5. Augustine, *The City of God,* ed. and trans. R. W. Dyson (Cambridge: Cambridge University Press, 1998), XXII:5, pp. 1113-14.

6. John D. Godsey, ed., *Karl Barth's Table Talk* (Edinburgh and London: Oliver and Boyd, 1963), p. 59.

publicly (John 7:4, 13). When he does so, it causes some of the people to note that his opponents are not arguing back. John even introduces a strongly ironic element when observers wonder whether the silence of Jesus' opponents indicates that they have become convinced that he is the Messiah. Though *parrhēsia* is sometimes used of Jesus, the New Testament typically uses it to refer to the apostles and other Christians.

Pentecost is the definitive instance of this role in enabling witnesses to come forward. The apostles did not actually *go and tell* (come forward and testify) until they received the Spirit at Pentecost. Until then, Jesus told them to stay in Jerusalem, where they were "all together in one place" when the Spirit came to them, at which point they were emboldened to come forward and proclaim the gospel (Luke 24:49; Acts 2:1). They received power *(dunamis)* and were immediately counted as witnesses (*martus,* Acts 1:8). Soon after that, when the religious leaders and Sadducees demanded that Peter and John give an account of the power *(dunamis)* by which a lame man had been healed on the steps of the temple, Peter was "filled with the Holy Spirit" and spoke to them (Acts 4:7-8). After their testimony, the people were impressed by their *parrhēsia:* "[W]hen they saw the boldness of Peter and John, and perceived that they were uneducated, common men, they wondered" (Acts 4:13).[7] Their power was from the Holy Spirit, both to heal the lame man and to risk testifying in front of those who had recently played a part in condemning Jesus. In response to being questioned about the source of this healing power, they displayed that very source of power in the answer itself, that is, in the manner of speech in which they gave the answer. The boldness that characterized their speech was *parrhēsia* — candidness, or outspokenness.[8]

Likewise, Peter described his ability to testify to the gathered crowds at Pentecost as *parrhēsia* (Acts 2:29). He knew his testimony was bold because he was contradicting the judgment of the crowd in speaking of the resurrection of "this Jesus, whom you crucified," and thus calling into question the legitimacy of their verdict (Acts 2:36). *Parrhēsia* is a major theme throughout Acts, and the book ends with Paul "preaching the king-

---

7. In response, the authorities had nothing to say, indicating that they both lacked boldness and a message. The *parrhēsia* of the apostles functions like a sign, given their lack of education, in the sense Augustine describes above. Jesus elicited the same reaction in John 7:15.

8. Heinrich Schlier, *"parrhēsia,"* in *Theological Dictionary of the New Testament,* ed. Gerhard Kittel and Gerhard Friedrich, trans. Geoffrey W. Bromiley (Grand Rapids: Eerdmans, 1964-76), 5: 871-86.

dom of God and teaching about the Lord Jesus Christ quite openly *(parrhēsias)* and unhindered" (Acts 28:31). But even this ending does not conclude the story that Acts begins to tell, because the whole book is really a kind of "program for the future task of the church."[9] The bold and frank speech of the apostles sets the church's agenda, the relationship between its message and its mission, and the orientation of the gospel's power to the worldly powers.

Elsewhere, Paul uses *parrhēsia* to describe how "we had courage *(parrhēsiazomai)* in our God to declare to you the gospel of God in the face of great opposition." Paul contrasts the *parrhēsia* that characterized their declaration with speech that flatters, deceives, or seeks glory (1 Thess. 2:2b-3). These and other instances give a sense for the specifically Christian use of *parrhēsia*.[10]

The boldness of the apostles' witness is not just an effect of the Holy Spirit's work as a corroborative witness, but is itself a way the Spirit corroborates. The words of the testimony and the boldness with which it is given are together two witnesses and not two aspects of a single witness.[11] Thus, in overcoming the dangers that proclaiming the gospel might entail, the very overcoming is itself part of the claim that what is proclaimed is true. Martyrs are those whose boldness — whose *parrhēsia* — is a risk unto death but, precisely because of that risk and death, they are spoken of as the paradigmatic witnesses of the Christian gospel (as in Rev. 17:6: *martus Iēsou*). The death of martyrs is part of their testimony, and their ability to risk their lives is the testimony of the Holy Spirit.[12] If, as I have observed above, witnesses do not present evidence but are God's evidence, martyrs are the first demonstration of how this is the case.

Yet Christian *parrhēsia* is not exhaustively described by boldness; it also signals free speech. This accords with Foucault's observations about

9. Stanley B. Marrow, SJ, "*Parrhēsia* and the New Testament," *The Catholic Biblical Quarterly* 44 (1982): 431-46 (esp. p. 442). Marrow further suggests that, between Peter's first usage of *parrhēsia* and the concluding reference to Paul, Acts portrays an overarching *inclusio* in which the gospel is freely proclaimed.

10. Marrow and Szakolczai both think that speaking of a specifically Christian notion of *parrhēsia* is justified.

11. See W. C. van Unnik, "The Christian's Freedom of Speech in the New Testament," in *Sparsa Collecta: The Collected Essays of W. C. van Unnik* (Leiden: Brill, 1980), 2: 284. This is particularly the case in John's Gospel.

12. The semantic association of *parrhēsia* with martyrdom in early Christian literature has its roots in 4 Macc 10:5: "Enraged by the man's boldness, they disjointed his hands and feet." See Marrow, "*Parrhēsia* and the NT," p. 437.

how it functions in the Greek polis among free citizens in the public assembly. Here the reference is usually to the gospel's outward expansion in disregard of obstacles. W. C. van Unnik notes that, in Acts, *parrhēsia* "is closely connected with the proclamation of the gospel; it denotes the freedom with which it is proclaimed by him who himself is there [in Rome] on trial. It is, however, not the profession in the law-court, but the missionary activity that is carried out with all clearness and without outward hindrance."[13] This points to one way that Christian *parrhēsia* differs from classical and Hellenistic *parrhēsia*. The freedom of speech exercised in the Greek polis falls within the assembly of the *ekklēsia*, the institutional locus guaranteeing free speech. Those with citizen rights would assemble and speak freely in pursuit of the good of the city. But according to Gerhard Lohfink, the Christian transfer of the true *ekklēsia* from the domain of civil law to the church makes "an extraordinary claim."[14] They were claiming — as a function of the Christian mission — to be the true public body in contrast to the others, driving the locus of free speech outside of the institutions of sovereignty and propelling it into the wider world. The Christian polis is thus asserted to be more decisive than any other polis, whether it be Athens, Jerusalem, Rome, or any other city. Similarly transformed is the Greek association of justice with truth that rested on the virtue of *parrhēsia* being exercised in the polis. Both aspects overturn the former association between truth and political sovereignty. When Luke describes *parrhēsia* that *is* in a legal setting (as with Peter and John before the Council in Acts 4), the reader is led to associate the *parrhēsia* with proclamation rather than legal protocol. The gospel is good news to the nations but not to the state.[15]

We see, then, the importance of the setting or locale in which *parrhēsia* operates. Christians were not only speaking the truth when there were no institutional reasons nor guarantees for them to do so, but they were also speaking the truth when it was not being spoken in the polis (that is, first in Jerusalem, then in Rome). The exceptional nature of the community of believers as an alternative polis was established beginning with the community's prayer in Acts 4. Up to this point, Acts does not refer to them as the church. But the first they are mentioned following their

13. Van Unnik, "The Christian's Freedom of Speech," p. 279.

14. Gerhard Lohfink, *Does God Need the Church? Toward a Theology of the People of God,* trans. Linda M. Maloney (Collegeville, MN: Liturgical Press, 1999), p. 218.

15. Of course, this is anachronistic. We might properly identify empires and governments as the states of the first century.

prayer, Luke calls them an assembly by using the word *ekklēsia* (Acts 5:11). S. C. Winter points to the significance of this shift: "In this way the narrative recognizes that they have separated from the Jerusalem polis and have constituted their own assembly under the authority of God."[16] Paul, too, extends the way that Christian citizenship in the *ekklēsia* of God relativizes their other citizenships by subsuming the latter within the former: "Paul chose [*ekklēsia*] to indicate that the assembly of those who followed Jesus, the assembly called together in a particular city in the name of the biblical God, was in competition with the local political assembly of the citizenry, the official *ekklēsia*. The world is meant to hear the claim that the congregation of Jesus, gathered in the name of the God of the Bible, is where the interests of the city in question truly find expression."[17] The church as *ekklēsia* is fully public. Like its other activities, its speech pertains to the whole good of human society, not just a private realm. And because it is aligned with the heavenly polis, it does not compete with other earthy poleis, but anticipates their fulfillment in a way that renders problematic any simple binary estimation of public and private, such as is familiar to members of liberal democratic societies.[18] Moreover, in being both whole and public, the *ekklēsia* exposes the inherently parochial nature of the earthly poleis, even those with the massive scope of empire. The very self-description that the Christians used to refer to their gathering was a challenge to the other kingdoms and their claims to universality, autonomy, and the pursuit of human goods apart from God.

It is worth observing one thing that this means for political theology generally. If the *ekklēsia* is the most genuine public as it is aligned with the heavenly polis, Christian political thought need not take as its starting point the existence of human governments as we find them nor the necessity of their ultimate survival as crucial to the attainment of human goods. It should instead begin with the reality of the church as a political body irrespective of whether and how it may have managed to accrue sovereign benefits in one instance or another. It is just as true and tedious as it is

16. S. C. Winter, "Parrhesia in Acts," in *Friendship, Flattery, and Frankness*, ed. John T. Fitzgerald (Leiden: Brill, 1996). Winter has in mind also a separation from the political life of the Temple as the paradigmatic locus of *ekklēsia*.

17. Dieter Georgi, *Theocracy in Paul's Praxis and Theology* (Minneapolis: Fortress, 1991), p. 57.

18. See William T. Cavanaugh, "Killing for the Telephone Company: Why the Nation-State is not the Keeper of the Common Good," *Modern Theology* 20, no. 2 (April 2004): 243-74 (esp. p. 267).

heartbreaking to acknowledge that the church in many times and places fails to live up to its status as a fully public *ekklēsia* that in seeking Christian goods is simultaneously most authentically seeking human goods understood in their broadest sense. But this is a failure to which Christianity must always resist growing accustomed. It certainly must not yield to pressures to solidify it into a first principle that mistakenly underwrites as necessary institutions, structures, and governments as the primary concern of Christianity's political thinking.

Where the existence of a political body called the *ekklēsia* of God is the starting assumption for political theology rather than its outworking, theorizing will follow from what is always first a concrete people. The church's life is its concrete existence as real gatherings in which the people of God are either present or represented. Their unity is actual and can be seen; it does not depend on an imaginary unity that follows from shared fantasies or fears. "God has built the Church of God not on principles, but on people."[19] The church's unity is physical and material, as Paul theorizes: "Because there is one bread, we who are many are one body, for we all partake of the one bread" (1 Cor. 10:17). The church's unity is eucharistic, as the early gatherings in Acts demonstrate (Acts 2:42-47).[20] This community does not preexist the bread in either the imagination or in fact, but is the body of Christ precisely in the breaking of the bread. Hence the Eucharist far surpasses the political importance of constitutions and related attempts to bring into being a people who did not exist before.

Foucault's near-total neglect of Acts is disappointing. One wonders how he would have interpreted the transformation of *parrhēsia*'s political referent displayed there. Still, the sense of *parrhēsia* that he discerns in

19. Lohfink, *Does God Need the Church?* p. 221. The language of imagination owes to Benedict Anderson, *Imagined Communities: Reflections on the Origin and Spread of Nationalism*, rev. ed. (New York: Verso, 1991), which he argues is characteristic of modern nations.

20. In a very interesting suggestion about the ideal size of a Christian gathering, Lohfink cites the initial gathering of 120 people in Acts 1: "[I]t probably expresses the experience that a community should not contain more than 120 people. Only at that size can it remain a concrete assembly in which no one is invisible, in which each member can be aware of the sorrow and happiness, the cares and the joys of the others. How could it be possible to share responsibility for the faith of the others in a huge community with hundreds of baptized persons? The figure of 120 is the upper limit in a community that is not to become an anonymous cultic society but remain a community of common life struggling to fulfill its prophetic calling" (pp. 221-22). One wonders whether the logistical problems that very large churches face when they celebrate the Eucharist actually also make a much more profound theological point.

early Christian literature does have some basis in the New Testament. In particular, its occurrences in Hebrews and 1 John denote a different kind of bold speech than appears in the Gospels and Acts. Such occurrences, for example, emphasize boldness in approaching God on grounds that Christians have a sympathetic high priest in Christ or else because they have examined their hearts and are convinced that they are free of a bad conscience (Heb. 4:16; 1 John 3:21). Self-examination and private prayer surely seem to lack the political element elsewhere in the New Testament and seem to support Foucault's thesis about Christian *parrhēsia*.[21] But it would be a mistake to think that the latter Christian uses constitute a departure or even a problematization of the earlier uses. In order to conclude this (wrongly), one would need to make two assumptions. First, one would need to separate the private and public spheres, where the gospel is boldly proclaimed in the marketplace, on the one hand, and where sins are privately confessed to God or a priest, on the other. Given the transformation of the political associated with *parrhēsia*, particularly in Acts, we might exactly expect that these two forms of speech, both of and in the new *ekklēsia*, would coincide.[22] A second assumption for Foucault's argument is that, had he investigated *parrhēsia* in Acts and the Gospels, he would have needed to associate those more overtly political uses with the earlier Greek uses, which he exegetes from Euripides leading up to Socrates. But again, this ignores the transformation of the polis. If there was a shift within Christian *parrhēsia*, as Foucault maintains, it is a change in emphasis rather than a change in kind. This bears further elaboration.

What is the significance of the suggestion that the boldness in approaching God is of one species with the boldness in approaching the world's unbelief in confrontation with other people or with power? The Christian witness as *parrhēsiastēs* does not fear the truth on account of confidence in God's goodness instantiated in the resurrection and vindication of Christ. When a Christian confesses sin, she is saying that the gospel is good; the resurrection and lordship of Christ permit confrontation with

21. Van Unnik even says that the meaning of *parrhēsia* in 1 John is "completely different" from the Gospels, and "1 John . . . leads over to later usage in which freedom of speech is the characteristic attitude of Christian prayer" (Van Unnik, "The Christian's Freedom of Speech," p. 288). This later usage is prominent in Origen and Isaac of Nineveh.

22. Arpad Szakolczai makes this critique against Foucault in *The Genesis of Modernity*, p. 236. Likewise, Winter notes how the public/private distinction is broken down in Acts, so that by the end of the book, Paul mentions having borne witness both in the *dēmos* and the *oikos* (Acts 20:20) (Winter, "Parrhesia in Acts," p. 200).

sin. It should not be surprising that the Christian confrontation with un-just rulers expresses the same virtue as when Christians confront the self's own injustices. If Christian *parrhēsia* were only the former, the *ekklēsia* would dualistically oppose the world, and Christians would be self-righteous. If it were only the latter, there would be no Christian polis, and sovereignty would be given over completely to worldly power. Instead, the parrhesiastic nature of confession is a reminder that determinative politics is not granted to the church except insofar as the church continues to speak the truth, both in its proclamation and its confession.[23]

Christian *parrhēsia* evinces several more features that I should briefly mention. Though it is displayed as a virtue, *parrhēsia* is neverthe-less a *gift* that is given and received.[24] The apostles are filled with the Holy Spirit and speak with *parrhēsia* only after having prayed for it: "And now, Lord, look upon their threats, and grant to thy servants to speak thy word with all boldness *(parrhēsia)*, while thou stretchest out thy hand to heal, and signs and wonders are performed through the name of thy holy ser-vant Jesus" (Acts 4:29-30). Here the gift of the Holy Spirit itself is coinci-dental with the gift of *parrhēsia*. Moreover, Christian *parrhēsia* seems al-ways to be tied to the content of what is being told and cannot be separated from that content. In contrast to the secular usage found in the Cynics and others, Christian *parrhēsia* in the Bible is never found on its own as a stand-alone quality used in speech generally. The Cynic is com-pelled by the need to speak freely and thus, according to Epictetus, "must be able to lift up his voice, and mounting the tragic stage, to speak like Socrates," denouncing the shameful acts of the people.[25] In contrast, the Christian witness is compelled by the gospel, that is, by what has been seen and heard. Put simply, Christian *parrhēsia* is not first a characteristic of witnesses, but a characteristic of the gospel. This explains why, even though most instances of *parrhēsia* in Acts are in the face of some danger, not all are: for example, the preaching of Apollos and Paul in Ephesus

23. This may explain why the ban has historically been practiced by those churches that have grasped this most clearly. Church discipline is not finally separable from the church's proclamation, though this is perhaps most evident to so-called sect-type churches.

24. Marrow, *"Parrhēsia,"* pp. 442-43.

25. Quoted in Lincoln E. Galloway, *Freedom in the Gospel: Paul's Exemplum in 1 Cor 9 in Conversation with the Discourses of Epictetus and Philo* (Paris: Peeters, 2004), p. 160. See also van Unnik, "The Christian's Freedom of Speech," p. 288: "When [the Christians] used 'free speech', they had not the pride of the Cynics who wanted to show their independence by reviling other people; they used it to bring to light the open mystery of God."

(Acts 18:26; 19:8).[26] There is more to the witness's bold proclamation than the risk he takes. Instead, boldness comes from the substance of the proclaimed message itself, regardless of whether or not there is danger involved in proclaiming it. This accords with the idea that the gospel is first a message of salvation and not condemnation.[27] Proclaiming the gospel often creates and precedes dangers insofar as the danger is a function of the world's unbelief.[28] But unlike Greek *parrhēsia,* Christian *parrhēsia* cannot be identified only by the criterion of risk.

Finally, Christian *parrhēsia* describes a condition of openness to God, others, and the gospel.[29] This openness "is what distinguishes it from mere freedom of speech in the political sphere, from the frankness and openness of amity and friendship, and from the cynic boldness of unbridled discourse and mindless criticism."[30] I will further explore this characteristic below in a discussion of patient witness.

Turning to consider the words of the testimony itself leads to the other role of the Holy Spirit. If the Spirit's first way of helping the witness is by acting as a corroborative witness, the second way is by speaking on behalf of the witness by giving her the words to say. Entailed in this role is more than speaking eyewitness evidence, since it points to the witness's composure and ability to trust God in the moment of crisis instead of merely a knowledge of facts. Clearly displaced is the Weberian charismatic whose charm wins over his hearers. The Spirit's promise to speak for the witness addresses the fear of not being clever or eloquent enough to be convincing; it also exemplifies how Christian *parrhēsia* is a gift that calls forth openness — in this case to the giver of the words.

At Pentecost, the Holy Spirit's role in speaking for the apostles is shown in their new speech, having received tongues of fire followed immediately by speaking "as the Spirit gave them utterance" (Acts 2:3-4). Jesus

26. Even though Apollos's preaching was incomplete, he is still described as "being fervent in the spirit." Paul's speech was also unhindered in Rome (Acts 28:31). See S. C. Winter, "*Parrhēsia* in Acts," p. 186.

27. Marrow, "*Parrhēsia* and the New Testament," p. 443. As Barth taught, "Confession is decisively action, and not — or only incidentally — reaction. It says Yes and not — or only relatively — No" (*CD* III/4, p. 81).

28. "It is not so much the opposition which provokes the 'freedom of speech' on the side of the Christians, but their parrhesia which provokes opposition and danger" (van Unnik, "The Christian's Freedom of Speech," p. 282).

29. Schlier, "*parrhēsia,*" p. 883.

30. Marrow, "*Parrhēsia* and the New Testament," p. 444.

himself likewise claims only to speak what the Father tells him (John 12:50). But the key text — anticipating much of the persecution the early church encountered — is part of Jesus' discourse in Mark 13:

> But take heed to yourselves; for they will deliver you up to councils; and you will be beaten in synagogues; and you will stand before governors and kings for my sake, to bear testimony before them. And the gospel must first be preached to all nations. And when they bring you to trial and deliver you up, do not be anxious beforehand what you are to say; but say whatever is given you in that hour, for it is not you who speak, but the Holy Spirit. (Mark 13:9-11).

Here the context is one of persecutions for the sake of Jesus and being called on to give an account before authorities who are hostile to the preaching of the gospel to the nations. This is a threat to the Christian mission, yet it comes with the reassurance that the gospel will be preached to all the nations, in spite of opposition.

These words find immediate fulfillment in Jesus' own trial and death. They also anticipate the apostles' opposition to authorities recounted in Acts, particularly in Paul's case (e.g., Acts 22:1-22; 25:8-11; 26:1-32; 28:23-31). Paul himself celebrates the fact that his opposition has actually ended up promoting the gospel, inspiring with confidence those imprisoned with him who are made "much more bold to speak the word of God without fear" (Phil. 1:14). He understands the bold and publicly displayed confidence to be an element of the very words they speak, since the words are gifts of the Holy Spirit. The gospel is already a bold message, and it is hence not only fitting that it should be proclaimed with boldness, but doing so is a witness to the Spirit whose message the Christian bears.

This second role of the Holy Spirit has another side as well, as Barth comments on this text's Matthean parallel (Matt. 10:19): "This is a reminder that, like faith itself, the word of faith is not something which is at the disposal of man, of believing man."[31] Barth has in mind the inadequacy of mere human words compared to what is given by God. "What is *adopted* and not *received* cannot be the content of the required confession."[32] The gospel must constantly be received; it is not everywhere the same message; it remains the speech of the Holy Spirit into the world. Its

---

31. Barth, *CD* III/4, p. 80.

32. Barth, *CD* III/4, p. 80 (emphasis added). In this passage, by "confession," Barth means testimony.

words are in motion, caught up in the give and take of real historical events, animated as living witness to the living Christ, who goes ahead and bids disciples to follow.[33] Christ's self-identity is the only coherence that the gospel message needs for those who are his as a continual and ongoing work. As a message, Christian proclamation may be welcomed or rejected by those who hear it just as it may be obstructed or allowed to flow freely by those who would witness to it. But the receptivity of witnesses to the Spirit's message is not incidental to their moral competence and ability to declare the gospel in the face of hostility. The medium and message coincide, just as do boldness and openness.

Furthermore, if the words of the witness do not ultimately *belong* to the witness but to the Holy Spirit, then the witness is not finally responsible for the outcome of those words. The witness is relieved of the functional and operative aspects of his task. This is the source of the idea that the preached word is sacramental, that it enacts what it signifies. The proclamation is part of the thing it proclaims as a performative speech-act, though it is much more satisfying to put the matter in theological language. When the claim "Jesus is risen" is made, the truth of these words is offered to God in hope that the Spirit will transform them, making of them something more than what they are on their own. The Spirit does not so much make them true as make them genuine and continual processions of God's Word, as themselves Christ's sacramental presence in the church within its narrating the present, risen life that Christ is living. When "this is true" is said of the gospel of Christ, the substance of this claim is enacted in its reliance on the Spirit's speech. Sacramentally, the witness proclaims something other than itself while, precisely by way of the proclamation, the witness is implicated by it without presuming to own it. Since the words of the proclamation belong to and derive from the Holy Spirit, the proclamation is the Spirit's witness to the Son. Nevertheless, the human witness must still come forward. Eberhard Busch summarizes the way that Barth thought of human witness to Christ as *mere* witness on this account, since the human witness differs from both Christ's witness to the truth and the Holy Spirit's witness to Christ while still participating in it:

33. The fact that the four canonical Gospels complicate rather than simplify the messages they portray is a benefit to a church that might otherwise imagine that its life together would be easier if we had only one Gospel. Insisting that these are all part of the church's Scripture and are all four witnesses to the story of Christ is the first exercise in fostering the spirited dispositions appropriate to the dynamic life of its central character.

That they, in contrast to him, are witnesses as called *sinners* demonstrates that they are so in another way than he is. They bear witness to the truth which is never identical with them, which is even alien to them, and which is only "guaranteed" to them. They are by all account mere *witnesses* to this truth . . . mere in the sense that they neither are nor possess the truth. They cannot control or manipulate it. They are dependent upon it, upon its constantly opening itself to them anew. When it opens up before them, they can only point to it. That is what they *can* do and *ought* to do. The truth is not made known to them as an "end in itself," let alone an "object of their self-seeking" . . . as if they were permitted to hoard it away from others, to conceal it and deny them access to it.[34]

The witness faces the temptation to limit the openness of *parrhēsia* and instead become an advocate. The advocate turns a witness's testimony into a compelling case by weaving together the testimonies of many witnesses and presenting them persuasively to the court. No single witness bears the burden of doing any more than giving testimony, because witnesses are not responsible for convincing hearers that their testimony is true. There is a legitimate way of speaking about the Spirit as both advocate and witness, but the *human* witness is never asked to be in a position to advocate his own case. Modern jurisprudence follows this pattern when it allows everyone accused to have access to a lawyer.[35] In the theological idiom, apologetics names the tendency to conflate the role of witness with the role of advocate, where the apologete can stand outside the truth by offering words not as testimony, but as evidence. Bruce Marshall rightly makes the point that the Spirit persuades people to hold Christian beliefs as true, but does not do so by adding more evidence or reasons beyond what is already available. The Spirit makes something attractive, and this something is the church's witness, that is, its testimony, which is its irreducible form of "evidence."[36] Evidence denotes how testimony is used and

34. Eberhard Busch, *The Great Passion: An Introduction to Karl Barth's Theology,* trans. Geoffrey W. Bromiley (Grand Rapids: Eerdmans, 2004), p. 146 (emphasis in original).

35. Plato reported the received wisdom that "even the wolf . . . has a right to an advocate." Plato, "Phaedrus," in *Plato in Twelve Volumes,* trans. H. N. Fowler, Loeb Classical Library (Cambridge, MA: Harvard University Press, 1982), 1:272c.

36. Bruce D. Marshall, *Trinity and Truth* (Cambridge: Cambridge University Press, 2000), pp. 204-5. Likewise, Yoder attests to how apologetics can be made to take the place of witness: "I by no means want to lack respect for the 'apologetic' mission of the faith commu-

made to function as part of an argument or case; this is made by the advocate and not the witness. Especially in its modern form, apologetics errs
when its resources are construed as evidence rather than testimony.[37]
Barth's famous claim that "the best apologetics is good dogmatics" directs
Christians away from presenting evidence and toward giving testimony.[38]

In contrast to the apologete, the martyr denotes the proper separation between advocate and human witness. The martyr stands within the
truth (or on account of the truth), even at great cost, since part of the
claim that the martyr's testimony is true is its self-involving character. If
the truth is true, the martyr is willing to suffer whatever implications follow from it.[39] Barth notes that the willingness to suffer the consequences
that testifying will bring tests whether the confession being made is genuine. "A declaration may be bold and clear, and centrally Christian . . . but so

nity, whereby believing thinkers encounter their neighbors' sense-making concerns.
'Making sense of the universe' is not a bad thing to do, nor a bad terrain on which to encounter our non-believing or otherwise-believing neighbors. Yet when taken alone
apologetics is not angular enough to produce testimony" (Yoder, "Christianity and Protest
in America," unpublished paper).

37. Richard Bauckham, in a perceptive discussion of witness in John's Gospel, concludes that "[a]s with all testimony, even that of the law court, there is a point beyond which
corroboration cannot go, and only the witness can vouch for the truth of his own witness"
(Bauckham, *Jesus and the Eyewitnesses: The Gospels as Eyewitness Testimony* [Grand Rapids:
Eerdmans, 2006], p. 411). Philip Kenneson describes this as our own situation, radically in-
tensified by postmodernism's exposure of the church's former reliance on apologetics simply to be a denial of its witnessing task. Philip D. Kenneson, "There's No Such Thing as Objective Truth, and It's a Good Thing, Too," in *Christian Apologetics in the Postmodern World*,
ed. Timothy R. Phillips and Dennis L. Okholm (Downers Grove, IL: InterVarsity Press,
1995).

38. John D. Godsey, ed., *Karl Barth's Table Talk* (Edinburgh and London: Oliver and
Boyd, 1963), p. 62. Academics often ridicule apologetics, but for the wrong reasons. Like witness, apologetics should not aspire to the status of an academic disciple; and condemning it
for not being one only reproduces an error of expectation. Wolfhart Pannenberg notes:
"Apologetics has had the task of raising the question of the truth of Christian doctrine. With
few exceptions dogmatics has dealt only with the content" (Pannenberg, *Systematic Theology*, trans. Geoffrey W. Bromiley [Grand Rapids: Eerdmans, 1991], 1:48).

39. Of course, a "martyr" may suffer for a lie, meaning that self-involvement does not
guarantee truth: this is merely consistent with saying that a martyr does not offer proof. But
we suspect that a truth that is unable to produce *any* martyrs cannot be true, suggesting that
martyrdom is necessary but insufficient for displaying the truth. Apologetics, if meant to
stand alone, risks not being able to produce martyrs. Possibly more problematically, I acknowledge that comments like these are more like apologetics than martyrdom. That is why
speaking is better than writing.

long as it remains theoretical, entailing no obligation or venture on the part of him who makes it, it is not confession and must not be mistaken for it. . . . A man confesses when with his Christian declaration he champions this cause before men, and especially before those to whom it is alien, disclosing the community and accepting the consequences of this disclosure, in his own person."[40] While for Barth there is no proclamation without witness, Wittgenstein understood how the very ability of someone to speak the truth depends on the extent to which one embodies it: "The truth can be spoken only by someone who is already *at home* in it; not by someone who still lives in falsehood and reaches out from falsehood towards truth on just one occasion."[41] A witness is someone who is at home in the truth, simultaneously open to its being something uncontrolled by the words used in speaking it and open to being formed according to what is true, so that speaking it may end up being an eminently surprising act.

Neither Wittgenstein nor Barth would have imagined that a martyr *proves* the truth. In fact, they might even have shared a certain agreement with Nietzsche's sardonic comment: "I would deny that any martyr ever had anything whatsoever to do with truth."[42] Nietzsche is rejecting the kind of "maximally pragmatist" logic that moves effortlessly from claiming:

      (1) if Jesus is risen, then saints will die for the faith
to (2) saints do die for their faith
      (3) therefore Jesus is risen.[43]

Such a move takes a description of a historical event as an argument for a proposition. It syllogistically discloses that it is more at home in logic and logical proofs than in the substance of whatever truth it claims to defend. Nietzsche recognized its absurdity when he declared that it is never necessary to refute a martyr.[44] Indeed, part of the reason a martyr's death does not need to be refuted is also a reason for martyrs to be killed: they expose the violence inherent in arguments that inevitably run out but are not

40. Barth, *CD* III/4, p. 85.

41. Wittgenstein, *Culture and Value* (Chicago: University of Chicago Press, 1980), p. 35e.

42. Friedrich Nietzsche, *The Antichrist*, in *The Portable Nietzsche*, ed. and trans. Walter Kaufmann (London: Viking Penguin, 1968), sec. 53.

43. Marshall, *Trinity and Truth*, pp. 188-91.

44. Nietzsche, *The Antichrist*, sec. 53. Even more to the point, he goes on to ask, "Is the cross an argument?" He was right to think the answer is no, but he was wrong to think that this means the cross has nothing to do with truth.

based on confidence in the truth itself. Nietzsche was wrong to think that martyrs have *nothing* to do with truth; they merely have nothing to do with apologetics understood as devotion to games of logic, since a martyr's death does not prove anything.[45] I will return to these issues in part III below.

A further failure of witness has to do with how the witness's identity relates to testimony. The way apologetics attempts to do without the witness by relying only on the advocate (or, perhaps better, by advocating rather than testifying from the witness stand) is similar to the way protection offered to a witness who hesitates about coming forward threatens the self-involving nature of witness. If a witness is given a new identity, his testimony becomes anonymous, and the words are separated from the person.[46] Words on their own (detached from the person of the witness) do not constitute testimony, because nothing is at stake for those who utter them. This names a perversion in which the church is an extrinsic instrument for, say, growth or making converts through preaching that fails to be completely honest so long as the church does not anonymously embody the substance of its preaching.

Plato understood the importance of embodying one's words. In the *Phaedrus* he critiques rhetorical forms that oppose this. Socrates holds that speaking is better than writing, since words do not contain wisdom on their own, separated from considerations of what kind of person speaks them. Writing breaks off the conversation that would allow the other party to discover this.[47] Therefore, the writer hides behind his words by writing them

---

45. David Bentley Hart, who is not a Barthian, approaches Christian rhetoric as the peaceful offer of martyrs rather than the proof of apologetics: "I want less to refute the position against which I have set my argument . . . than to point toward another grammar, an alternative rhetoric, a fuller vision, whose own inner rationality can argue for itself" (Hart, *The Beauty of the Infinite: The Aesthetics of Christian Truth* [Grand Rapids: Eerdmans, 2003], p. 31; see also p. 441). James K. A. Smith argues, in concert with Hart, that apologetics is always linked to a kind of coercion inasmuch as it relies on the necessary logic of disinterested rationality that makes unbelievers irrational (Smith, "Questions About the Perception of 'Christian Truth': On the Affective Effects of Sin," essay presented at the American Academy of Religion, 2005).

46. I do not mean to imply that witness protection programs are somehow not a "good thing," but only to indicate how hard it is to speak a risky testimony and also mitigate the risk, since all testimony has value only insofar as it is embodied historically. The most obvious mode of historical embodiment is having to live with the consequences of testifying under threatening circumstances.

47. Plato, "Phaedrus," 275c.

down and summarily ducking out of the way. When Socrates argues against those who say in court that persuasion is more important than speaking the truth, he is making a similar point. Just as writing can only remind one of what one already knows, those who prize rhetoric that is convincing, regardless of the truth of what is said, also depend on *probability,* saying what most people think. The things that will be convincing to the most people will no doubt be things they already believe. "For sometimes one must not even tell what was actually done, if it was not likely to be done, but what was probable, whether in accusation or defense; and in brief, a speaker must always aim at probability, paying no attention to the truth."[48] Plato is opposed to this, of course, and for the same reason that he thinks speaking is better than writing: words must be used in modes that enhance the involvement of their user in the consequences of those words.

Nevertheless, there is more than one way to avoid the kind of rhetoric that gives Plato such cause for concern. Even spoken testimony can never guarantee the involvement of the witness. What matters is who bears responsibility for the speaking, the speaker or someone else? It is important to note that when the New Testament describes what I have here identified as the second role of the Holy Spirit in witness, it does not describe the Spirit's speaking on behalf of the witness in a way that the witness disappears. Rather, in being given words to say, the witness is nonetheless the one who speaks herself. Consider how it might be otherwise. In contrast to how Christianity understands the Holy Spirit's speaking witness when it follows the New Testament in the matter, James Scott describes a fascinating example of how, in certain ecstatic moments, the fear of a witness is mitigated in spirit possession rituals that allow the speaker to be anonymous. His example involves how low-caste servants in south India give voice to their grievances against their superior-caste counterparts in a way that nevertheless affords the speakers a certain amount of protection. The words spoken can be attributed to the spirit and not the speaker.

> In the case of spirit possession, a woman seized by a spirit can openly make known her grievances against her husband and male relatives, curse them, make demands, and, in general, violate the powerful norms of male dominance. She may, while possessed, cease work, be given gifts, and generally be treated indulgently. Because it is not she who is acting, but rather the spirit that has seized her, she cannot be

---

48. Plato, "Phaedrus," 272e.

held personally responsible for her words. The result is a kind of oblique protest that dares not speak its own name but that is often acceded to if only because its claims are seen to emanate from a powerful spirit and not from the woman herself.[49]

Even though the woman speaks, her identity is nearly irrelevant to the testimony, and she is not held responsible for it. However, this example serves as a contrast for our purposes. The identity of the Christian witness is crucial to the testimony, because the meaningfulness of the words uttered (and therefore their truth) depends on who is speaking — as well as the total context of the speech. It is difficult to see why someone who may be absolved of incendiary testimony due to a spirit speaking for them would ever be killed for it. Moves that preserve the anonymity of the witness such as gossip, rumor, and spirit possession are refusals to come forward fully.

A contrast to such anonymity is the silence of martyrs. The anonymous witness has words but no identity; the witness to Christ, however, has the identity made known by coming forward and a testimony that exceeds her own speech, even in the silence of death. That God continues to speak despite silenced witnesses is the content of Revelation's scroll. God not only promises to raise up fallen martyrs, joining them to the glory of the risen Christ, allotting them a share in unmediated fellowship within God's eternal city; but those whose enduring faith leads even to death are also promised that their witness will, despite all probability and patent explanation, help bring about the conversion of the nations.[50] After enduring the hatred of the world in response to their testimony against it, their silence and dead bodies are trophies to the power of some to destroy God's messengers and silence God's word of judgment (Rev. 11:1-13).[51]

49. James C. Scott, *Domination and the Arts of Resistance: Hidden Transcripts* (New Haven: Yale University Press, 1990), p. 141.

50. Richard Bauckham, *The Theology of the Book of Revelation* (Cambridge: Cambridge University Press, 1993), p. 84.

51. The definitive confrontation between the powers of this world and the power of the gospel is located here. Recalling the second clause of the Lord's Prayer, the repentance of the nations marks a realignment of power, such that the seventh angel declares, "The kingdom of the world has become the kingdom of our Lord and of his Christ, and he shall reign for ever and ever." I will say more about "the powers" in the next chapter, some of which is based on Barth's commentary on the second clause of the Lord's Prayer. Here it is worth noting that the exercise of what Barth called rebellious powers (in the Pauline sense) can come to an end, in fact, through repentance, and that the witness to which they respond is the political and missionary task of the church.

Martyrs do not strive for anonymity in order to allow their message to do what they themselves cannot. Instead, their very deaths and silence are also witnesses to the testimonies they bear. These even continue to bear witness against those who kill them, since God has promised in time to raise them up. However, the promise is even more profound than this, because their deaths will not only be vindicated by being united to Christ's; their testimonies are also vindicated by bringing about, in fact, what their deaths appear unquestionably to thwart: their message of repentance (and not just condemnation) lives on and finds some who are able to welcome it. In other words, the ability of a witness to come forward is not just a function of the belief that martyrs will be raised with Christ, but that their testimonies continue in their dying and rising — and the nations repent as a result.

$$* \qquad * \qquad *$$

The above observations may be left somewhat crudely general, yet they are sufficient to show that those who bear witness to Christ have a seemingly paradoxical relationship with their testimonies. On the one hand, they speak the testimonies with boldness — that is, fearlessly and confidently. On the other hand, the witness does not possess the testimony nor control its truth, patiently remaining open to the truth even while speaking it boldly. It is important to deal with this apparent paradox. If openness were absolute, being open *to* or *for* something would be excluded. The effort here is to qualify absolute openness according to its object, Christ. Robert Jenson chides a clear paradox to which Bultmann (unlike Barth) was susceptible in holding the specificity of faith's object at bay in his critique of religion and instead giving an abstract account. Jenson exploits what is deficient about this strategy: "To believe, to exist authentically, is to be unconditionally open to the future. But to *what* future?" In imagining that the resurrection removed Jesus from history and placed him in eternity, Bultmann disallowed a temporal future that might be Jesus' future. The future could only be an abstraction that, when one is open before it, exists as something other than the open future of Jesus himself. So, as Jenson asks, *What* future? Merely, he adduces, a future that is fully open to the future.[52] This may yield patience, but it is difficult to see how it will yield boldness for anything other than its own endless deferral.

52. Robert W. Jenson, *Systematic Theology: The Triune God* (Oxford: Oxford University Press, 1997), 1:170-71.

Instead, Jenson follows Barth in insisting that the future that demands openness is the concrete and material future of fellowship with Jesus, whose historical specificity resists those species of being open that
themselves attempt to defy all history. Put differently, only as the proclamation of Jesus takes a narrative form will it be able both to attest to the
full historical reality of his life, death, and resurrection, and to look to the
future anticipated by that narrative as well. Even more strongly, the way
the witness's proclamation is open to Jesus' future is its hope that God is
fulfilling Jesus' story in part through this proclaiming activity.[53]

The witness does not circumscribe the truth, because any such line
would function to specify in advance the determinate expression and form
the truth might take, closing it off; yet this is not truth as an abstraction
but the freedom of Jesus to express himself as the free action of God. The
paradox comes apart when alleged claims to truth can rise above the vaga-
ries of creaturely existence and set at bay the ways that being temporal beings limit our capacities to know in any other ways than simply as creatures. As creatures who exist by contingent gift, excess of Trinitarian love,
and superfluity rather than out of necessity, need, or compulsion, our
claims to know must not outpace our ability to receive what we are with
gratitude. When it does, we are dealing with power rather than truth, corrupt idol-making rather than knowing.[54] Such claims are at odds with the
testimonies of witnesses.

Consider an analogy. The practice of witness instantiates the Christian relationship to the truth in the same way that the practice of stewardship shows Christians how to relate to possessions. Stewards do not own
their possessions; their masters do. Yet stewards make use of the masters'
possessions in buying and selling. As Christians practice stewardship, they
come to see that, not just possessions, but, in fact, everything that
creaturely existence entails, exists to us by the grace of contingent gratuity.
The Sabbath similarly teaches Christians and Jews how to relate to work, as
Barth makes clear by placing the fourth Mosaic commandment at the
front of his discussion of "special ethics."[55] The Sabbath is not just a pause
of activity, a negative static space opened up within the undulations of

---

53. Thus Jenson: "[Jesus Christ] is the Word of God because he is the narrative content of the word-event that is the Word of God" (*Systematic Theology*, 1:171).

54. Miroslav Volf, *Exclusion and Embrace: A Theological Exploration of Identity, Otherness, and Reconciliation* (Nashville: Abingdon, 1996), p. 248: "If truth is imposed there can be
no gain in knowledge, but there can be gain in power."

55. Barth, *CD* III/4, p. 54.

otherwise ceaseless labor that does not threaten the ascendancy of production. The Sabbath is a positive activity in its own right that relativizes all other human action. It shows that one's work does not exercise an ability one has attained and therefore owned, but that it is a gift. Sabbath locates all labor around worship, not worship around labor. Consequently, human work should not be taken as determinative, but only as the procession of grace through the realization that all work is first praise.

The same is true of truth. To the extent that Christians bear true witness, they function not as truth's owners but as truth's stewards and recipients through grace. They make use of it, find it on their lips, but have no claim to it as a possession since it always remains a gift. As we have seen, this is one of the distinctive features of Christian *parrhēsia:* "Giving what you've received as gift can then only be done as a servant . . . or a herald . . .: in these roles you pass on the master's goods or the judge's words to others. The goods and the words aren't yours: you didn't make them and you don't control them. You have them only in the sense that you can pass them on to others."[56] It is a mistake to think that the truth of the gospel belongs to the herald who is thus authorized to operate it. However, just as the steward moves the master's belongings around but does not himself control the substance of the transactions, the witness shares received gifts, not ownership. Just as the Sabbath relativizes labor, so nonpossessive witness relativizes all other discourse. All of this suggests that Christians do not just *learn* how to relate to the truth through witness, but the practice of witness is already itself a practice of relating to truth nonpossessively.

There are at least two reasons that the testimony of witnesses cannot be possessed. One relates to the idea of possession as such, the other to the substance of the testimony. First, though it may not be immediately evident, the idea of possession nonetheless implies death. It trades on the sharing of goods that cannot be shared in return. Items that are possessed no longer undergo exchange, because the reciprocity that made possession possible has been cut off.[57] Once the other party dies, possession takes the form of a one-way donation to the party who remains alive. If the testimony about Christ has passed to his witnesses, it could only be possessed by them if Christ were dead. But this is absurd, of course, because the very

---

56. Paul J. Griffiths, *Lying: An Augustinian Theology of Duplicity* (Grand Rapids: Brazos, 2004), p. 90.

57. Oliver O'Donovan, *Desire of the Nations: Rediscovering the Roots of Political Authority* (Cambridge: Cambridge University Press, 1996), p. 288.

ground for the testimony itself is precisely the opposite: that Christ is not dead but that God has raised him up. This is why the testimony about Christ is always accompanied by the Spirit of truth. Both the Spirit and the testimony witness to the ongoing, nonpossessive nature of the gospel. God gives the Spirit, which makes the testimony about Christ possible but, as with the testimony, the Spirit cannot be possessed, because this would imply that God, as the giver, is dead.[58]

Second, the substance of the testimony refuses to be circumscribed by possession. The testimony is meant to be shared, and thus the act of possessing it is at variance with its most essential impulse, and it refutes what it claims to say. The testimony can either be true or possessed, but not both. What does it mean to possess testimony? For Augustine, speech that is possessed and owned is typified by lying. One commentator on Augustine calls the process of abandoning the lie *disowning speech.*[59] Speech is a gift from God and is for giving back to God in adoration and confession; thus it remains a gift as it persists, precisely as it is continually given and received. Therefore, speech that is possessed rejects the divine gift by foreclosing on the purpose of speech, making speaking the truth impossible. The proper use of speech renounces, surrenders, and "disowns" itself through giving itself back to God for the service of God.[60] What makes a lie a sin, therefore, is precisely this rejection of the divine gift. Moreover, just as telling the truth in its purest form is to speak of God, which arises from rejoicing in the truth itself as participation in the truth of God, so also the purest lie is told simply for the utter joy that comes from telling it. The disordered and corrupted joy that issues in lying exemplifies the rejection of the genuine joy that rejoices in the truth precisely by sharing what is true.[61]

58. "No man *has* the Holy Spirit. . . . They can only pray and wait for Him" (Barth, *CD* III/4, p. 320).

59. Griffiths, *Lying,* chap. 5, "Disowning."

60. Griffiths, *Lying,* p. 90.

61. Reinhard Hütter notes how possessing the truth limits its sharing, since those who are self-absorbed "want to grasp and own what can only be received as a gift: the gift of a self transparent to the truth that it owes its existence not to itself, but rather to the Giver of Life. Honoring this truth in its constant reception is what makes the self open to the other, to genuine hospitality" ("Hospitality and Truth: The Disclosure of Practices in Worship and Doctrine," in *Practicing Theology: Beliefs and Practices in Christian Life,* ed. Miroslav Volf and Dorothy C. Bass [Grand Rapids: Eerdmans, 2002], p. 209). One who grasps the truth and refuses to show hospitality by sharing it indicates that he believes the truth is a scarce resource.

We may go further than this. Saying that lying is a sin can mislead us into making too strong a conceptual separation between the two, since it suggests that sin is a prior category to which lying belongs. For Augustine, however, "all sin is a lie."[62] To lie is to sin; but more so, to sin is to lie. Imagining that human happiness can be found apart from God leads to refusing the divine gift. Though this actually leads to greater misery, it is not the consequence (that is, the misery) that makes the refusal sinful. It is, instead, the *lie* that is at the root of it all. Overcoming the lie is not just a matter of disowning speech, though it involves that. It must, in its acts of speaking, actually disown the truth by refusing to control it either through forceful obtrusion or through the elevation of a higher principle — such as goodness or justice. Augustine argued against a version of this when he taught that "he who says that some lies are just, must be judged to say no other than that some sins are just, and therefore some things are just which are unjust: than which what can be more absurd?"[63] Augustine rightly saw that, as with justice, any goodness could not actually be goodness if it were set over against truth, since the truth is good and goodness is true. Joseph Fletcher represents a more recent attempt to elevate another principle over truth, which I will discuss in chapter 9.

Speech and truth are disowned through confessing Christ. For a deeper understanding of such claims and their consequences for Christian witness, we must return to the qualities of the *parrhēsiastēs* with which we began.

---

62. Augustine, *City of God,* XIV, chap. 4.
63. Augustine, *Contra Mendacium,* trans. H. Browne, Nicene and Post-Nicene Fathers, ed. Philip Schaff, (Edinburgh: T. & T. Clark, 1988), 3: sec. 31.

CHAPTER 6

Christian Witness as Patient Protest

Having considered the distinctive shape of Christian *parrhēsia* in the previous chapter, I want now to look more carefully at how some of the features particular to Christian witness enable protest and resistance. No theologian has grasped with such clarity the challenges and implications of what I have here described as the parrhesiastic nature of *coming forward,* as has John Howard Yoder. Yoder's account of Christian witness is remarkably similar to Foucault's truth-teller; but in the end it surpasses Foucault's. Like Foucault, Yoder emphasizes the importance of the truth-teller as a decisive moral agent whose activity precedes an assessment of epistemological certainty: "We believe 'news' when we hear it because those who tell it know whereof they tell. They are accredited by their status as witnesses, not because we run their report through our *a priori* grid."[1] Any guarantees assuring us that they will tell the truth make them redundant. No assurances are more forceful than the trust and confidence we place in the witnesses' reliably telling us what they saw. Moreover, Yoder helps to show how the ability of the witness (*parrhēsiastēs*) to speak the truth to those who possess sovereign power is bound up with the nature of the truth to which his testimony corresponds.[2] In a short unpublished article entitled "Christianity and Protest in America," Yoder proposes some

---

1. John Howard Yoder, "On Not Being Ashamed of the Gospel: Particularism, and Validation," *Faith and Philosophy* 9, no. 3 (July 1992): 285-300 (p. 291).

2. However, the language of "correspondence" between truth and testimony may be too theory-laden to allow for how the witness relates to the testimony.

prerequisites for radical critique that suggest how Christians might relate to the truth.[3]

To *pro-test* is to take a stand *for* something: it is to engage in a positive testifying activity that does not just denounce but promotes an alternative. The protester has something else in mind beyond the simple condemnation of what she is against. The positive alternative is the place where the protester stands and from which she is critical of the system whose representatives will hear the testimony. Rather than merely castigating the king, the protester endorses another kingdom; she does not simply rebuke the governor with feckless invectives, but commends another government altogether. And yet this opposition countenances no appeals to transcendent universals (Platonic or otherwise) of the kind that Foucault rejected with such resolute devotion. The protester's place to stand is not contingency-free, but is another particular place. "There is no non-particular place to stand."[4] The place to stand is rather the socially coherent community of the church embodied as a political, worldly (i.e., terrestrial) form of life.

The particular life and story of Jesus is, for Christians, a communally embodied existence. In marked contrast to those whose commitment to speaking the truth requires them to stand at a distance, the witness-as-protester strives more authentically to inhabit the life of which she speaks. She depends on a community that, like all of God's creations, exists by sheer contingency and, in claiming to speak what is true, they themselves witness to the God whose gift creation is. The story of Jesus is given to the world, and when part of the world comes to include itself in that story, we refer to it as church. This means that when witnesses appeal to the story of Jesus when it confronts worldly power, it is calling for the conversion of that power. Witness dismisses the strengthening of a case for the truth of what is seen if it involves primarily making use of the abstract and the general. And it is only on the basis of the *ekklēsia*'s political sociality that the abstract ideation of truth-as-such may be refused without contradiction.[5]

---

3. Yoder presented this essay in November 1991 at a conference on "Christianity and Democracy" at Emory University Law School.

4. Yoder, "On Not Being Ashamed of the Gospel," p. 289.

5. Foucault, no doubt, follows Nietzsche in being an antimetaphysician. One wonders what Nietzsche would have thought of Yoder's theology; he certainly did not allow for anything like it when he remarked that, presumably because they share the same metaphysics, "Christianity is Platonism for the people" (Nietzsche, *Beyond Good and Evil*, trans. R. J. Hollingdale [London: Penguin, 1990], preface). Yoder's is a theology (though by no means the only one) that does not share Plato's metaphysics of truth.

I have already shown how too strong a commitment to liberal social forms can lead some to fail to get at the heart of Foucault's constructive proposal. As a consequence, then, so long as the ideal polis takes a certain (often liberal) form, the *ekklēsia* may simply not be recognizable to these thinkers.

Why has the church in the modern West found it so difficult to resist the pressures that evacuate and diminish its political and social aspects? Liberalism's ideal polis is, by definition (and therefore originally rather than just ideally), marked by unity-generating loyalties that limit the role of Christianity. The *ekklēsia* often willingly embraces its diminished role in public and external life for the sake of good citizenship among the other communities, divergent loyalties, and diverse allegiances that characterize the liberal political situation. But the liberal solution to the problem of diversity famously disguises its own heavy-handedness by disallowing the kind of parochial, politically external living for communities on which it in fact depends.

It is possible to put a fine point on this by looking at a chief question of liberal thought. Who are the people who comprise the diverse community for which liberalism is the solution? Yet, phrasing the question this way smuggles the answer into the question itself. The people preexist the choices with which they are faced — of how to live peaceably in some manner that will not threaten their existence as a people. Unlikely to be asked are questions such as: Who are these people? On what basis are some included and some excluded? Who excluded them? The makings of a national identity are therefore implicit in, rather than derived from, the life of a people. The American founding, for example, assumes a "we" who are able to claim "We the people . . ." in the very act of constituting the nation that includes them in it. Of course, part of what allows modern liberal states to claim legitimacy is precisely their disinclination to claim any manner of social unity (linguistic, religious, ethnic) as foundational to the unity that they alone aim to provide. Nevertheless, the most effective way to provide that unity is to make use of a collective perception that something other than the state itself — something more substantive, less fragile — in fact unifies. Ernest Gellner notes that "[n]ationalism is not the awakening of nations to self-consciousness: it *invents* nations where they do not exist."[6] There are no preexistent people whose unruly lives display the lack of consensus that national congregations, in their invoking of dubious

6. Quoted in Benedict Anderson, *Imagined Communities: Reflections on the Origin and Spread of Nationalism* (New York: Verso, 2006), p. 6.

state-of-nature stories, intend to overcome. Benedict Anderson adduces, in opposition to Gellner, that the fact of invention itself is more significant than the idea that invention implies falsehood. For Anderson, it is enough to call the bluff of communities that organize themselves around tacit or explicit accounts of their own existence by drawing attention to the work of their imaginations. The mere fact that doing so exposes what is otherwise unspeakable indicates that the imagination also works to disguise its own activity by invoking substitutes.

The risk that makes liberalism an inherently unstable solution is that it must manage the invention of a people who attribute their community membership to something else without allowing the latter to be rewarded with ultimate loyalties. As a consequence, liberal discourse must constantly seek both to fill and to evacuate its claims. It will supply content with one hand and then remove it with another. It must communicate solidity and permanence that outstretches and overreaches its ability to provide it, since its securing a hearing as a legitimate authority depends on modestly presenting itself as neither solid nor permanent. This is the reason no modern state will claim to wage war on behalf of its own interests. Its interests can only ever be so modest that they are always threatening to disappear altogether. But they may wage war on behalf of those things that are more universal, meaning natural to humanity simply as such: freedom, justice, and so on.

There is an inverse, as I have been saying. This is a liberal reticence to identify strongly substantive accounts of the universals it otherwise claims (freedom, justice), because doing so renders them no longer fit for securing unity around them. They must be deliberately left empty if they are to bring a people together who share nothing else in common. Therefore, the liberal ethos in which the *ekklēsia* of God finds itself among and within modern Western nations involves strong temptations toward abstraction for the sake of concord and societal peace. These temptations are intrinsic to the ideology of such nations. This is not to say that there cannot be a nonliberal nation. It is rather to say that a nonliberal nation is very difficult to conceive in theory and that in practice it would be doubly vulnerable, lacking both the legitimacy that derives from its ability to unify a people around a common identity and the security that such unity exhibits in the context of the modern West.

Against this background, it is crucial to recognize that Christianity is distinctively both universal and particular. The particulars of Christianity and of the story it tells are set against powers whose ascendancy is as unstable as the insecurity it is designed to keep at bay. Moreover, Christianity posits Christ as the goal of human existence, the measure of true humanity as himself a particular man. Christ is thereby also simultaneously universal and particular. He is, within and as himself, consummate humanity *as* an individual human being.

A christological account of human community is likewise both universal and particular. If the *ekklēsia* is the body of Christ, then it is not merely a self-serving, inward-focused community that ponders the goods it has discovered for itself and for the flourishing of its communal life. Rather, its discovery of the communal possibilities that Christ makes for his body is itself the recognition that authentic human goods are precisely identical with them. God's will is to make the whole world the church. Therefore, the more authentically the church inhabits the goods of the life it has been given through grace, the more its doing so testifies to its conviction that these are genuine goods for all people. This is not to say that the human goods that Christianity identifies and endeavors to live are achieved effortlessly or that they may be fully enjoyed by those whose living is not enriched by the gifts that the church makes available in its worship. But so long as the Christian witness is also an invitation for others to join it, it will also point to the virtues and practices that characterize the life that dwells amid those goods.

The same goes for the goods that Christians have not yet discovered. The Christian community will most authentically inhabit the goods it celebrates when its life together is marked by an openness to God's reality that has not foreclosed on the fullness of the world or of God's gifts in the mistaken belief that what has been seen is all there is to see. One of the witness's skills is the ability to say, "This is what I saw" in a way that elicits cries of "let's see what else there is" rather than "now we can stop looking." This is a skill that, in its reporting of the past and in its keeping alive the memory of those who have gone before, is also decidedly oriented toward the future. It loops back over the past again and again in the hope that there is ever more to witness. It is convinced that no single pass is definitive and final, meaning that its orientation toward the past is itself future-directed. This is because to be *ekklēsia* is not to be marked by possession but by expectation. A people who has received good things from God will expect more to follow. Their grasping at what they have already received will in fact keep them from willingly and repeatedly opening themselves to further gifts, meaning that they are not only deficient of faith, but of generosity. The gifts one has already received are meant, in turn, to be gifts to others.

Therefore, not only does the critical domain of Christian witness abjure abstraction, but the substance of testimony is itself also irreducibly particular. The gospel is not a set of abstract truths but concrete, historical (and hence particular) claims to which the believing community is entitled insofar as its life is formed by them.[7] Neither the life nor its habits of speech may evade one another with impunity. Nor may they take flight into the inviolability of generality. Foucault was close to this kind of positive program when he endorsed the Cynics over against the Platonists. Nevertheless, the Cynic cannot escape being permanently oppositional. The Cynic makes of antagonism toward foes a first principle and a necessary aspect of an identity that elides every argument and social form. As a consequence, the drama of cynical practices limits itself merely to mimicking the practices it attempts to defy. This is why Cynics are always rude. But the urgency of the Cynic surely needs to be contrasted with the patience of the witness.

*   *   *

I have already shown how openness to God, to others, and to the gospel is a characteristic of Christian *parrhēsia*. The witness's patience is disposed toward discovering how to let the truth speak for itself.[8] Patience first comes with the confidence that the truth *can* speak for itself. It need not resort to propaganda and other illicit supports so characteristic of ideologies that would fall without them. Efforts to disguise, sell, or modify the truth into something other than what it is represent a loss of confidence in the power of truth in its confrontation with rulers and others whose possession of power is more plain and is more clearly able to produce desired effects

---

7. "What the herald reports is not permanent, timeless, logical insights but contingent, particular events. If those events are true, and if others join the herald to carry the word along, they will with time develop a doctrinal system, to help distinguish between more and less adequate ways of proclaiming; but that system, those formulae, will not become what they proclaim" (John Howard Yoder, "The Disavowal of Constantine," in *The Royal Priesthood: Essays Ecclesiological and Ecumenical,* ed. Michael G. Cartwright [Scottdale, PA: Herald, 1998], p. 256).

8. See John Howard Yoder, "'Patience' as Method in Moral Reasoning: Is an Ethic of Discipleship 'Absolute'?" in *The Wisdom of the Cross: Essays in Honor of John Howard Yoder,* ed. Stanley Hauerwas, Chris K. Huebner, Harry J. Huebner, and Mark Thiessen Nation (Grand Rapids: Eerdmans, 1999), p. 28, n. 9. More generally, see Romand Coles, "The Wild Patience of John Howard Yoder: 'Outsiders' and the 'Otherness of the Church,'" *Modern Theology* 18, no. 3 (July 2002): 305-31.

when that power is flexed. But, as Barth remarked, "One should note that truth needs no propaganda and does not engage in it. As the truth, it simply speaks for itself and opposes falsehood. Propaganda is a sure sign that what is at issue is not the truth but an ideology which needs it. . . . If only we could say of the church that it does not engage in propaganda! To the extent that it does it makes itself unworthy of the truth to which it must bear witness."[9] Patience orients itself with what is true against the odds. It commits itself to a true description of things against all likelihood that a false reality may be a more persuasive one. It confronts the very real possibility that a world that is put in terms other than what it truly is would lead to greater benefit for those who need it or to a more readily acknowledged flattery among those well-placed to apportion welfare. Why patience? Because these commitments require the ability to see past short-term results and expediency, awaiting vindication instead. Christian *parrhēsia* displays this distinctive feature.

The Christian confidence in the truth's ultimate triumph also frees the witness from rushing the events that lead to that victory and from violently interposing one's zealous agenda in order to bring it about. If victory could be brought about by the temerous intervention of the witness qua protester, it would not be a victory for the truth.[10] (One should never lose sight of the fact that killing a witness does not kill the truth.) Therefore, enduring to the end is not a matter of idleness but of waiting on the truth against the odds. It is crucial that patience waits *for something,* meaning that it is opposed to idleness. In contrast, the pure energy of the cynic soul is only a constantly surging force whose interventions randomly submit to chance possibilities and privative victories. The cynic will consider his activity more important than any positive program. It is true that a witness may be inactive for a time, engaged in a positive hope that can do nothing

---

9. Karl Barth, *The Christian Life: Church Dogmatics IV,4, Four Lecture Fragments,* trans. Geoffrey W. Bromiley (Grand Rapids: Eerdmans, 1981), p. 227.

10. Frederick Christian Bauerschmidt says as much by drawing on Aquinas's commentary on Jesus before Pilate in John's Gospel: "Speaking truth to earthly power is no guarantee that you will not be killed, for the power of 'physical' rulers is essentially the power of coercion, which reaches its extreme measure in the death of those who will not comply. But the noncoercive power of truth accomplishes the purposes of truth more inexorably than the purposes of any earthly rule. A martyr for truth can resist an earthly ruler to the point of death, and thus beyond the limits of the ruler's power, but the power of truth has no limits" (Bauerschmidt, "Aquinas," in *The Blackwell Companion to Political Theology,* ed. Peter Scott and William T. Cavanaugh [Oxford: Blackwell, 2004], p. 54).

but wait. Perhaps in contrast to the worldly *parrhēsiastēs* (certainly in contrast to the cynic), the risk the witness takes is not so much being hated by the opposition but having no effect. When the testimony is protest, it will always be tempted to take into its own hands the direction the protest will go, the outcome its speaking will have, and the influence of these things on future events. Resisting the temptation lets go of all of this. It remains true to itself even when others are not persuaded, and it is cautious about adapting its message in order to gain a wider hearing if the only way to do so is to betray the life from which it speaks. A testimony's openness to God and others stands as a reminder that any eschatology that does not issue in patience is really utopian.

Nevertheless, Christians are subject to a great temptation to be irrefutable. As I discussed above, one resists "disowning" the truth and opts for possessing it in a manner akin to lying, though not by directly speaking falsehood. Mastering the contingency that inevitably means some others will choose not to believe the gospel, ordering the imbroglio of what others will affirm, diminishing the odds that some will reject the offer — the lure of these can be temptations too strong to resist. This is clear enough from history. We fear the vulnerability that comes from allowing human freedom to flourish and express itself, since there is always a chance it may express itself in rejection of what we take to be most important. The contingent other may repudiate what we see, diminish or positively ignore what we have come to understand as vital, and simply refuse to believe.

> We want what we say not only to be understandable, credible, meaningful. . . . We want people to *have* to believe us. We hanker for patterns of argument which will not be subject to reasonable doubt. We are impressed by the power to convince which we see exercised by demonstrations in mathematics and logic, in the natural sciences, and in documented history . . . and we want our claims about God or morality to be similarly coercive. We think that truth must somehow be made irresistible. . . . We become "apologetic," ready to decrease the vigor of our claims, if that will decrease their vulnerability to rejection.[11]

An imperialistic *coming forward* wields power with sovereign authority. Our desire for what we say to be invulnerable discloses our base hunger for

---

11. Yoder, "On Not Being Ashamed of the Gospel," p. 287 (emphasis in original). It is worth pointing out that "apologetic" need not always entail the diminishment that Yoder claims.

power, not only over our interlocutor but over the truth itself. Christian *parrhēsia* is both a bold and patient witness in its vulnerability to refutation.

Connected to this is the gospel's particular ethic for friends and enemies. But the good news about Jesus does not simply have *implications* for peaceful social relations. Rather, the ability to declare it as true (that is, the availability of the option to do so, its condition of possibility), despite its repudiation of force in the very declaration of its truth, is what it means to call it good.[12] Its truth is its goodness. Its free proclamation in the face even of great risk is a witness to the conviction that the truth is corroborated by its goodness rather than the force it might use to meet that risk on an equal footing. Therefore, communicating the gospel coercively not only compromises its goodness but compromises its truth as well. Its claim to be good news is threatened when it is proclaimed less than freely. The true witness simply cannot be guaranteed that the gospel will be welcomed by those who hear it.[13] Bearing witness to the gospel of peace implies peaceful witness: "The truth claim of the herald or witness must remain noncoercive if it is to be valid. You never *have* to believe it."[14] It is important that Christians find themselves needing to relate to the truth without violence for reasons that arise out of a decisive confidence in the truth as a peaceable gospel and not out of an uncertainty about the status of truth claims or an indifference to people's commitment to what is true in the name of peace and social concord — postmodern, liberal, or otherwise.

Protest is funded by this confidence. Christian witness is a positive activity with determinate content, meaning that it has something to say even when it is not being *against* something. Therefore, any critique or protest will always depend on whether what is entailed in the proclamation of the gospel happens to engage critically with society and its leaders. It is possible that in some settings and some situations, proclamation may

---

12. The coordination of the message and the medium also attests to the *newness* of the good news (Yoder, "Meaning After Babble," *Journal of Religious Ethics* 24, no. 1 [Spring 1996]: 125-38, esp. p. 135).

13. Yoder, "But We Do See Jesus," in *The Priestly Kingdom: Social Ethics as Gospel* (Notre Dame, IN: University of Notre Dame Press, 1984), p. 55: The gospel is good news "because hearing it will be for them not alienation or compulsion, oppression or brainwashing, but liberation. Because the news is only such when received as good, it can never be communicated coercively; nor can the message-bearer ever positively be assured that it will be received." Though Yoder is surely right about this, I worry about any construction of the form "the gospel is good *because* . . ." since it can imply a reductive account of the gospel whereby it is reduced to goodness, liberation, or some other good thing.

14. Yoder, "The Disavowal of Constantine," p. 256.

not do so, though an authentic proclamation of the limitations of worldly power will very often (and more so than is often assumed) enrage the powers. The point is only that, while the gospel is an outrage to the kingdoms and powers of the world, its proclamation is not first and foremost characterized by denunciation but is only so secondarily. Christianity does not run out of things to say when it has finished its censures. This surely contrasts with the politics entailed in Foucault's commendation of the truthteller. For him, it seems that the powers are necessarily unjust and that this is the precise *ground* for political protest. The account here reveals a distinctive aspect of Christian truth according to which the powers just happen to be unjust. Because they are not necessarily so, proclamation is always good news before it is resistance. And its ability to also be resistant is a function of its goodness. The state, on the other hand, overdetermines its relationship to social formations and processes in an effrontery against the reign of Christ, which renders the powers subject. When one understands the state according to the New Testament designation of "principalities and powers," it is clear that a reason the powers cannot be unjust out of *necessity* is that the state has no ontology except in reaction to the reign of Christ in his victory over the powers and in reaction to the sociality of the church, whose life is made possible according to a politics unconstrained by the kingdoms of the world. This point bears some elaboration.

It is sometimes assumed that, for Yoder (and, following him, Stanley Hauerwas), the state is *necessarily* coercive, idolatrous, and demonic.[15] But this misreads Yoder (and Hauerwas), for whom the state is only these things contingently and descriptively, paralleling Foucault's account of the state as an "epiphenomenon." Necessity implies too strongly an ontology of the state. Yoder's may indeed be a negative view of the state; but he might insist that it is not negative in theory but realistic in observation, like Jesus' description of Gentile rulers who "lord it over you" (Matt. 20:25). As an empirical observation rather than a normative claim, it is more the stuff of journalism than political theology. It resembles the advice that journalist I. F. Stone would give students to always remember: governments lie. In his most considered treatment of the powers, Yoder describes their condition repeatedly with the descriptive words "we find them," rather than with stronger, normative words, for example: "[W]e find them ruling over the lives of those who live far from the love of God (Eph. 2:2); we find them

15. For example, Oliver O'Donovan, *Desire of the Nations: Rediscovering the Roots of Political Authority* (Cambridge: Cambridge University Press, 1996), pp. 151-52.

holding us in servitude to their rules (Col. 2:20); we find them holding us under their tutelage (Gal. 4:3)."[16] The adjectives we apply to the state (evil, coercive, unjust) may often matter less than the way they are attributed — necessary, contingent, a tendency that "we find" they have. (And while Hauerwas admittedly does not very often show how the church's identification with state power to accomplish its ends is problematic *historically*, I think his theoretical commitments should lead to this kind of analysis; certainly Yoder's own commitments do.) This is why Yoder insists on pointing to Constantine as a historical case even though "Constantinianism" also primarily functions as a heresy.[17] The injustice of the powers is a function of their coercive overdetermination in opposition to Christ's reign to which they are subject. As such, they are not necessarily unjust.

Further to this point, it is also true that Yoder's account suffers from a lack of clarity regarding the nature of the powers. His usual characterization is that the powers are fallen but relatively good.[18] They were a part of God's good creation, but now they are fallen and in rebellion against God. As a consequence, they can no longer properly be understood according to the "orders of creation." This is a delicate formulation, since it can too easily sound tragic: the powers are just good enough to warrant submission — after all, they bring order — but just evil enough that they are bound to persist in their intransigence and tyranny (or more mildly resisting constitutions and mechanisms of reform). This is surely a common surface reading of Yoder, and Hauerwas often gets implicated in this logic. However, I think Yoder would be unhappy with this conclusion because it takes the fallenness of the powers to be determinative, and all but ignores the work of Christ in overcoming them. Instead, Yoder thinks that the work of Christ and not creation or the Fall should define how we think about the powers (and ecclesiology), something for which he criticized Reinhold Niebuhr.[19]

---

16. John Howard Yoder, *The Politics of Jesus*, 2nd ed. (Grand Rapids: Eerdmans, 2000), p. 141.

17. For a critique of the way Constantine has been made to serve as an ahistorical abstraction, however, see J. Alexander Sider, "Constantinianism Before and After Nicea: Issues in Restitutionist Historiography," in *A Mind Patient and Untamed: Assessing John Howard Yoder's Contributions to Theology and Peacemaking*, ed. Ben C. Ollenburger and Gayle Gerber Koontz (Telford, PA: Cascadia, 2004), pp. 126-44.

18. Yoder, *Politics of Jesus*, esp. p. 141. Yoder depends heavily on Hendrik Berkhof, *Christ and the Powers*, trans. John Howard Yoder (Scottdale, PA: Herald, 1977).

19. For example, John Howard Yoder, "Reinhold Niebuhr and Christian Pacifism," *Mennonite Quarterly Review* 29 (April 1955): 101-17.

The defeated powers belong to the order of redemption and not creation. This is where contingency comes in. We may ask whether the injustice of the powers is contingent on the fall or whether it is historically contingent, something that would require particular investigation into actual political and other structures as they actually exist.

The conflict of Jesus with the powers (which Christians experience, at the very least, as a tension of conflicting political and ecclesial loyalties) is not some kind of generalized conflict-as-such that lazily blankets all human interactions and their interactions with structures. It is rather a historical encounter between the historic person Jesus and the historic field of the powers, within which Jesus does not operate.[20] "If we ask whether the early Christians rejected the state as such, we cannot answer. There was and is no such thing as a *state as such*. The state as such is an intellectual construct that is helpful for later purposes, but it is not present in early Christian thought. Therefore we cannot ask that question except hypothetically."[21]

Barth similarly taught that the godlessness of the powers is not ontological since, after all, their independence from God and hence their attributing to themselves godlike status *is* their claim to be absolute, something that is exposed in Christ as manifestly a ruse.[22] God is not only the limit to their exercise of power, but, in making use of them, he makes them bend to his lordship over them. They are neither ontological in the sense of how they are characterized (they are not absolutely godless) nor in existing out of necessity. "Troublesome though they are," says Barth, "they are only contingent and relative determinations" (p. 215). Their power is only relative to Christ's, which is another way of saying that they are not absolute. They cannot have more than a "pseudo-objective reality," since they are actually profoundly imaginary. We therefore must resort to referring to them using language that is "consciously mythological" rather than concrete (p. 216). Furthermore, they are part of the background and "negative presupposition," even "the target" of Christian proclamation of the gospel (p. 217). Barth cites Ephesians 3:10-11, where the church directs its procla-

---

20. Here I am drawing on some insights and ways of formulating Yoder's position in Daniel Barber, "The Particularity of Jesus and the Time of the Kingdom: Philosophy and Theology in Yoder," *Modern Theology* 23, no. 1 (January 2007): 63-89.

21. John Howard Yoder, *Christian Attitudes Toward War, Peace, and Revolution* (Grand Rapids: Brazos, 2009), p. 46 (emphasis in original).

22. Barth, *Christian Life*, p. 215 (hereafter, page references to this work appear in parentheses in the text). See also Hauerwas, "Pacifism: Some Philosophical Considerations," *Faith and Philosophy* 2, no. 2 (April 1985): 99-104 (esp. p. 104).

mation of Christ's lordship, not only to the human world, but also in bold confrontation with the principalities and powers. When Christians cry, "Thy kingdom come," they are also making a negative entreaty for "the gracious unmasking, overcoming, and ultimate abolition of these absolutisms that rule us *per nefas*" (p. 219).

The openness of *parrhēsia* will, in its Christian expression, need to carry over into the openness of discovering new and less obvious powers, expressions of godless rebellion that are less than overt, and closer to home. This discovery may especially come from within the church and implicate her most cherished aspects, esteemed theologies, and treasured practices. The line between church and world is notoriously difficult to draw; but the one between church and the powers may be impossible to draw, except when it is only traced with the intent of fostering more discovery. Therefore, we will have to observe every structure and relationship to see, in the conflict between Jesus and the powers, whether it is a power in the sense that Jesus defeated.

Nicholas Wolterstorff addresses these questions in a lecture entitled "Fallen Powers," where he criticizes Yoder for removing a consideration of political power from the order of creation in favor of the order of redemption. Citing Thomas Aquinas and John Calvin on the worth and dignity of the "kingly office" and the "office of the magistrate," Wolterstorff notes in Yoder "a very different mentality."[23] For the latter, the order of redemption is where the rebellious powers were defeated and their sovereignty broken. Wolterstorff credits Barth's influence for shifting the main emphasis in much of twentieth-century Protestant political theology from creation and preservation to redemption. Yet he questions whether Barth would approve of the direction the theology has gone since then, arguing that Barth was primarily interested in reassociating what Reformation theology had notoriously separated into two kingdoms: divine justification (the spiritual realm) and human justice (the temporal realm). Against a longstanding tendency to make the case that these two are not at odds with each other, merely governing — as they do — independent spheres that are within themselves proficient to the required exercise of power, Barth refuses to believe that there is no genuine and important connection between them.[24]

---

23. Nicholas Wolterstorff, "Fallen Powers" (unpublished essay, presented in 2007 at Yale University), p. 3.

24. Karl Barth, "Church and State," in *Community, State, and Church*, trans. G. Ronald Howe (Eugene, OR: Wipf and Stock, 2004), p. 102.

The event of divine justification in Christ has political implications that speak something additional to what can be said on the basis of creation-preservation. What is this?

Yoder follows Barth in locating the fullest theological analysis of the powers within the work of Christ's triumph over them on the cross. He understands the powers, which include political structures, to be in some sense indispensable to the lives of society, something that indicates their original salutary function within God's good creation. "There could be no society or history, there could not be humanity without the existence above us of religious, intellectual, moral, and social structures. *We cannot live without them.*"[25] Even though they are fallen and in rebellion, they still serve something of their original good purpose in providing order to a society. Even though their pretense has been unmasked and their rebellion thoroughly exposed in Christ's defeat, they continue to function within God's providential ordering of creation. They do so, however, not as necessary in the sense that God somehow needs them, but according to God's patience in letting them endure until God's kingdom is the only one. Until then, God uses the powers (such as particular political structures and states) to accomplish his good purposes.

The powers are thus fallen but still subject to providential control, which God exercises in freedom and independence from them. Jesus brought the "original revolution," breaking as necessary the natural and imagined ties and worldly structures of the state, church, law, society, family, honor, and religion. That God is able to make good use of what Barth calls "the lordless powers" vindicates the way that, in Christ, God enlists them short of utterly destroying them. In being independent of them, God does not need them in order to accomplish his purposes. But if this is true, why claim, as Yoder does, that we cannot live without them? In saying as much, Yoder implies that they are more necessary than they should be.

Consider what a precarious situation we are in, according to Yoder: "Our lostness and our survival are inseparable, both dependent upon the powers."[26] What would it mean to be dependent on what Christ has defeated? Where the powers are states, are they necessary evils (something Wolterstorff thinks Yoder has committed himself to)?[27] If so, surely it is

25. Yoder, *Politics of Jesus,* p. 143 (emphasis in original). Yoder is using the nomenclature of "structures," though it is not a designation essentially different from "powers."

26. Yoder, *Politics of Jesus,* p. 143.

27. Wolterstorff, "Fallen Powers," p. 19.

more than God's mere patience that allows them to continue to exist until God's kingdom comes in fullness. Is there some necessary function they serve?

I suspect that part of the confusion arises from the question of how God makes providential use of the powers. Both Yoder and Barth make statements to this effect. Wolterstorff does not disagree, though he thinks we can say more about them than this, as Thomas and Calvin do, particularly when it comes to the secular state.[28] Becoming clear on what God's providential use means, however, involves coming to terms with the meaning of God's sovereignty. It is one thing to claim that God makes use of something, quite another to say that he is committed to working through and with it. And God's using something says nothing about that thing's goodness. For example, Isaiah bore witness to God's "use" of Assyria in his judgment against Israel for exploiting the poor and widows and neglecting the needs of the society's most vulnerable members (Isa. 10). God is said to "command" the Assyrians, "the rod of my anger," and "the club in their hands is my fury" (vv. 5-6). Even though Assyria intended imperialistic world domination and not divine judgment on Israel for straying from her covenant, God nevertheless made sovereign use of Assyria in the same way that one wields a tool like an axe or a staff (v. 15). Likewise, Scripture describes Pharaoh and Pilate as instruments of God's sovereign will and purposes.

Wolterstorff seems to have more than this in mind when he says, "Not only is the state an indispensable component of God's providential rule of human life. God also uses states as a means to the achievement of God's redemptive purposes."[29] Wolterstorff wants to be able to draw conclusions about power and authority of states (and empires and so on) from his use of them. But God makes redemptive and sovereign use of the Assyrian army as he does any evil, including suffering and tragedy. God is not the cause of earthquakes that kill thousands. Nevertheless, God providentially may make use of unspeakable tragedy. He can and does bring good things from unimaginable catastrophe. This does nothing to exonerate the evil situation nor to declare the earthquake (or wars or school shootings) a surprising good. These are still hideous evils and part of the

---

28. Some aspects of the secular state that Wolterstorff emphasizes and critiques Yoder for not so much as mentioning are its exercise of positive authority and its pursuit of social goods, such as justice (Wolterstorff, "Fallen Powers," pp. 20-21).

29. Wolterstorff, "Fallen Powers," p. 20.

reason that the fallen creation still yearns for the consummation of God's redemptive work.

Despite Yoder's misleading formulations concerning God's use of the fallen powers, I am convinced that this is Yoder's genuinely considered position. God is autonomous from the powers and does not need them; his use of them in the exercise of his sovereignty over them exposes, for those with the eyes to see it, their subjugation and humiliation short of their final destruction. God's use of evil things is the consistent witness of the cross as itself a subjugation to powers of destruction. Resurrection overcomes Christ's death at the hands of the powers, signaling their defeat. Our allowing them to continue to reign has nothing to do with their goodness or their promised benefit to human existence and flourishing. They are simply not necessary for such things. God could just as well use something else, something just as evil, fallen, rebellious, and defeated, and he very often does. That powers and political structures such as states are not simply left on their own to accomplish their own stated ends through their own devices means that God has not left the pretense of the powerful to its own grandiose imagination. But neither does God's using them make them praiseworthy. They are still to be condemned along with Pharaoh, the Assyrians, Pilate, and the cross of Jesus.

What does it mean to conceive of the powers according to Christ's work of redemption? We noted a key aspect of Christian *parrhēsia* above: the true polis undergoes a radical revaluation in Christian thought, beginning with the New Testament. The church as the *ekklēsia* of God emerges as the decisive, genuine political body, since true politics is not found where there are sovereign rulers whose vaunted benevolence makes them the legitimate exercisers of authority. Instead, true politics is where the truth is spoken freely and appeals for justice made openly, even in the face of every attempt to silence them.

Like Foucault, Yoder refuses a positive account of the state, but for different reasons. Yoder appeals to *another social reality*, a more definitive political body, something that can be found only cryptically at best in Foucault's attempt to dismiss the state on grounds that its authority is manufactured.[30] For Yoder, only the church exists by necessity (though,

---

30. The trick is in not reformulating the nonreality of the state in such a way that the state is given over to necessary descriptions, since this only reintroduces a kind of positivity through the back door. Even though O'Donovan is right that Yoder sometimes makes this mistake himself, it is merely a function of sloppiness and not a fundamental tension in his work.

since it is created out of gratuity, it always remains contingent in a certain sense). This accords with the transformation of the *ekklēsia* that Acts takes as the definitive locus for parrhesiastic activity. As such, the *ekklēsia* is decidedly political. The new options for human community made possible in the kingdom brought by Jesus require a social response that is first constitutive of and displayed in the church. Insofar as the state refuses to be the church, it adopts for itself a private existence that it nevertheless arrogates to a false ultimacy. To put it differently, the first politics consists of that public that perceives the humiliation and public example of the powers that Jesus made by triumphing over them (Col. 2:15). That public is the church.

It is important to notice how this first politics does not owe a correspondence to the foundation or establishment of the church as an entity but to its ongoing activity of proclaiming the gospel. The domination of worldly power came to an end in the crucifixion and resurrection of Christ. "The power that they exercise in defeating their enemies, the national possessions they safeguard, these are now rendered irrelevant by Christ's triumph."[31] The realization that the powers are in this devastated state in the aftermath of Christ is enacted and given positive political form where the cross and resurrection are proclaimed. And the church's proclaiming these things is itself part of its realizing them. The pentecostal establishment of the church as a speech-imbued social body was only ever instituted by the Holy Spirit to the extent that the church's proclamation is both its precise mission and — necessarily, inseparably — its existence as given and received. In other words, the activity of proclaiming this saving event testifies to the fact that this event saves, and that it somehow saves in the moment of confrontation with the defeated powers. This is an indication that Christian *parrhēsia* as the proclamation of the gospel is the very ground for relativizing the power claims of every other polis. To reiterate: the proclamation makes the church a determinative polis; the Spirit makes the church by enabling this proclamation.

On this basis, one can entertain the otherwise counterintuitive thought that the positive activity of proclamation actually constitutes the most decisive resistance to disobedient principalities after all. A form of life that does not depend on the tragic interface with worldly power does not mean there will not be clashes with worldly power. It means only that those clashes will not *finally* be tragic, even when they fail to be effective. Their

---

31. O'Donovan, *Desire of the Nations*, p. 151.

nontragic nature is not a function of short-term appearances of success. Foucault taught that every mode of resistance will be circumscribed by the logic of what it resists, allowing "nonresistance" to be something other than mere passivity in the face of the powers. Rather, nonresistance signifies a determination to live independent of them, resisting them precisely by *not* resisting them, that is, by living as demonstrations of the kingdom's worldly possibility. This is why, for example, martyrs praying for the emperor is an act of defiance. "[T]he very presence of the church in a world ruled by the powers is a superlatively positive and aggressive fact. All resistance and every attack against the gods of this age will be unfruitful, unless the church herself is resistance and attack, unless she demonstrates in her life and fellowship how men can live freed from the powers."[32]

One such mode of *non*resistance-as-resistance occurs when the testifying community refuses to use its gospel testimony as part of a strategy for accomplishing something else. Yoder's preferred nomenclature for this is "effectiveness," according to which he identifies a fundamental tendency of countless formulations of Christian social ethics. These formulations take the Christian message to be effective *for* something. They make strategic use of ethical action instrumentally to bring about a state of affairs considered desirable: a more just social order, greater democracy, the overthrow of a tyrant, and so on. Yoder writes:

> One way to characterize thinking about social ethics in our time is to say that Christians in our age are obsessed with the meaning and direction of history. Social ethical concern is moved by a deep desire to make things move in the right direction. Whether a given action is right or not seems to be inseparable from the question of what effects it will cause. Thus part if not all of social concern has to do with looking for the right "handle" by which one can "get a hold on" history and move it in the right direction.[33]

Yoder is well known for teaching that the "handling" of history, so much taken for granted in social ethics, is the outcome of a particular course of events in which the church aligned itself with sovereign power in order to accomplish what it took to be good ends. This "Constantinian" shift saw the church go from a position of weakness to one of power. Historically, the reference is to Constantine's fourth-century conversion to Christianity

---

32. Berkhof, *Christ and the Powers*, p. 51.
33. Yoder, *The Politics of Jesus*, p. 228.

and the subsequent identification of Christian institutions, offices, goals, and means with the power of the emperor. In this decisive shift, the faith of the invisible church was separated from the social strategies of the visible church, which was now aligned with the state. Since the power of the state was on the side of the church's social agenda, that agenda's temporal ends reflected the urgency that the empire placed on its actions as an empire, such as the waging of wars and — closer to our own time — the alleviation of social problems. In Yoder's diagnosis, the faithfulness of the church became identified with its ability to be effective toward these ends.

Nonresistance understood in these terms differs from nonviolent resistance used as a tactic to bring about change. Yoder declares that this signifies secular thinking, even in its ostensibly Christian form, where it is nevertheless divorced from Christian practices and spiritual disciplines.[34] True Christian nonviolence is not merely tactical or in the first instance concerned with effectiveness, but with the way that the logic of the powers is challenged. Yoder's principled pacifism can make him appear absolutist with regard to violence — as well as against effectiveness in principle. He is really neither, as can be shown by two points.

First, Yoder claimed several reasons for not being an absolutist. Chief among them is *patience,* as I observed above. Christian patience recognizes "considerations which call for purported 'absolutes' to be mitigated, yet without justifying the dominant alternative constructions, usually called 'relativist' or 'realist,' of moral logic."[35] The main challenge usually put to Yoder does not come from relativists but realists. One response to realists like Reinhold Niebuhr and Paul Ramsey is to point out that the ground they identify for making exceptions wrongly assumes that all obligations must be brokered by principle and the hierarchical ordering ahead of all actual encounters. Patience is the appropriate virtue in the face of situations that lead some to formalize exceptions since no set of possibilities

---

34. John Howard Yoder, *Nevertheless: The Varieties and Shortcomings of Religious Pacifism,* rev. and expanded ed. (Scottdale, PA: Herald, 1992), pp. 52-55. Yoder is inconsistent in what he says about Gandhi. In one place he asks whether Gandhi took violence always to be wrong or simply "usually unwise and ineffective" (p. 54); but later in the same book he acknowledges that "both Gandhi and King rejected the pragmatic justification of means by ends. They chose a worldview according to which, in the long run, because the cosmos is in the hand of God (despite the presence of sin), we reap what we sow" (p. 126). He is more accommodating to Gandhi and King in *The War of the Lamb,* ed. Glen Stassen et al. (Grand Rapids: Brazos, 2009).

35. Yoder, "'Patience' as Method in Moral Reasoning," p. 25.

can ever be known in advance. Patience looks for more options than there appear to be, including miracles and martyrdom, two options that are generally left out of exception-making for nonviolence. Still, one cannot even know ahead of time whether miracle or martyrdom is called for.[36] The real absolutist, then, is the one who impatiently claims to know in advance, thereby interweaving a priori exceptions with prohibitions (of martyrdom, miracle, or something else) in the form of institution or theory. One form that this takes is the assumption that violence denotes something clear, objective, and univocal. Hauerwas explains:

> Ramsey and Niebuhr betray their commitments to an ahistorical account of violence and nonviolence that is presumably simply part of the human condition. Such a theory is necessary because they lack any sense that nonviolence is one of the characteristics of a historical community. Such a community has no stake in the assumption that a hard-and-fast distinction can be or needs to be made between what is violent and what is not. Rather, it is pledged to constantly explore, through internal as well as external challenges, how practices that at one time may well have been nonviolent have in fact become violent. . . . Christian nonviolence, in short, does not begin with a theory or conception about violence, war, "the state or society," and so on, but rather with practices such as forgiveness and reconciliation. Only by learning how to live through such practices can we as a people come to see the violence, often present in our lives, that would otherwise go unnoticed.[37]

Yoder is therefore principally interested in generating a patience in which the violence we took for nonviolence will be noticed. This orientation led Yoder to constantly look for new forms of Constantinianism in history and to refuse to assume that the work involved in identifying it is the straightforward work of theory.[38]

Second, Yoder is not against arguments from effectiveness in principle, but against the shortsighted way that arguments from utility get made.

---

36. Yoder, "'Patience' as Method in Moral Reasoning," p. 33.

37. Stanley Hauerwas, *Dispatches from the Front: Theological Engagements with the Secular* (Durham, NC: Duke University Press, 1995), p. 130. Here Hauerwas is defending Yoder's and his own position. See a similar argument in Hauerwas, *Performing the Faith: Bonhoeffer and the Practice of Nonviolence* (Grand Rapids: Brazos, 2004), pp. 169-72.

38. See John Howard Yoder, "Christ the Hope of the World," in *The Original Revolution: Essays on Christian Pacifism* (Eugene, OR: Wipf and Stock, 1998).

His critique of effectiveness is really just a way of addressing short-term justifications. Suffering nonviolently is not effective in the short term, but it is effective in the long term since it accords with and anticipates the triumph of Jesus. This anticipation can only be truly anticipatory when it does not rush the arrival of the thing it waits for, though it still may groan in anguish. "The church will be most effective where it abandons effectiveness."[39] Of course, this reference to eschatological effectiveness will be a matter of faith rather than calculations for optimizing consequences.[40] By clinging to the belief that they are being faithful to God's promises, Christians may find themselves needing to refuse even violence that could be used to prevent injustice. This is a witness to the eschatological belief that the unjust powers are under God's judgment. It is a declaration of "freedom from needing to smash them since they are about to crumble anyway."[41] The need to smash the powers comes from an abortive imagination that asserts itself in the name of responsibility: "When it *seems* to me that my unjust deed is indispensable to prevent some much greater evil being done by another, I have narrowed my scope of time, or of space, or of global variety, or of history. I have ruled some people out of my Golden Rule, or have skewed the coefficients in my utility calculus."[42] But these corruptions take the life and work of Christ as nonessential to an ethic of responsibility since such an ethic cannot see how acting responsibly extends beyond my own power to shape the present. Put simply, a truth that needs to be fought for must be less than true. Instead, "[t]he most effective

---

39. Yoder, "The Otherness of the Church," in *The Royal Priesthood*, p. 64. "As Yoder emphasized, the use of violence accords with the view that we are masters of our historical destiny, with the corollary assumption that we must take 'responsibility' through the use of force in order to prevent undesirable outcomes; in contrast, the nonviolent disciple, who believes that the crucified Christ is lord of history, conforms herself to Christ's nonviolent example, confident that by so doing, she is eschatologically effective" (Alain Epp Weaver, "Unjust Lies, Just Wars?" *Journal of Religious Ethics* 29, no. 1 [2001]: 51-78, esp. p. 73). I believe that Yoder assumed that nonviolence would almost always be ineffective but felt the challenge to deal with prominent exceptions such as King and Gandhi. He may have been tempted to think that the successes of their movements proved that they were more tactical than principled in their nonviolence, though, as I pointed out in an earlier footnote, he was sometimes able to resist this.

40. Samuel Wells, *Improvisation: The Drama of Christian Ethics* (Grand Rapids: Brazos, 2004), p. 55: "Faithfulness is but effectiveness measured against a much longer timescale."

41. Yoder, *The Politics of Jesus*, p. 187.

42. Yoder, "The Hermeneutics of Peoplehood," in *The Priestly Kingdom*, p. 38.

way to contribute to the preservation of society in the old aeon is to live in the new."[43] The Christian ethic in the present confesses that Christ is also lord of the future.

We hear clear resonances of Foucault in these remarks about the future, the new aeon. But there is a difference: Foucault's anti-utopianism too crudely precludes an eschatology that would enable him to speak about the possible future terrain opened up by present questions and critique. This makes his comments about a future "we" strangely aloof, because any such future polity is always uninhabitable for him in the present. Despite hopes that his books would shape the future, Foucault could not point to a people whose future living derived from their present way of life. Yoder preserves Foucault's insight that no present social arrangement is finally determinative of transcendent notions, either in its own positivity or by correspondence to an ideal metaphysic. But he surpasses Foucault by insisting that the contingency of Christian witness extends all the way through to the new humanity that exists only by sheer promise.[44] After all, promise is the only way that faith knows about the future ahead of time and, consequently, is the only epistemic ground on which the prophet stands.[45]

One way that Yoder developed a critique of Constantinianism is through a critique of ethical method.[46] What Yoder calls "methodologism"

43. Yoder, "Peace Without Eschatology," in *The Royal Priesthood*, p. 165. Of course, this is true only by promise. "Not being in charge of the civil order is sometimes a more strategic way to be important for its survival or its flourishing than to fight over or for the throne" (Yoder, "On Not Being in Charge," in *The Jewish-Christian Schism Revisited*, ed. Michael G. Cartwright and Peter Ochs [Grand Rapids: Eerdmans, 2003], p. 172).

44. See Yoder, "Meaning After Babble," p. 134, where he argues against Jeffrey Stout's attempt to rescue ethics from "Babel," or modernity's use of univocal, transcendent moral norms. Stout's attempt in *Ethics After Babel: The Languages of Morals and Their Discontents* (Princeton, NJ: Princeton University Press, 2001) is to suggest that, even though there is a plurality of contingent moral worlds, we can nevertheless hold up "slavery is always wrong" as a timeless truth. Yoder thinks this shows that Stout is really nostalgic for Babel and suggests instead: "The locus of the validity of the wrongness of slavery, or of killing, is then not a Platonic superworld, not even the mere millimeter thereof which Stout wants to keep, but the future common world which we begin to live toward in hope every time we run the risk of entrusting ourselves and what we claim to believe to the language of a moral community other than our own" (Yoder, "Meaning After Babble," p. 134).

45. See Robert W. Jenson, *Systematic Theology: The Triune God* (Oxford: Oxford University Press, 1997), 1:68.

46. See Chris K. Huebner, "Can a Gift Be Commanded? Theological Ethics Without Theory by way of Barth, Milbank and Yoder," *Scottish Journal of Theology* 53, no. 4 (2000): 472-89.

is the general temptation to develop intellectual systems that reduce the moral life and theology to uniform arrays of meaning by fitting them into totalizing, coherent structures. This is most problematic — though perhaps least conspicuous — when talking about God in this way. For example, in its metaphysical form, the god of the philosophers exhaustively defines the limits and meaning of every conception of the divine, transmuting into an idol astonishingly more pernicious than the idols of wood and stone mocked by the biblical prophets, more pernicious exactly for being nearly impossible to recognize. The idolatrous schema sets the terms under which God will be discovered.[47] In its ethical form, methodologism takes the validity of types of argument to be decisive for the soundness of the arguments themselves. The importance lies with knowing whether the argument being made is one from duty or from utility, and the ethicist helps to clarify the debate by making explicit how both sides are reasoning. Yet even though this is a typical academic exercise, it represents for Yoder a Constantinian move that endeavors to control and manage the debates by abstracting them from the communities and traditions that give rise, not first to styles of reasoning, but to real decisions about how to live. In these latter settings, which are more conscious of the ebb and flow of communal life and are therefore less homogeneous in their approach to that life, there is no need for the ethicist to take control of the debate in methodological terms. In fact, her role will be quite the reverse: helping the community identify that its ethical decision-making is irreducible to one kind of reasoning, and that it instead displays elements of duty, principle, virtue, and utility.[48]

The lure of master-methodological approaches lies in their apparent ability to resolve tough questions *ahead of time* (apart from promise) and *in the abstract,* which is to say, at a distance from the concrete encounter of the people asking them in the places they ask them. Typically, ethical method represents universal forms that later get filled with particular content. Answering questions in this way means having the luxury of deliberating from a point of view from which there is not much that directly turns on the answers. In conference addresses and lectures, Yoder routinely refused to address certain questions if he thought that the only way to an-

---

47. John Howard Yoder, "Walk and Word: The Alternatives to Methodologism," in *Theology Without Foundations: Religious Practice and the Future of Theological Truth,* ed. Stanley Hauerwas, Nancey Murphy, and Mark Nation (Nashville: Abingdon, 1994), p. 89.

48. Yoder, "The Hermeneutics of Peoplehood," p. 36.

swer them was at the expense of concrete reasoning communities. In one such instance, after raising questions about the implications of a radical Protestant approach to moral reasoning, he concluded: "The questions are proper; my inability to resolve them *a priori* is proper as well. The stories can be told of how they have been answered before. The trust is not unreasonable that they can be answered again; yet this is not true *a priori*. It is true only in the actual encounter between a believing community and the next challenge. The only way to see how this will work will be to see how it will work."[49] But Yoder does not just think that methodological strictures violate the boundlessness of knowledge in general. He believes that the power of the gospel requires methods and languages for expression that are as polyvalent as the people and communities that receive, embody, and communicate that power. "Pluralism as to epistemological method is not a counsel of despair but part of the Good News. Ultimate validation is a matter not of a reasoning process which one could by dint of more doubt or finer hair-splitting push down one story closer to bedrock, but of the concrete social genuineness of the community's reasoning together in the Spirit."[50]

*   *   *

My aim in this section has been to show that when truth confronts power, it is authorized to do so on the basis of what is true, that this truth spoken "from below" constitutes a relativization of the claims of sovereign power, and that this is evinced in the boldness and patience of the truth-tellers. By way of contrast, when the relationship between truth-telling and power is construed only as a matter of responsibility of rulers or of rights of subjects, this takes for granted a set of options limited by Constantinian assumptions. Not only are the options Constantinian in their assumption that Christian ethical reflection is for those who hold the power (since it assumes that Christians will hold the power), but also in the methodological structure of the problem as a theoretical one to be solved in the abstract by *a priori* means.[51] By discussing, with the help of Foucault and Yoder, how

49. Yoder, "The Hermeneutics of Peoplehood," p. 45.
50. Yoder, "Walk and Word," p. 83.
51. Though I believe that there are good reasons for being skeptical about the possibility of a Christian emperor generally, following Yoder, all I am challenging here is the assumption that a Christian emperor is a normative condition for Christian ethics. "I am not arguing that the Christian must avoid being in a position of power, nor that there is nothing

witness as a practice does not presume the control otherwise thought necessary for bringing about a desirable state of affairs by putting the truth to use, I have attempted to avoid this delimiting construction. The paradigm for thinking about truth and power is a patient demanding the truth from a doctor, not a doctor weighing arguments for when to lie to patients.[52] (In how many ethics classrooms is it assumed that students are more likely to be faced with doctor dilemmas rather than patient dilemmas?)

We may further submit the following conclusions. The importance of truth is not best understood through appeals to a noble ideal that can be made to function politically, but first as the gospel of Jesus, who is risen. As such, the truth is always already political before it is epistemological or personal. Because it is rooted in promise, the truth of the gospel does not enlist fighters but witnesses. In doing so, it enables the possibility of radical protest in a political climate that knows only violence. The political significance of the new *ekklēsia* is found in the fact that only a witness who refuses coercion can think alternatives to it. The free speech exercised in the heavenly polis of God supersedes the earthly polis by including it rather than eradicating it. Free, bold, and open speaking is not limited to the citizens of one nation or kingdom, but it has been opened up to everyone that God's kingdom reaches. This is part of the news the gospel proclaims as good. The freedom of Christian speaking is exercised in a tenaciously principled apathy concerning the legal and sovereign safeguards for preaching the gospel. Christian free speech is enacted and realized in the proclamation of the gospel itself, by Christians proclaiming it quite irrespective of whether or not it is allowed by the powers that be.

Foucault helps us see what is central in refusing the privilege of assuming sovereignty and helps us appreciate that this situation is also increasingly a reality for Christians after Christendom. Since Christians today can no longer rely on the power of the sovereign, *parrhēsia* as an activity that comes from below has reemerged as a real possibility. New options for truthful speech are brought about by emancipating Christian practice from assuming the exercise of power; principal among these options is the proclamation of Christ as noninstrumental and thus as a si-

---

to say about how rulers behave. . . . What I reject is (a) considering the ruler as the primordial mover of history, and (b) modifying the content of moral obligation in order to approve of the ruler's doing things which would be wrong for others" (Yoder, "Ethics and Eschatology," *Ex Auditu* 6 [1990]: 127, n. 12).

52. Plato thought that only doctors and rulers were permitted to lie, not private citizens or laypeople (*The Republic*, 389b).

multaneously bold and patient witness. Even for kings, the activity of
parrhēsia as Christian mission displaces sovereign power, meaning that
those on thrones are now no longer exempt from fulfilling a parrhesiastic
role themselves.[53] Thrones no longer denote resistance to critique, even
critiques of their own exercise of power. This helps us understand why
Christian kings had confessors and why Origen thought that, by praying
for the emperor, Christians are engaging in an eminently political act. After all, Christians can pray, "God save the queen," because the gospel shows
that even the queen needs to be saved — and she cannot save herself.

All of this suggests that the message Christians bear as witnesses to
the lordship of Christ makes them much more than protesters, more than
cynics. Nevertheless, when Christian witness *is* protest, it is not because it
is negatively set against one or more specific sets of lies, but because it is a
positive message about how the world has been made possible for those
who would insist on being told the truth. A tragic doctrine of human existence may enable protest against lies but can only issue in Foucault's cynics
for whom witness is impossible since there is no resurrection in a tragic
universe (a point Nietzsche would have understood). With their witness,
Christians describe and inhabit a way of life that does not depend on the
comfort lies bring — not because lies do not bring comfort, but because
those who have seen the risen Christ can no longer be satisfied with easy
consolation. Truth-telling embodied by such witnesses scoffs when Caesar
lies.

53. I owe this point to Janet Soskice.

PART III

TESTIFYING

This is the truth speaking for itself. It is not an argument.

Karl Barth, *Church Dogmatics*

He who saw it has borne witness — his testimony is true, and he knows that he tells the truth — that you also may believe.

John 19:35

He bears witness to what he has seen and heard, yet no one receives his testimony.

John 3:32

CHAPTER 7

The Witness of Witness

The previous sections have addressed the ways that bearing true witness involves seeing clearly and coming forward to testify. This section concerns the act of testifying itself, of proclaiming and speaking the truth. For the first time, we will permit ourselves to address lying in its ordinary sense (chapters 8 and 9). It will partly be the burden of this section to give an account of lying as, quite literally, bearing false witness. More to the point, however, I will want to give an account of the reverse: truthful speech as true witness. Bonhoeffer taught that lying is bound up at the most fundamental level with the repudiation of God and contradicting the Word of God that discloses the reality about the world. "[T]he lie is the denial, the negation and the conscious and deliberate destruction of the reality which is created by God and which consists in God. . . . The assigned purpose of our words, in unity with the word of God, is to express the real, as it exists in God."[1] Truthful speech is first marked by testifying that all that is real exists in God. Even silence testifies to this when our words fail to be adequate to this reality and the most truthful thing to do is not to speak at all. Speech and silence are both witness. Even though Bonhoeffer never completed the essay in which he suggests that witness is paradigmatic for truthful speech (and though we will only occasionally make specific reference to him in what follows), I will nevertheless extend this insight throughout the whole of the present section.

My argument in this chapter is bold in its claims about the theological

1. Dietrich Bonhoeffer, "What Is Meant by 'Telling the Truth'?" in *Ethics*, trans. Neville Horton Smith (London: Touchstone, 1995), p. 364.

and christological nature of truth, and it finds a natural interlocutor in Karl Barth. In an important section of *Church Dogmatics,* Barth discusses proclamation within a larger context of a discussion of freedom.[2] Among other things, Barth wants to indicate how taking up "the invitation and obligation to bear express witness to God" means engaging in a free action that cannot be justified by any consequential reasons. For Barth, there is no goal to be achieved by speaking the truth about God — not proving the sincerity or courage of the witness, not satisfying some other personal need, not even instructing or bringing about salvation of others. The believing community neither testifies for the sake of recruitment nor for social change. There may be nothing wrong with intending some of these things in other respects. Barth insists that if they are achieved at all, it is because they arise from testimony that is given without any consideration of aims or goals. The only *explanation* for testifying is the honor of God, but this hardly counts as a reason in the sense that is usually demanded.[3] Instead, giving testimony is a species of praising God, an action that is likewise gratuitous.[4] God is honored in praise by receiving back what he has given to his creatures, not by accepting anything that does not already belong to him. As Augustine taught, this is the reason that we have speech and mouths — to praise God.[5] No consequence of praise can be given as a prior justification of its exercise. Inasmuch as mouths and speech are fulfilling their nature by praising God, and that praise gives expression to joy, the proclamation of the gospel is secondary only to God's prior love for humanity through creation and redemption.

2. Barth, *CD* III/4, pp. 73-86 (hereafter, volume, part, and page references to the *CD* appear in parentheses in the text and notes).

3. Explanations differ from reasons, but even explanations are second order with regard to testimony that is primarily narration, as John Milbank observes: "'Narrating' . . . turns out to be a more basic category than either explanation or understanding." Testimony tells a narrative that is *temporally structured,* and, while it usually cannot point to its necessity on the basis of universal laws and first causes, it can point to antecedent causes, purposes, and what has (contingently) followed from them (Milbank, *Theology and Social Theory: Beyond Secular Reason* [Oxford: Blackwell, 1990], p. 267). If we could draw conclusions from what went before (i.e., without narrating subsequent developments in plot), we would not wonder, What happened next? See Stanley Hauerwas and David Burrell, "From System to Story: An Alternative Pattern for Rationality in Ethics," in *Truthfulness and Tragedy* (Notre Dame, IN: University of Notre Dame Press, 1977), pp. 28-29.

4. In *Political Worship: Ethics for Christian Citizens,* trans. Margaret Kohl (Oxford: Oxford University Press, 2004), Bernd Wannenwetsch argues that all worship must resist instrumentalization, but that it is "ethical" for precisely this reason.

5. See Augustine, *Confessions* X.2.

Barth treats the proclamation of the gospel in a section called "Freedom before God." What did Barth mean when he spoke about the witness's "freedom"? He meant that the witness who testifies is not bound by anything that might impinge on the time, place, or way that that testimony is given. There are no external reasons why the gospel ought to be proclaimed other than that the truth of the gospel is so compelling that it must be told.

> In order that God's glory may shine forth, the history of the covenant must also be related, proclaimed and therefore imparted. Man is made responsible for this. As God wills man to be free before Him, He always has in view the freedom of those who have something to relate about Him, the freedom of confessors [i.e. witnesses] who cannot keep silence but must speak of Him, their freedom to expose themselves to His glory, to commit themselves to His honour with clear and definite words, to be serviceable to Him in and with these words, to be His declared and decided partisans. (*CD* III/4, 75)

Barth sees no tension in claiming that the witness is simultaneously free *and* made responsible for proclaiming the gospel. The compulsion by which the witness cannot keep silent is not a compulsion against his freedom precisely because any freedom to act is made possible by God and is contained within the grace by which God upholds all of creation. Against modern notions of freedom, Barth asserts a radically theological equation of the pure obedience to God's command with the absolute freedom of human beings (see, e.g., Barth, *CD* I/2, p. 879: "freedom as true obedience and obedience as true freedom"). A person who is free before God is "free in the execution of his responsibility before Him!" (*CD* III/4, p. 73) Owing to his pure obedience to the Father, Christ was revealed truly to be free. Likewise, the command to bear witness to God is not only compatible with human freedom, but, if human freedom is understood first as freedom to trust God and to participate in divine work, then obedience to such a command is freedom's highest expression.[6]

Even so, the first characteristic of this obedience is still freedom. As freedom, it is marked by a gamelike and songlike lightness that calls into

---

6. Barth notes how Christian witnesses share in the freedom of Christ precisely by being witnesses in his service (*CD* IV/3.2, p. 602). Herbert McCabe also shows how Aquinas had a compatible notion of freedom: God brings about my free actions without making those actions any less free (McCabe, *God Matters* [London: Continuum, 2005], p. 11).

question those who would make testifying into too serious an activity. The proclamation of the gospel, precisely because it does not try to accomplish anything, is freed from the severity it might otherwise have if there were anything at stake. But since *coming forward* is purged of fear, the witness can *testify* without fear with the "risk of being ludicrous which its utterance runs" (*CD* III/4, p. 78). As an example of this fearlessness, Barth points to David's half-naked display of dancing and celebration when the Ark of the Covenant was brought up to Jerusalem (2 Sam. 6). Even though he was accused by Michal of being undignified, David's reply that he will play before the Lord constitutes, for Barth, the kind of lightness of the witness in the face of danger and lack of faith. The dance of celebration that is the testimony of the witness is the response to the witness's seeing the risen Christ. Such witness is only secondarily posed in contradiction to the forces of unbelief and is in no way driven by confrontation, nor by what may be gained through conflict. There is no original opposition between the foolish dancer and the laughing crowd. Instead, the witness is first captivated by the joy that made David dance and is no less unmoved by whatever consequences may follow.

Nietzsche, whose landlady occasionally saw him dancing naked as she peered through the keyhole, portrays the sad Zarathustra, who surpasses Michal but, pathetically, never becomes like David.[7] Zarathustra wants to dance, but instead only muses about dancing. When he comes across girls dancing in a forest, they stop, recognizing him. He encourages them to keep dancing, uttering profundities about the goodness of lightness: "the devil is the spirit of gravity." But his words keep him from joining the girls and Cupid. He is more captivated by the instrumental use of language, even to the point of exceeding irony, than he is by the substance of his words. Had it been the reverse, he would simply have danced. The wisdom of life is not life itself, Zarathustra discovers, as he laments the distance on which his wisdom has insisted. Having driven away the dancers (representing pleasure, the livers of life) he wonders why he is still alive, suspecting that perhaps he has just proven that he is not.

Life is a dance that is always threatened by well-meaning justifications for dancing. Just as they will keep one from actually dancing, Barth resisted all attempts to justify proclaiming the truth. Truth is more natu-

---

7. Friedrich Nietzsche, *Thus Spoke Zarathustra*, in *The Portable Nietzsche*, ed. and trans. Walter Kaufmann (London: Viking Penguin, 1968), 2nd pt., "Dancing Song." See Craig Hovey, *Nietzsche and Theology* (New York: T. & T. Clark, 2008), chap. 7.

rally attuned to the movements of joy and celebration than to the many ways we have found to codify and analyze it. In general, these are ways of justifying, proving, and deciding on what is true. Barth worried that doing so implies that there are reasons for deciding whether God's truth is true ahead of an encounter with it. The temptation to ground the content of dogmatics in an epistemology, for example, relies on the logic that produced theological prolegomena in the modern period for which the content of theological knowledge could not help but become secondary to its form. Wolfhart Pannenberg, like Barth, cautions against the discontinuity of form and content and summarily counsels rejecting every design in which "the truth of Christian doctrine must be established in advance of all discussion of its content."[8] The substance of Christian dogmatics, insofar as it is known by revelation, is not knowable under the category of *revelation* apart from what is revealed, because it is impossible to know what constitutes revelation-as-such. "Knowing" revelation-as-such can easily take its place as theology's first task. However, the question of whether revelation can be true (or reliable or trustworthy) cannot be addressed before the substance of revelation itself, just as the gospel must be allowed to precede any subsequent formalization.[9] To put it simply, there is no epistemology behind Word for Barth. This is why Barth refused to produce a prolegomenon to dogmatics: the Word of God is sui generis (*CD* I/1, esp. secs. 2, 5.4).[10]

However, Barth did not just reject such epistemologies for theoretical reasons. Doing so would only risk reproducing yet another epistemology. Instead, he acknowledged as early as the Barmen Declaration (1934) that the recourse some make to epistemology really evinces a more profound political problem.[11] As long as there are other sources for the

8. Wolfhart Pannenberg, *Systematic Theology*, trans. Geoffrey W. Bromiley (Grand Rapids: Eerdmans, 1991), 1:47.

9. Here revelation is in the form of *presuppositional* grammar rather than *propositional,* so the language of "content" (and "substance") may not be quite right. Still, presupposition is more like content than it is like form. Perhaps it is better to say that grammar is the form of the content that can only be evinced insofar as that content is allowed to be expressed.

10. Barth equally refused the confidence engendered by a revelational positivism, elaborating the mystery of the Word before the knowledge of the Word in a memorable dialectic (sec. 5.4f.). In particular, "the self-presentation of God in His Word is not direct, nor is it indirect in the way in which a man's face seen in a mirror can be called an indirect self-presentation of this man" (*CD* I/1, sec. 5.4, p. 165).

11. Terry Eagleton notes how "questions of epistemology are deeply bound up with

church's proclamation apart from the Word itself, they do not merely function as justifications for God's revelation. They actually go much further by taking its place. Barth's opposition to Hitler was a function of how he understood the christological core both of revelation and its grammar or revealability.[12] The German churches not only supplied foreign grounds for understanding revelation, but supplanted the Word of God *as that revelation* in the process. Hendrikus Berkhof reports his firsthand testimony using the language of the powers: "While studying in Berlin (1937) I myself experienced almost literally how such Powers may be 'in the air.' At the same time one had to see how they intruded as a barrier between God's Word and men. They acted as if they were ultimate values, calling for loyalty as if they were the gods of the cosmos. . . . [The Powers] let us believe that we have found the meaning of existence, whereas they really estrange us from true meaning."[13] This may be an inevitable feature of any ideology that makes room for the truth of its own description of reality before supplying it in the attempt to ensure that it will be accepted.

Barth notoriously established a sharp contrast between natural theology and theology of revelation in order to make clear the distinction between revelation and revealability. Eberhard Busch summarizes Barth's position in the following way:

> In a theology of revelation . . . we know God because he *has given* and *still gives* himself to be known, and only in following that sequence can we attempt to understand the extent to which it is "possible." Natural theology reverses this direction by constructing a general possibility of the knowledge of God or of "revelation," thereby giving humanity a standard by which to measure what may or may not be counted as true. "Revelation" must [then] subject itself to this standard and is accountable to the humans who wield it. It can be regarded as only *one*

matters of political history" (Eagleton, *The Illusions of Postmodernism* [Oxford: Blackwell, 1996], p. 13). Eagleton is talking about how we remember and retell the past, but with Barmen, we are reminded that questions of epistemology extend themselves also, if not first, into how we talk about the present.

12. I borrow the word "revealability" from Jacques Derrida's discussion of Heidegger in "On the Gift," in *God, the Gift, and Postmodernism*, ed. John D. Caputo and Michael J. Scanlon (Bloomington: Indiana University Press, 1999), p. 73. I owe this term to Daniel Barber, "The Particularity of Jesus and the Time of the Kingdom: Philosophy and Theology in Yoder," *Modern Theology* 23, no. 1 (January 2007): 63-89.

13. Hendrikus Berkhof, *Christ and the Powers*, trans. John Howard Yoder (Scottdale, PA: Herald, 1977), 32-33.

among many possible approximations of the constructed concept of the possible knowledge of God. Its reality depends upon the validity conferred by those who are equipped with the standard. In that the human determines in advance who God "can" be for him, he may well thereafter worship a God. But is he bowing down to anything other than his own product?[14]

Even though it is likely that these lines between natural theology and revelation are ultimately unwarranted and overdrawn, they nevertheless mark out how Barth thought about the relative priorities of the conditions for revelation and revelation itself.[15] The reference here to a standard against which human knowledge of God gets compared in order to know if that

14. Eberhard Busch, *The Great Passion: An Introduction to Karl Barth's Theology,* trans. Geoffrey W. Bromiley (Grand Rapids: Eerdmans, 2004), pp. 68-69. In Barth's own words, "By 'natural theology' I mean every (positive *or* negative) *formulation of a system* which claims to be theological, i.e. to interpret divine revelation, whose *subject,* however, differs fundamentally from the revelation in Jesus Christ and whose *method* therefore differs equally from the exposition of Holy Scripture" (*Natural Theology: Comprising "Nature and Grace" by Professor Dr. Emil Brunner and the Reply "No!" by Karl Barth,* trans. Peter Fraenkel, intro. John Baillie [London: Geoffrey Bles, 1946], pp. 74-75).

15. So holds the school of interpreters of the "New Aquinas," including Fergus Kerr, David Burrell, Victor Preller, and Eugene Rogers. For an analysis of Aquinas on *synderesis* that follows the lines of this "new" interpretation, see Craig Hovey, "Forester, *Bricoleur,* and Country Bumpkin: Rethinking Knowledge and Habit in Aquinas's Ethics," *Scottish Journal of Theology* 59, no. 2 (July 2006): 159-74. This interpretation sees much more in common between Barth and natural law than was seen by both traditional Thomists and Barth himself. Barth was wrong about Aquinas but right about the priority of revelation. Still, it is not clear that Barth would be happy with a construal of his position as endorsing something *natural,* as he wrote against Brunner: "[M]y soul is innocent of ever even have dreamt of the idea that it was a task of our theological generation to find a way back to a 'true *theologia naturalis*'!" (Barth, *Natural Theology,* p. 70). Nevertheless, Barth goes on to defend the Roman Catholic doctrine (owing to Aquinas) by distinguishing it from Brunner and nineteenth-century Protestants. For the former, "a true knowledge of God derived from reason and nature is *de facto* never attained without prevenient and preparatory grace" (p. 96). Earlier, Barth noted how Anselm's *Monologion* was wrongly understood as a cosmological proof of God's existence (and thus an instance of natural theology) "on account of the memory of Thomas Aquinas," while it should have been seen as "biblical-ecclesiastical-dogmatic" (*Anselm: Fides Quaerens Intellectum,* trans. Ian W. Robertson [Richmond, VA: John Knox, 1960], pp. 57-58). But, of course, this *memory* of Aquinas may be wrong, as the new interpreters insist that Aquinas's "proofs" were not really proofs. See, for example, David Burrell, *Aquinas: God and Action* (London: Routledge and Kegan Paul, 1979), and Eugene F. Rogers, Jr., *Thomas Aquinas and Karl Barth: Sacred Doctrine and the Natural Knowledge of God* (Notre Dame, IN: University of Notre Dame Press, 1995), esp. pp. 55-56.

knowledge is true names an epistemology that attempts to insert itself in advance of the action of God. Any such standard will inevitably supplant what it is meant to measure. This is because, in order to say anything about its being adequate to the purpose, one will imbue it with an authority that does not belong with the same intensity to what it evaluates. This erects an idol of self-fascination (what Busch calls humanity's "own product") because, insofar as any standard precedes God's action of addressing us, we will only see and hear what we expect, what we *want* to see and hear based on our fears. Therefore, God's action is either not free or not a recognizable event, two aspects that correspond to skills of a witness (that is, coping with God's freedom and recognizing him). This was part of the argument of part I.[16]

I am not concerned here with whether or not Barth adequately characterizes his opponents, even though I think it is certain that he does many of them a disservice. My main interest is how Barth's *constructive* thesis bears on the questions that concern us. As I argued in the last section, the only ground for theological discourse (and indeed any truthful speech) is the presence of the church as a reasoning, witnessing community. But as a condition of possibility for a hermeneutical encounter with knowledge of God, the church is already implicated in that knowledge and does not precede it. This is because revelation itself supplies the conditions for coming into contact with humanity (*CD* I/1, p. 29).[17] Although Barth had a notoriously underdeveloped ecclesiology, we nonetheless elaborate on solid Barthian themes when we insist that the existence of the church is part of the content of what that church proclaims. The church does not precede the gospel as an antecedent human institution, and it does not follow from the gospel as an implication. Instead, as the church lives its life of praise and service, it is not acting out a previously justified way of life, nor is its way of life justified by anything it achieves through living this way. Just as David danced for love of God — in contrast to Zarathustra, who forgot to dance while proclaiming his love of dancing — ecclesial life is evangelical before it is self-consciously theological. Christian proclamation is theol-

---

16. Barth also refused to allow doctrines to be derived from theological systems: "The doctrine of the Trinity, like all other doctrines, is preceded by the fact of revelation itself and as such" (*CD* I/2, p. 879). We might only add the reminder that the "fact" of revelation is not able to be checked against any prior criteria.

17. This is against Brunner, for whom such a "point of contact" was the human capacity for revelation simply by virtue of being human, meaning that it is not the *product* of revelation, but precedes it.

ogy's only legitimate prolegomenon. The church's life in this regard precedes the lives of theologians by informing the theological task through its prayerful disciplines. Its life begins with taking the existence of the church as the product of God's creativity. Only after it has begun to live this way can it answer questions about the knowledge it has. "It can only venture to embark on this way, and then on this way, admittedly perhaps as its first task, yet genuinely on this way, concern itself with the knowledge of the correctness of this way" (*CD* I/1, p. 42). Apart from the life of the church, there is no general human experience nor basic anthropological starting point for making theological assessments. The church is a presupposition for any proclamation it makes. Even "nature" is enfolded within ecclesial proclamation that the world is *creation*, since the presuppositional grammar for knowledge of nature cannot simply be in "nature" itself.[18]

To assess the truth of Christian witness ahead of engaging in the way of life that includes and produces witnesses is to prioritize some other standpoint, theory, principle, or standard of adjudication above the truth of the gospel. The difficulty, as Barth saw, was that that standpoint, theory, principle, or standard of adjudication becomes (impossibly) more true than the truth.[19] For the same reason, the Christian practice of bearing witness to Christ, itself a practice of truthfulness, does not follow from a prior understanding of what makes something true. The truth of Christ becomes redundant in the face of an account of truth that is prior to Christ and is therefore also, as we have seen, prior to the church's practice of witness.[20] For his part, Pannenberg is reluctant to follow Barth in locating the possibility of theological knowledge and the ground of dogmatics in the church, thinking that this suffers from the kind of religious subjectivism from which Barth wished to escape (in which the experience of the individual constituted one such prior principle, as Barth thought it did for Schleiermacher and Bultmann). But Pannenberg takes the church to be an

18. I am grateful for Peter Ochs's insight on this point.

19. Augustine made a similar point against those who elevated the mind as the sole determiner of what constitutes true knowledge (*De Trinitate*, XIV.13). I am unsure whether this makes Barth Augustinian on this point.

20. Barth commends the Scottish Confession for condemning "the error according to which knowledge of God is a theory, the contemplation of an object which imposes no obligation and does not affect our existence, a theory which must then be followed by practice." For Barth, to know God is to obey God, and vice versa (Barth, *The Knowledge of God and the Service of God According to the Teaching of the Reformation* [London: Hodder and Stoughton, 1938], p. 115).

idea rather than the concrete, historical starting point in time: "For the *concept of the church* . . . must itself be developed in the course of dogmatic reflection."[21] In other words, for Pannenberg, as long as the church is an idea or a concept, it must arise out of theology, and thus theology precedes the church. But this differs significantly from Barth, who grounded theology in the life of the church as a reality, as a present time-bound sociality with habits of behavior for being in the world and in contrast to any conceptual scheme that makes reference to some incontrovertible ground of reference preceding it. No idea, not even the idea of the church, can be more fundamental than the church itself, which is why, after epistemology, truth is only adjudicated by witness.

Recalling De Certeau's distinction between tour-type and map-type descriptions of space (chapter 3), we can say that Christians are those people who insist on continuing to give tour-type descriptions of their lives. Put negatively, this is what witness is: the refusal to hand over its task to a mechanical process that, by its very mode of operation, can only tell the world what the world already knows, recalling to mind what it has already seen before. Just as the architect who designed my house but has not lived in it cannot tell you what it is like to live there, Christian witnesses are neither privileged seers nor tellers. They only speak with a knowledge afforded them by living a particular way, among a particular people. But if this helps us know what a witness is, we need to acknowledge what seems like a paradox. The contingent nature of reality, especially the reality and uniqueness of Christ, requires that there be witnesses, since contingent things cannot be known by theory. But at the same time, witness cannot be a *requirement* of necessity, because it does not seek to accomplish anything, since this, in turn, would imply that whatever is accomplished by telling the truth about Christ is better than the truth about Christ.[22] This would allow speaking the truth to become instrumental, something Barth provides good reason to resist. Witnesses are required by contingency; but witnesses cannot be required by anything other than witness. Surely this is a paradox.

Yet the paradox is irresolvable at the level of theory — the level of

21. Wolfhart Pannenberg, *Systematic Theology*, trans. Geoffrey W. Bromiley (Grand Rapids: Eerdmans, 1991), 1:45 (emphasis added).

22. Putting the matter this way shows that Lessing's infamous ditch is not in fact a ditch at all, but only a monument to his prejudice. Lessing tried to solve the so-called problem of the universal and the particular without considering how the truth might be found in the particular.

this essay's analysis, if you like. It accords with the antitheoretical orientation taught by Barth and others. We can only get so far before we have to observe with Wittgenstein that some things cannot be said but can only be shown. The witness of Christ's witnesses can only be shown, since by any theoretical account it literally should not exist (since if you could give a theoretical account of them, you would have demonstrated that they are replaceable and made superfluous by theoretical accounts). But Christ's witnesses do exist, not as arguments, nor as defenders of the idea of truth, nor as theoretical propositions, but as a people who are irreducible even to the most exalted ideas. This is the witness of witness.

*   *   *

If natural theology (at least as Barth understood it) is insufficient to do the work of witness, we may extend the discussion further since, even apart from explicitly theological considerations, it is common to misconstrue the relationship that truth and truthfulness share. Within philosophy, debates about theories of truth deal with epistemological and ontological matters (the difficulty of knowing what is the case), while truthfulness is usually discussed separately as a moral matter. Truth is something to know; truthfulness is what we do with it. This construction fails to connect truth-telling with the truth and, from the ethical side, cannot help but set aside questions of the truth in favor of the ethics of truthfulness.[23]

On the moral accounts, truth is taken either to be self-evident or unattainable, but not ultimately crucial to the moral heart of the matter.[24] Neither positivists nor skeptics have made much connection between the truth and truthfulness; even people who have their doubts about "the Truth" do not want to be lied to. "Even the most nihilistic of postmodernists whine when their books receive a bad review."[25] This tension need not

23. This is the argument in Bernard Williams, *Truth and Truthfulness* (Princeton, NJ: Princeton University Press, 2002).

24. James Fodor, *Christian Hermeneutics: Paul Ricœur and the Refiguring of Theology* (Oxford: Clarendon, 1995), p. 50, n. 13.

25. Carl E. Braaten, "Sins of the Tongue," in *I Am the Lord Your God: Christian Reflections on the Ten Commandments,* ed. Carl E. Braaten and Christopher R. Seitz (Grand Rapids: Eerdmans, 2005), p. 210. Some philosophers use the capital-T "Truth" to denote a kind of ideological totalitarianism or hidden Platonic metaphysical objects, or both. For example, Richard Rorty writes that the recourse to Platonic notions is an attempt to escape humanity. The alternative course of action he commends is "to abandon the Platonic no-

indicate a contradiction, since it corresponds to two strands of the Enlightenment: the tyranny of oppressive "panoptical" systems and liberal critique.[26] Suspicion makes use of the second strand (valuing truthfulness) to deconstruct the first strand (distrusting truth). Therefore, this suspicion owes more to the Enlightenment than it often admits under the banner of postmodernism. Nevertheless, a separation of truth from truthfulness fails to yield an adequate conception of either one, and it even risks outright distortion.[27] In order to appreciate the complications, we will consider what Nietzsche thought about it.

Nietzsche speaks of the will to truth, by which he means the desire to know the truth at all costs. He sees that even if we conclude that we could do without the will to truth, that conclusion would no doubt be the outcome of a line of reasoning propelled by the will to truth, hence actually verifying it. Nietzsche gave a genealogical answer to the question "Why is the truth important to us?" But he recognized that, regardless of the answer, there is still a more basic drive that causes us to ask it. One cannot simultaneously conclude that the will to truth is dispensable and attach any value to it as a conclusion. We would have to admit: "We pursued this line of thought because we wanted to know the truth about the will to truth." To be sure, the will to truth is not the same as either truth or truthfulness, but here Nietzsche is frustrated by his own inability to overcome the will to truth, given his commitment to rejecting all metaphysical truth — Pla-

---

tions of Truth and Reality and Goodness as entities which may not be even dimly mirrored by present practices and beliefs, and to settle back into the 'relativism' which assumes that our only useful notions of 'true' and 'real' and 'good' are extrapolations from those practices and beliefs" (Rorty, *Philosophy and the Mirror of Nature* [Princeton, NJ: Princeton University Press, 1979], p. 377). In previous chapters I have already addressed the kind of representationalism Rorty is arguing against, and I have drawn on resources other than Rorty's pragmatism (though I might have adopted his approach with modifications). I draw attention to this Rorty quotation only to show how he uses words such as "truth" and "goodness" in different senses. Elsewhere, Rorty remarks that the capitalization of *Truth* is meant to indicate a use in which truth is "something identical either with God or with the world as God's project" (Rorty, *Contingency, Irony, and Solidarity* [Cambridge: Cambridge University Press, 1989], p. 5). Another way of putting the point with regard to truthfulness is that skeptics who deny God are still provided by philosophers like Rorty with a way of articulating the possibility of resisting lies (or, perhaps more mundanely, the possibility of there *being* lies) that does not depend on the equation Truth = God.

26. See Williams, *Truth and Truthfulness,* chap. 1. On truthfulness, see Michel Foucault, "What Is Critique?" in *The Politics of Truth,* ed. Sylvere Lotringer (Los Angeles: Semiotext(e), 1997).

27. Fodor, *Christian Hermeneutics,* p. 36.

tonic and Christian. His first step is to recognize how the will to truth transmutes into not lying:

> This unconditional will to truth — what is it? Is it the will not to let oneself be deceived? Is it the will *not to deceive?* For the will to truth could be interpreted in this second way, too — if "I do not want to deceive *myself*" is included as a special case under the generalization "I do not want to deceive." But why not deceive? But why not allow oneself to be deceived?[28]

Nietzsche agrees that we do not want to be deceived (despite what we have already said about self-deception). But there are *reasons* that can be given for not wanting to be deceived: "One does not want to let oneself be deceived because one assumes it is harmful, dangerous, disastrous to be deceived." Yet, he goes on, what if it is not all these things? How do we know that all of these terrible things attend to letting ourselves be deceived? In asking these questions, Nietzsche shows the problem of the truer-than-true thing we noted above — the thing (such as revealability for dogmatics) that Barth denied and hence refused to engage in a dogmatic prolegomenon. It is the thing by which we know what is true or, in this case, by which we can account for the fact that the will to truth somehow knows for certain that it is less harmful, dangerous, and disastrous not to let ourselves be deceived. Nietzsche uses the "knowing in advance" language of prolegomena to ask, "What do you know *in advance* about the character of existence to be able to decide whether the greater advantage is on the side of the unconditionally distrustful or the unconditionally trusting?"[29] The answer is that, while the reasons given for wanting to be told the truth (namely, prudential reasons, reasons from utility) can explain some instances of truthfulness, these same reasons can also be used to support other instances of *un*truthfulness. Often it is more useful to believe what is false or to tell lies. So far as *reasons* are concerned, telling the truth and telling lies warrant the same kind of justification.

---

28. Friedrich Nietzsche, *The Gay Science,* trans. Josefine Nauckhoff (Cambridge: Cambridge University Press, 2001), sec. 344. Subsequent citations are from this part of *The Gay Science.* I have been aided by Bernard Williams's introduction to that work. Williams's discussion reappears in *Truth and Truthfulness,* chap. 1.

29. Emphasis added. We should not be thrown off by the appearance here of the language of trust. Nietzsche is not changing the subject, but only using distrust and trust as substitutes for "wanting to be deceived" and "wanting to be told the truth."

The difficulty for Nietzsche is that this does not go very far toward explaining the will to truth: the belief that the truth is more important than anything else, that it has unconditional value. Nietzsche concludes that the will to truth "must have originated *in spite of* the fact that the disutility and dangerousness of 'the will to truth' or 'truth at any price' is proved to it constantly." Utility is not a strong enough principle as a truer-than-true thing to explain the emergence of the will to truth. "Consequently, 'will to truth' does *not* mean 'I do not want to let myself be deceived' but — there is no alternative — 'I will not deceive, not even myself'; *and with that we stand on moral ground.*" Recall that Nietzsche meant something different when he spoke of lying in the extramoral sense. Here, "on moral ground," he is speaking of lying in its ordinary sense — plagued by the perturbing realization that he himself is driven by the will to truth seemingly against his will. These reflections come in a personal section of Nietzsche's book that he titles "In what way we, too, are still pious." His pride in having jettisoned truth as a metaphysical idea runs up against the intractable will to truth. "[Y]ou will have gathered what I am getting at, namely, that it is still a *metaphysical faith* upon which our faith in science rests — that even we knowers of today, we godless anti-metaphysicians, still take *our* fire, too, from the flame lit by the thousand-year-old faith, the Christian faith which was also Plato's faith, that God is truth; that truth is divine." Nietzsche worries that the metaphysical faith that accounts for the unconditional will to truth involves another, unreal world, separate from the real, natural world we live in and in which history is played out. Because of the other world, he reasons, this world is summarily denied and commitments to it are enfeebled. Nietzsche does not want to deny this world; rather, he wants to affirm it in every detail. His later doctrine of eternal recurrence, which he called "the heaviest weight," is meant to do exactly this. The *Übermensch* is able to will that his present life in every detail, including its terror and suffering, should be lived again and again an infinite number of times. Such was Nietzsche's desire to affirm absolutely everything in this life.[30] Yet he finds the fact that the will to truth resists sufficient explanation in terms of consequences for this world to be at odds with his antimetaphysical sensibilities. As a consequence, he wonders if the will to truth is not based finally on a lie.

30. This doctrine first appears in *The Gay Science,* sec. 341. See also Friedrich Nietzsche, *The Will to Power,* trans. Walter Kaufmann and R. J. Hollingdale, ed. Walter Kaufmann (New York: Vintage, 1968), sec. 576.

I have noted how Nietzsche wrongly conflates Christian and Platonic thought, demonstrating how a version of Foucault's narration of a nonmetaphysical account of truth-telling (though not without critique and modification) can inform a suitable account of Christian witness. For the purposes of the discussion here about having reasons for telling the truth, consider how Nietzsche sees that truthfulness cannot actually be independent of truth and that any account of truthfulness that depends on consequential reasons does not tell the whole story. Likewise, separating truth from telling the truth is incompatible with a Christian understanding of what is involved in being a true witness, or so I shall argue here. The proposal that will continue to unfold in the next two chapters is that a better way to approach the question of truth and truthfulness is in a more specific form: What does the gospel of Jesus Christ have to do with telling the truth? In Christian theology, the relationship between truth and telling should not be understood in the abstract terms of, say, matching the truth of statements to the truth of beliefs; but it is better understood in terms of the specific good news of the Christian gospel, in which — following Barth — the truth is so compelling that it must be told. Telling is intrinsic to its status as true.[31]

The book of Acts narrates how Stephen's proclamation is a participation in the divine vision. Stephen tells the mob about his vision of the heavens opening up and of Jesus standing at the right hand of God, and he is subsequently stoned to death. Stephen's vision was taken to be a legitimate sighting of the risen Christ, as Paul's words later in the book indicate (Acts 22:20). As a result of the ensuing persecution of the Jerusalem church, witnesses were scattered into Judea and Samaria, in initial fulfillment of Jesus' earlier missionary charge (Acts 1:8). Perhaps Stephen should have known that he would only confirm the mob's suspicion of blasphemy when he told them about his vision (the charge of blasphemy was first brought by false witnesses in Acts 6:13). Stephen is not only the first martyr but also a model of a true witness since, having seen the glory of God, he could not keep silent about it.[32] He then died, calmly forgiving his perse-

---

31. This is different from saying that telling *makes it true,* which is only a version of the mistake I am opposing. Closer to the point is to say that the truth is told *because* it is true, though I worry that the "because" implies a reason external to the gospel itself.

32. That Stephen was the first martyr and a model witness does not mean that he was the first witness *(martys),* since not all witnesses are martyrs in that sense. What makes Stephen a model is his testimony and not his death: his death is part of his witness, meaning that he needed to be willing to suffer for his testimony, but he did not need to be killed to be

cutors, having abandoned efforts to determine the utility of his spoken witness for making converts or securing for himself a favorable verdict. Ironically, the so-called witnesses who made up the crowd "stopped up their ears," refusing Stephen's true witness (Acts 7:57). False witnesses not only do not know the truth when it is presented to them; they positively refuse to hear and see it. Stephen was the only one who saw the vision, not because he was privy to an esoteric secret meant just for him; indeed, anyone could have seen it. But just as the crowd refused Stephen's witness, they also refused to see God, that is, they could not bear that Stephen's testimony might be true. Stephen, in contrast, participated in the vision of the risen Christ by telling about it; to see it was to speak it.[33]

All of this suggests that the evangelical nature of gospel's truth means that it is simultaneously good news *and* compels proclamation. As such, proclamation is the paradigmatic mode of speech for Christians who have heard the good news. This does not mean that all speech is subsequently in the form of proclamation; far from it. Nevertheless, the proclamatory mode becomes the standard communicatory deportment against which all other modes are to be assessed and compared. "Not all human talk is talk about God," remarked Barth. "It could be and should be. There is no reason in principle why it should not be" (*CD* I/1, p. 47).[34] What is paradigmatic in proclamation is not an ethical or metaphysical

---

a witness. Barth cites H. Strathmann as saying that Stephen "is not called a martyr because he dies; he dies because he is a witness of Christ" (*CD* IV/3.2, p. 611). Moreover, as James McClendon reminds us, *living* witness entails manifold expression, "going, telling, persuading, baptizing, teaching" (McClendon, *Witness: Systematic Theology* [Nashville: Abingdon, 2000], 3:348). In other words, witness as living is first mission; the miracle is that in death it is mission still.

33. It is also possible to approach the giving of testimony from the other side and adduce that speaking is part of how Christians come to know what they believe. Stephen Webb comments that "Christians do not know what they really believe until they publicly witness to their faith" (Webb, *The Divine Voice: Christian Proclamation and the Theology of Sound* [Grand Rapids: Brazos, 2004], p. 17). In this he follows Barth, who describes how bearing witness to the content of faith is the way that "cognizance" becomes "knowledge" (*CD* I/1, p. 188). Likewise, Augustine (*Confessions* X.5) took confession to be a matter of speaking both what we know and what we do not know, since by confessing what we do not know, we come to know it as it is shown to us by turning to God. In other words, confessing allows God to disclose to us what we do not know because our ignorance is part of what we confess.

34. Barth goes on to teach that, due to sin, it is not really the case that all our speech is about God. He insists that preaching is the first mode of proclamation. My point here is different, but probably parallel: that proclamation is the first mode of speech.

norm (apart from Christ himself) but a stance or posture, a way of speaking, a manner of relating to what is said.

> God and the world are comprised in this name [Jesus Christ]. In Him all things consist (Col 1.17). Henceforward one can speak neither of God nor of the world without speaking of Jesus Christ. All concepts of reality which do not take account of Him are abstractions.[35]

If Christians speak truthfully about Christ, they are better able to speak truthfully about the world. Even though not all speech is proclamation, proclaiming the good news is nevertheless the most basic mode of discourse for Christians, their right and proper diction.

35. Bonhoeffer, *Ethics*, p. 192.

CHAPTER 8

The Difficulty of Lying

In an unfinished article on truth-telling, Dietrich Bonhoeffer made a curious claim: "How very difficult it is to say what actually constitutes a lie."[1] Why would Bonhoeffer say this? Is lying not a fairly straightforward affair? Perhaps philosophers are prone to unduly complicating it, but the liar surely finds it easy enough in practice. Still, if the argument of this section is correct, then the ability to identify something as false depends on the antecedent ability to identify something as true. False things pretend to be true and always compete for the commitments of those who would assent that they are. They play on our fundamental desire that the truth be something other than it is, that reality conform more simply to our hopes for what is real.

However, what is false can only be revealed against what is true, injecting a great number of complications, some of which I have explored in previous chapters. For now, consider how truth and falsehood may be seen to be related in one of two ways. I think it is helpful to conceive of the relationship in a way analogous to the relationship between goodness and evil.[2] Like evil, the fact that falsehood exists at all suggests the necessary existence of its opposite. If there really is to be such a thing as "correcting falsehood," it will depend on there being nonfalsehood, which is truthfulness. Two divergent ways that have been suggested for understanding how evil depends on goodness are prismatic for our purposes.

---

1. Dietrich Bonhoeffer, "What Is Meant by 'Telling the Truth'?" in *Ethics*, trans. Neville Horton Smith (London: Touchstone, 1995), p. 363.
2. D. Stephen Long summarizes these two positions in *The Goodness of God: Theology, Church, and the Social Order* (Grand Rapids: Brazos, 2001), chap. 1.

The first of these ways sees falsehood and truthfulness as equal participants in a tragic dialectic in which one cannot exist without the other. In yin-yang fashion, good and evil are involved in an eternal interplay, depending on each other, one occasionally but only briefly outpacing the other, only to be brought back to a harmonious stasis of equals. On this model, truthfulness is defined in opposition to falsehood, and vice versa. Both are necessary parts of the way the world is, though each constantly tries to overwhelm the other. The second way differs by positing an unequal relationship. It takes truthfulness to be independent of falsehood, but falsehood as dependent on truthfulness. Falsehood is denied a separate ontological status, meaning that truthfulness can exist in itself but falsehood cannot. This second, unequal notion is just a variation or extension of the Augustinian doctrine of evil as privation, in which evil is privative on goodness. Evil cannot exist on its own, nor does it exist by ontological necessity. Defining evil this way means that, if it is present, evil is always accompanied by goodness. Evil is a corruption of the good, but it does not have its own existence. If we think about evil without goodness, Augustine argues, we could not actually be thinking about evil; we would simply be thinking about nonbeing. This is because existence itself is good (even where it is fallen and sinful), being the creation of a good and gracious God, whose love not only extends to all creatures but does so first in his calling them into being. Goodness in something could not be completely overtaken by evil without in the process wiping out the thing itself. This idea, however, is not reversible: goodness can exist without evil, as it does in God. How does this analogy, then, help to illuminate the corresponding claim that falsehood cannot exist in the total absence of truth?

First, it unfolds in light of affirming that in God there is no falsehood but only truth. Falsehood cannot exist by necessity, but is a contingent condition inseparable from the created order that participates in God's being. Truth exists in a way that falsehood does not. Second is a corresponding epistemological affirmation: falsehood cannot be known or identified except against the "background" of truth.[3] This problematizes the assumption that falsehood is self-evident, so that all that pertains is to root it out. Furthermore, the epistemological consequence suggests that, in addition to the status of falsehood being reframed in terms of privation, *knowledge* of it is similarly reframed. Third is a related consequence of falsehood's privation that corresponds to the virtues engendered by the

---

3. As I show below, Charles Taylor speaks of backgrounds in this way.

epistemological priority of truth. The habits of mind that make it possible to identify falsehood as false are cultivated through positive practices to which truthfulness is internal. If lying is a form of falsehood, then the existence of an action called "lying," if it is to be an identifiable human action, depends on a correlative "nonlying" practice that is definable on its own terms. In other words, all lying in language requires the true and truthful language itself: that is, without coherent speech, no speaking could be incoherent.

Wittgenstein said as much from a linguistic standpoint: "Lying is a language-game that needs to be learned like any other one."[4] The ability to lie is correlative to speaking a language properly, because you surely cannot learn a language in disregard of speaking truthfully; but you must learn that language is something that can be used to tell a lie, that it can be falsified against how it is supposed to be used. There are rules that govern the successful lie. But these rules derive from and are secondary to the rules that supervene on nonlying discourse. This is because it is impossible to imagine a language constituted exclusively by lying. No one would continue to use it if they could no longer count on others telling the truth most of the time. After all, a lie only ever succeeds if there exists something truthful that the lie imitates and that can fool others into thinking that the lie is really the truth. Not only does falsehood depend on truth in order to be intelligibly false, but telling falsehoods depends on telling the truth.

It is possible to sum up the dominant view of truth-telling with the simple exhortation: "Do not lie." This is particularly true of deontologists, but also of virtue ethicists.[5] Yet there is a difficulty with this. In identifying truth-telling negatively rather than positively (where a positive notion identifies what should be done), lying becomes logically prior through a natural-law-like appeal to the evident nature of what constitutes lying. (I acknowledge that this comment is not fair to the best that natural law has produced.) However, lying cannot be logically prior if it is really the case that, as I have been arguing, lying depends on telling the truth, and the liar knows the truth and tries to convince others that what she speaks is true. And if the truth of witness is insufficiently assessed by natural means, then so is the falsehood of lying and deceit.

4. Ludwig Wittgenstein, *Philosophical Investigations,* trans. G. E. M. Anscombe (New York: Macmillan, 1953), sec. 249.

5. Rosalind Hursthouse, *On Virtue Ethics* (Oxford: Oxford University Press, 1999), chap. 4.

Someone may rightly object that it is possible to think of situations in which the liar does not actually need to know the truth. She may, after all, be misinformed or deceived. Usually, though, we do not call someone a liar who merely passes on misinformation. Nevertheless, even one who is deceived and hence does not know the truth must acknowledge that *something* must be true in order for something else to be a lie; the reverse is not true. This suggests that the association of truthful and false speech is not limited to statements. Moreover, a cynical person who makes clever though false use of the truth needs to know the truth in order to use it falsely with benefit. An exception to these general observations might seem to be what Harry Frankfurt calls "bullshit."[6] Unlike the liar, who has some kind of definable relationship to the truth, the bullshitter simply does not care whether the listener is deceived into believing the truth or not. He is instead apathetic and could not care less whether his speech is true or is a lie; it may be either one or a combination of both. His carelessness makes him a bullshitter. As an exception (if he really is an exception), the bullshitter contradicts Augustine's observation that "no one wants to become such a liar as to lose all awareness of what the truth is."[7] A common next step would be to decide whether the bullshitter is actually a liar or not, whether his intention to be believed despite his lack of concern to deceive warrants designation as a particular species of falsehood, and so on.

However, I am not convinced that a taxonomy of falsehood and lies is desirable, particularly as it often begins with what I consider to be a dubious assurance of *what falsehood is.* Taxonomies should only ever strive to be suggestive rather than exhaustive. If falsehood lacks its own essence (apart from truth), it is impossible to say how many different kinds of falsehoods there are. The best taxonomies are thus open-ended and incomplete. I detect in Bonhoeffer's words — "how very difficult it is to say what actually constitutes a lie" — openness to the idea that new forms of falsehood may always be possible.

This chapter follows Bonhoeffer's insight and looks at what can be gained by considering truth-telling as the positive practice of testifying, of bearing true witness to the gospel of Christ. If telling the truth is paradigmatically proclamation, then it is, in the first place, a liturgical act of celebration and praise, a songlike dance of joy, as Barth suggests. It is

---

6. Harry G. Frankfurt, *On Bullshit* (Princeton, NJ: Princeton University Press, 2005).

7. Augustine, *Confessions*, trans. Henry Chadwick (Oxford: Oxford University Press, 1998), X.41.66 (p. 218).

less a calculated move designed to manage consequences and more a species of doxology and (because proclamation is closer to singing than assertion) a sublime work of hymnody. The one who rejoices in the truth celebrates the truth and cannot keep silent about it. He refuses to keep it under wraps but instead speaks it openly and freely. This is the most basic statement about the human encounter with God's truth.[8]

Recall that Barth locates his discussion of gratuitous witness within a larger discourse on human freedom before God. He countenances freedom as *for* obedience to God. Witness as a positive activity correlates to Barth's positive notion of freedom. If human freedom were merely negative as freedom *from* God (indeed from any restraint), there could be no obligation to speak anything in particular, and we would only be left considering how *not* to speak. We would be left with what I will call a negative notion of truth-telling: do not lie. By negative truth-telling, I have in mind an inability to state what truth-telling is except in terms of not lying. We need to consider the relationship between human freedom and truth-telling in greater detail in order to see whether and how a positive notion of telling the truth is possible.

In his essay "What's Wrong with Negative Liberty," Charles Taylor distinguishes two notions of freedom.[9] The first he describes as an "opportunity-concept," an essentially negative view of freedom where to be free means to be independent from the interference of others (whether governments, corporations, or private persons). As an opportunity-concept, it is concerned with the opportunities open to the unhindered and uncoerced individual.[10] In contrast, the second view of freedom is essentially positive, where to be free means that the individual participates in the collective control over the common life of the people of whom he is a member. Taylor characterizes this as an "exercise-concept." One *becomes* free only by exercising control over the shape of one's life, by actively mak-

---

8. This is despite what I said earlier about silence, since the point before was that the silence that recognizes the inadequacy of words to their object is also a form of witness. But such silence is no less songlike for its lack of words.

9. Charles Taylor, "What's Wrong with Negative Liberty," in *Philosophy and the Human Sciences*, Philosophical Papers 2 (Cambridge: Cambridge University Press, 1985), pp. 211-29.

10. Taylor associates this view mostly with Hobbes, though he suggests that there are also some affinities with Bentham. Hobbes defined freedom as "the absence of Opposition; (by Opposition, I mean externall Impediments of motion) . . ." (Hobbes, *Leviathan* [London: Penguin, 1985; first published 1651], chap. XXI, p. 261).

ing choices that accord with what one takes to be of fundamental importance.[11] Exercising this second kind of freedom requires enough self-understanding to know what one's true desires are, against which freedom must be determined. In some forms, this requires that individual freedoms be discovered as mediated through communal practices in pursuit of the good — through the political life of the community. Those freedoms that communal life dictates define what it means to be free.[12]

Taylor argues that the former, negative view of freedom is not tenable. He makes his case in part by showing that a strict version of the negative view — freedom from all external infringements — is its least tenable version since, even in the absence of external barriers, there are always also likely to be *internal* barriers. These barriers might be psychological phobias, such as a fear of public speaking, that keep someone from pursuing a certain career. In this case, overcoming the fear of public speaking would make a person more free. But once internal barriers are brought into consideration, a difficulty arises for how to discriminate between different kinds of barriers. On what basis, for example, do we conclude that the fear of public speaking should be abandoned and the desire for the career requiring public speaking should remain? Taylor argues that making such discriminations requires a high degree of self-understanding and self-realization.

Even if a defender of the negative view conceded that internal constraints should also be considered, Taylor thinks that self-knowledge would need to be infallible in order still to maintain a negative view of freedom. A negative view could not account for self-deception without admitting to factors that would jeopardize the negativity of the view itself. It would then have to become a positive view of freedom after all. The logic of self-deception means that, although we may be doing what we want

11. Foucault observes this kind of freedom when he describes Greek sexual behavior as seeking to "stylize a freedom," where the free man is free exactly in the exercise of his activity (*The History of Sexuality 2: The Use of Pleasure,* trans. Robert Hurley [London: Penguin, 1984], p. 97). Taylor explicitly associates this view with Marx and Rousseau, though it also appears in the thought of Hegel to the extent that, for him, the state subsumes civil society (Hegel subsumes Kant's distinction between the two) such that only within the state can the "idea of freedom" be fulfilled. See Adam Seligman, *The Idea of Civil Society* (Princeton, NJ: Princeton University Press, 1992), pp. 50-51. Hegel was not definite on this point, however, and expressed his reservations about a state's actually achieving this.

12. William Werpehowski describes the Marxist version this way in "Ad Hoc Apologetics," *Journal of Religion* 66 (July 1986): 282-301 (esp. p. 294).

(having come to identify our desires), we cannot point to doing so as proof that we are free. In fact, we might simply be extending our lack of freedom without knowing it. This happens when we want what is contrary to the grain of our "basic purposes." Since there are clearly degrees of self-knowledge that admit relatively to grasping what these basic purposes are, we are always subject to deceiving ourselves concerning the nature of our wants. Since we cannot be trusted to be the final authority on the authenticity of our desires, Taylor concludes that pursuing freedom will always involve cultivating the self-irony necessary to keep ourselves in check by engaging in a rigorous, self-directed second-guessing.[13]

All of this suggests that there are reasons for abandoning both an extreme version and a milder version of the negative view of freedom. Defending a positive view, Taylor points out that freedom is only ever a human good at all because humans are "purposive beings": there are certain actions that are more significant than others, and these arise from beliefs about what matters more or less to us. Thus can internal fetters be identified as, in a sense, *not ours* to the extent that we recognize how they fail to reflect what we take to be of importance. They may appear as "brute desires," but they cannot be accepted as given realities on their own. Instead, they can only ever be the object of critical inquiry by our weighing them against our overall goods. We are not only subject to first-order desires, but also second-order desires, "desires about desires."[14] Because desires are always subject to self-deception to a greater or lesser degree, freedom consists partly in the ability truly to recognize which purposes are most important.[15] This surely makes freedom much more than an opportunity-

13. Taylor, "What's Wrong with Negative Liberty," pp. 215-16.
14. Taylor, "What's Wrong with Negative Liberty," pp. 219-20.
15. In this essay, Taylor stops short of linking the positive view of freedom he endorses with the attendant recommendation of the leading defenders of the positive view, namely, that freedom is only possible and recognizable as such within a certain kind of society. The nature of a society determines the ability to fulfill one's potential, for example, by furnishing notions of the good from which individual potentials derive and against which they are measured. Many, like Isaiah Berlin, fear that just such a view justifies totalitarianism (such as Stalinist communism) in the name of liberty (Berlin, "Two Concepts of Liberty," in *Four Essays on Liberty* [Oxford: Oxford University Press, 1969]). Nevertheless, it does seem to follow that if a positive notion of freedom is to be embraced, then a political notion of the good will need to, in some sense, mediate collective notions of what it means to be free. In turn, individual notions of freedom will take their cues either from the social goods that find expression on the individual level or from the individual goods that are open to description and "second-guessing" because of purposes that can be located beyond the extension of the indi-

concept. The relative importance of goods with the relative liberty to embrace them will determine whether one is truly free or not. Where judgments concerning goods are unavailable, ignored, or considered irrelevant, freedom will be politically incoherent. In practice, people who seek liberation of any kind do so in order to have access to and fulfill particular things that they judge to be personal, social, or general human goods. "Freedom from" may serve the interests of the most abstract political philosophies, but it is difficult to imagine that it is something that could be lived.

We should notice that we have arrived at a connection point between truthfulness and freedom. If Taylor is right that true freedom must be positive in order to have any meaning, then being free will involve engaging in those activities that are most important. This explains the way Barth speaks about bearing true testimony. When he locates testifying by the Christian witness within freedom, it is within a substantive, positive freedom of the Christian life that not only allows for the possibility of obedience to God's command, but is in fact constituted by it. Taylor's argument illuminates how the freedom of the witness would not actually exist if it were not for the mission that God has given, which is the mission that makes witnesses in the first place. "There is no freedom except when what we are, and do, corresponds to what has been given to us to be and to do."[16] Christian freedom does not depend on liberal rights or on the positive subjectivity of individuals who have made a connection with their deepest desires. Rather, the new social reality that announces the *possibility* of a new social reality as its mission of Christian witness becomes the very locus of freedom: it is a freedom to obey Christ's command to speak the truth of the gospel by recalling and proclaiming a past ("he was crucified and raised") that changes present and future societies and the loyalties they would call forth. The insight of negative liberty is that the gospel liberates, but it does so for the sake of a positive option that exceeds mere liberation. The liberated discourse of the new polis — the divine speech of the *ekklēsia* — does more than demand that others turn from old lords, because it does so by demonstrating alternative citizenship as a paradigm. Such speech is both an invitation to, and a sign of, a new possibility.

---

vidual subject. On these grounds alone, of course, it is not possible to rule out totalitarian force except inasmuch as the political goods themselves in fact preclude it. But this could not be spelled out ahead of time in formalistic terms. It is easy to see how the negative theorists feel compelled to retreat to the formalistic security of their view.

16. Oliver O'Donovan, *Desire of the Nations: Rediscovering the Roots of Political Authority* (Cambridge: Cambridge University Press, 1996), p. 252.

If, as I suggest, truthfulness is a normative, positive practice on which falsehoods such as lying are parasitic, what are we to make of the injunction against bearing false witness in the Decalogue? Indeed, most of the Ten Commandments are phrased negatively, making them appear as mere prohibitions. As such, Nietzsche took them to be arbitrary and given without reasons. Therefore, he saw them as an assault on human rationality.[17] Similarly, ethics of the "divine command" often go out of their way to make clear that no further justification beyond the command itself is necessary to warrant obeying it. Yet the mere fact that these commands are negative need not suggest that there are practices that can be sustained in their own negativity. We might instead be led to a different set of observations about them. For one thing, it is surely an obvious point that there can be no negative practices at all, because *not* doing something does not tell you what to do when you are not doing what you should not be doing. Cessation is not a practice on its own. But more to the point, every positive practice can be formulated imperatively, albeit in a negative way, without threatening the positive nature of the practice. Rules only derive their intelligibility from a prior knowledge of what constitutes the practices they modify. For example, Martin Luther noticed that in order for there to be such a thing as stealing, there must exist antecedent practices of generosity rooted in trusting God.[18] Similarly, there could be no adultery apart from faithful marriage. The injunctions against stealing and adultery in the Ten Commandments, therefore, do not need to stand on their own as self-evident categories since they rely for their intelligibility on prior, positive practices to which they implicitly appeal.

Nevertheless, they only have such positive meanings as they are claimed by the particular history of Israel and the church, as communities of faith for whom what is denied them as prohibitions rests on what is previously given them as the possibility of an adamant historical persistence.

17. Friedrich Nietzsche, *Human, All Too Human,* in *The Portable Nietzsche,* ed. and trans. Walter Kaufmann (London: Viking Penguin, 1968), sec. 48, p. 68.

18. Martin Luther, "Treatise on Good Works," in *The Christian in Society I,* Luther's Works, trans. W. A. Lambert (Philadelphia: Fortress, 1966), 44:109. Bernd Wannenwetsch observes how the negative commands are easier to keep than the positive ones because, though the negative commands presuppose positive practices, they do not specify the shape of those practices on their own (Wannenwetsch, "You Shall Not Kill — What Does It Take? Why We Need the Other Commandments If We Are to Abstain from Killing," in *I Am the Lord Your God: Christian Reflections on the Ten Commandments,* ed. Carl E. Braaten and Christopher R. Seitz [Grand Rapids: Eerdmans, 2005], p. 150).

As such — and only as such — does the Decalogue list virtues.[19] "[I]t happens that each Commandment (except perhaps the first and the last) has its place in connection with a *powerful practice* in the community of Israel. . . . For example, honoring a father (the Fifth Commandment) makes no sense except in a community where there *are* fathers, where, that is to say, a kinship system makes fathers (and other relatives) socially visible. . . . So to issue the Commandment is both to *presuppose a practice* and to show a way of conduct with regard to that practice."[20] Such practices are important in order for commands to resist being translated into vague (though positive) clichés, such as "be humane." The problem is not that there is something wrong with humaneness, but that earnest admonitions like this are, on their own, never sufficient to elaborate what humaneness consists in. Apart from the practices that supply that content, such directives are empty and meaningless.[21] Of course, there may be political reasons why a people actually prefer empty slogans to ones full of content, as they may more readily secure agreement among people whose unity would surely dissipate before more particularistic content. But a people who claim such slogans and clichés for themselves usually do so in order to disguise their dependence on other things for knowing how to live. A people who claim to live by "be humane" may not be able to derive an ethic from it, but their understanding of humaneness will come from somewhere to fill the void. It goes without saying that the operative ethic that rushes in may not be altogether reputable or able to be acknowledged consciously and openly without raising further problems (such as the ones the slogans were meant to help avoid).

19. Robert W. Jenson, *Systematic Theology: The Works of God* (Oxford: Oxford University Press, 1999), 2:207.

20. James McClendon, *Ethics: Systematic Theology* (Nashville: Abingdon, 1986), 1:180 (emphasis added in the last sentence). Barth also exhibited this same logic in his treatment of the command not to kill: "[W]e shall better understand the negation expressed in this command if we first turn our attention to the positive fact which, although not expressed, is undoubtedly contained in it" (*CD* III/4, p. 344). Barth concludes similarly about the Sabbath (*CD*, III/4, pp. 62-63). See also John Paul II, *Evangelium Vitae*, sec. 75.2: "[T]he negative moral precepts have an extremely important positive function."

21. McClendon, *Ethics*, p. 181. Nietzsche, too, thought it was impossible to correct for negative prohibitions using "nonsensical" imperatives such as these ("Fragment on Ethics, 1868," in *The Portable Nietzsche*, p. 31). And, of course, negative clichés ("I cannot tell a lie"), though dependent on practice for their intelligibility, often disguise that dependence because of being both negative and being clichés. Below I discuss the status of *rules* prohibiting lying.

In the same way, for our purposes, not bearing false witness presupposes the positive practice of bearing *true* witness. Commenting on this commandment, Luther asks, "What does this mean?" He answers: "We should fear and love God, so that we do not falsely accuse, betray or slander neighbors, or spread evil rumors about them, but rather excuse them, speak well of them and interpret everything about them in the best sense."[22] Where do these positive injunctions come from? In a community that is formed by the right worship of God as prescribed by the first table of the Decalogue, the prohibition of false witness presupposes fearing and loving God for the positive work of speaking well of others. At the very least, this suggests interrelationships among the commands that collectively point to a broader, more positive and comprehensive ethic governing the life of the people whose worship of God obligates them to include themselves in that way of life. Likewise, Calvin argued that to the prohibition against false witness "is linked that we should faithfully help everyone as much as we can in affirming the truth."[23] Aquinas took the acts of love of God and neighbor to be more basic than not bearing false witness.[24] Therefore, what is pernicious about lying is much more than the violation of a negative command; it goes against *positively* loving God and neighbor.

In his sermons on the Ten Commandments, Calvin thought that the commandment not to bear false witness was actually redundant, given the prior commandment not to take God's name in vain. This is because he noticed a strong connection between the loss of confidence in truthful testimony concerning one's neighbor and the loss of confidence in the significance of God's name. The one who wrongly invokes the power of God's name is not appropriately possessed of the power of what he beholds in that name. Calvin is thinking about how oaths work for witnesses, something I consider in detail below. In essence, a false witness does not fear the God of the oath he takes. As lack of faith, this is, for Calvin, a more basic and prior sin compared to a lie that is told to the detriment of one's neighbor. Put differently, the idolatry in lying about God — making God less than God — is a metaphysical mistake linked to the heart of all other lying. This concurs with Augustine's insistence that virtue is only possible

<hr>

22. Luther, "Die zehn Gebote," *Kleiner Katechismus,* 16 (quoted in Jenson, *Systematic Theology,* 2:207).

23. John Calvin, *Institutes of the Christian Religion,* ed. John T. McNeill, trans. Ford Lewis Battles. Library of Christian Classics, vols. XX and XXI (London: SCM, 1960), II, 19:47.

24. Aquinas, *ST,* II-II.110.4, reply to obj. 2.

through true worship.[25] Where there is right worship of the true God, the Second Commandment is fulfilled; where there is subsequent virtue in truthfulness, the Eighth Commandment is fulfilled.[26]

Christians both anticipate and participate in the realization of a kingdom marked foremost by permissions rather than prohibitions, on account of the freedom for fearing and loving God brought by the resurrection of Christ. This positive freedom, even when it comes in the form of a command to bear witness (and perhaps especially then), is a gift of permission since it comes from God who, as our creator, knows what is right for us. As Robert Jenson observes, "In the church, moral commands tell what we may reasonably do because Christ is risen, which otherwise could be thought irresponsible. Insofar as it is the gospel that enjoins us, we do because we may, not because we ought."[27] According to Jenson, the Christian ethic proceeds originally and more substantively from the permission that Christ's freedom makes possible first for himself, and only on this basis, for those who share in his risen life. If this is the case with the moral commands of the church, it is especially the case with its mission to bear witness to the nations. The *grounds* for the mission is the *task* of the mission. Its one condition of possibility is its only claim: the resurrection of Christ as a reality makes possible the command that grants permission to the church to proclaim this as its message. Oliver O'Donovan notes that the moral life of the church springs from the gladness that the gospel brings: "Church morality is an evangelical morality" that is "not added to it as a preface . . . or as a postscript."[28] It does not merely follow from the gospel, where the gospel provides *reasons* for acting one way rather than another. Of course, the gospel has implications, but the celebration of the kingdom feast is not one of them, since such celebration is itself the realization that the good news is good. The church's mission both springs from its gladness and fulfills the divine command precisely because that

---

25. Augustine, *City of God* XIX.

26. I am using the Catholic and Lutheran convention in numbering the Ten Commandments.

27. Jenson, *Systematic Theology*, 2:209. Likewise for Barth, "[t]he form by which the command of God is distinguished from all other commands . . . consists in the fact that it is permission — the granting of a very definite freedom" (*CD* II/2, p. 585).

28. O'Donovan, *Desire of the Nations*, p. 182. Similarly, Barth notes that thankfulness is the origin of every good action in the Christian life (Barth, *The Knowledge of God and the Service of God According to the Teaching of the Reformation* [London: Hodder and Stoughton, 1938], p. 123).

command is nothing less than permission to do the very thing for which we have been given freedom.[29] This way of putting the matter can admittedly sound paradoxical. But it is only truly a paradox if the freedom of creatures is a negative one, if it is maximally achieved by escaping obstacles. (But the language, of course, already betrays its reliance on its own circularity: obstacles to what? To freedom.) Freedom is not negative for creatures of the God of Jesus Christ.[30] It is in the nature of the gospel to extend into proclamation. There is no gospel without witnesses and no witnesses without the gospel, though even the rocks and the stars cannot help but bear witness when God's people refuse to do so. The kingdom feast fulfills creation and thus entails the joy original to God's creative purposes, which means that if there is no joy, God has not really set the table and invited all to come to it. Supposing, as I have been urging in these pages, that truth-telling were understood in these terms, then the truth of the gospel can be seen as fashioning the Christian character of the relationship to truth by good news that cannot help but call forth truthfulness in those who are captivated by it. Witnesses cannot imagine being anything less than truthful since this would deny the gospel.

✳ ✳ ✳

Up until now, we have considered some of the problems with understanding truthfulness negatively. The problems have largely been associated with

---

29. The "because" in this sentence is by way of giving explanation, not of giving a reason.

30. Jenson reminds us that angels are creatures, though not human, and their witness differs from the witness of human creatures in some respects but not others: "God creates and sustains all things by speaking. What the angels' speech witnesses *to* is itself again speech, God's speech, and so the angelic witness belongs to the action to which it testifies. Thus the angels' witness participates in bringing to pass the content of the witness. . . . That a Virgin conceives is not merely what Gabriel talks *about* but is the very reality of Gabriel. Again, that the Lord is risen is not merely a contingent content of the angelic witness; the only describable earthly events of the Resurrection . . . were the appearances of the angelic witness" (Jenson, *Systematic Theology,* 2:125). Humans are not as exalted as the angels, and so the church's witness does not bring to pass the content of its witness. But like the angels, the church exists by virtue of the same call (the response to which brings the church into being) that it heralds as an extension of the angelic witness. In this way, we can say that overzealous witness tries to create rather than testify to the fact that God creates. Since this overestimates human status and perverts the angelic witness, would we be justified in calling it demonic? We are reminded how it is that witness does not seek to accomplish anything — least of all bringing about the incarnation or return of Christ, or the construction of the City of God.

privation and freedom. Nevertheless, because falsehood and lying have often been granted the elevated status afforded them by such negative formulations, the discourse on lying has taken on two related characteristics.

First is what Bernard Williams calls "fetishizing assertion," by which he means taking the assertative mode of speech to be more sacrosanct than other modes. He observes an obsession with giving careful definitions of lying in order to distinguish it from other forms of deception, usually with the intention of prohibiting lying absolutely, but not other forms of deception. As an example, Williams notes how Aquinas prohibited all lying but also allowed for the truth to be masked in clever ways.[31] Williams thinks this is absurd hairsplitting, since he cannot see what it matters that one form of deception is called a lie while another is not. He notes that this kind of discrimination only becomes necessary if you grant an exalted status to assertions as a mode of speech. Here Williams mainly accuses Kant (though he also accuses Aquinas on similar grounds) of fetishizing assertion owing to the latter's insistence that the point (the natural end) of assertion-in-general is the accurate communication of thought and that, insofar as this involves the natural, rational use of a human faculty, it is bound up with what it means to be a human. Kant used rather strong words to express this: "But communication of one's thoughts to someone through words that yet (intentionally) contain the contrary of what the speaker thinks on the subject is an end that is directly opposed to the natural purposiveness of the speaker's capacity to communicate his thoughts, and is thus a renunciation of his personality, and such a speaker is a mere deceptive appearance of a human being, not a human being himself."[32]

Kant's near-hysteria aside, Williams notes that this kind of teleology is now dead (presumably following the announcement from Nietzsche's Zarathustra that Kant was "running on borrowed time"). Instead, Williams thinks we should strive to develop a naturalistic account that is free from teleological assumptions like Kant's reliance on the functions of universal reason from which we can derive a rational morality concerning things like prohibiting false assertions. But this alone does not exhaust what Williams means by fetishizing assertion. He also has in mind the essentializing of assertion-as-such devoid of the content of any particular assertion whatsoever. "The [teleological] doctrine makes the assertion

31. Williams, *Truth and Truthfulness* (Princeton, NJ: Princeton University Press, 2002), pp. 102-6. One such reference in Aquinas is *ST* II-II.69.1-2.
32. Quoted in Williams, *Truth and Truthfulness*, p. 106.

into a fetish by lifting it out of the context in which it plays its part and projecting onto it in isolation all the force of the demand for truthfulness."[33] In other words — and this will be the essential point for my purposes — the *form* of assertion is made to bear all the weight of the subsequent construction of a morality quite apart from the *content* of what is asserted.[34]

Related to this is the second feature that marks truth-telling in an environment where lying is inordinately elevated. If lying is prohibited absolutely, then the other forms of deception that are less heinous than the simple lie of a false assertion yield a kind of loophole casuistry. In order to avoid lying on the understanding that it violates reason or some other condition by which assertion-as-such might otherwise be kept pure (through an absolute prohibition), nonlying forms of deception were not always justified, even though they may have been distinguished from lying. (For example, Aquinas did this in order to distinguish relative severity and to identify which kinds of lies were mortal sins and which were venial sins.) A priest who equivocates in order to protect what he has heard in the confessional does not lie in a strict sense. Instead, he speaks in an ambiguous way that could easily be taken to mean something other than the truth; indeed, this is its aim. Nevertheless, since the possibility exists that it *could* also be taken to mean what is the truth, the speaker is innocent of lying.[35] Williams thinks that it is arbitrary to insist that one of the speaker's possible meanings needs to be the true one since the whole point of equivocating is that the assertion be believed in its *false* meaning. He concludes, as before,

33. Williams, *Truth and Truthfulness*, p. 110.

34. Alasdair MacIntyre makes a similar point by following Peter Geach in observing, "[T]he notion of assertion cannot be explicated independently of that of truth. It must therefore be the case . . . that any attempt to give an account of assertion cannot be explicated independently of that of truth" (MacIntyre, "Moral Relativism, Truth and Justification," in *The MacIntyre Reader*, ed. Kelvin Knight [Notre Dame, IN: University of Notre Dame Press, 1998], p. 211). Against neopragmatists like Robert Brandom, MacIntyre wants to show that, when an assertion is made, it is made because it is thought to be true; but also that this holds for different (nonassertive) uses such as conditionals. The meaning of sentences is not sufficiently captured by recourse to the form of the sentence, namely, assertion, since there are many kinds of true sentences. True *assertative* sentences are true independent of their assertative form. I am sure MacIntyre is right in this, but I worry that he would be satisfied with too formalistic an account of truth.

35. For a survey of such casuistry, see Albert R. Jonsen and Stephen Toulmin, *The Abuse of Casuistry: A History of Moral Reasoning* (Berkeley: University of California Press, 1989), chap. 10.

that such a condition intends to preserve the sanctity of assertion, often on the same or similar grounds as those Kant gave.[36]

I think Williams is right to reject Kant's decontextualizing of form from content. Even so, I think it is a mistake to abandon teleology altogether. Just as we noted that Barth rejects dogmatic prolegomena on the grounds that no formal categories can be derived from an epistemology prior to Word, Kant's reasonable and natural designation of the right use of speech for truthful communication makes just this kind of move. It should be summarily rejected on the same (Barthian) grounds, because it matters what is being said. Stanley Fish puts it this way:

> You assert, in short, because you give a damn, *not about assertion* — as if it were a value in and of itself — *but about what your assertion is about.* It may seem paradoxical, but free expression could only be a primary value if what you are valuing is the right to make noise; but if you are engaged in some purposive activity in the course of which speech happens to be produced, sooner or later you will come to a point when you decide that some forms of speech do not further but endanger that purpose.[37]

Lying, like restrictions on free speech, is not something that one can define simply as an abuse of assertion; it requires the background of true speech. In turn, as Fish insists, true speech is not an abstract category (again, not assertion-as-such), nor even a "value in and of itself." Rather, it is a way of talking about what exists prior to that description, namely, the "purposive activity in the course of which speech happens to be produced."

I think Fish's comments certainly enrich how we understand Christian speech. Witness is a purposive activity, and the person of the witness "gives a damn" not primarily about reason or assertion, nor communication, nor even the general practice of telling the truth, but about the specific practice of relating the gospel of the kingdom come in Christ. And what is speech for? Augustine argued that its purpose is the praise of God.[38] Following that insight, we can further claim that truthful speech is ordered first by its use in bearing witness to Christ. As Barth claims, language and speech have been given by God in order that, as faculties, they

36. Williams, *Truth and Truthfulness,* pp. 102-3.

37. Stanley Fish, *There's No Such Thing as Free Speech* (Oxford: Oxford University Press, 1994), p. 107 (emphasis added).

38. Augustine, *Enarrationes in Psalmos,* 98.8.

may be summoned for a specific purpose: "It is certainly not a demand that he should merely speak," but that "in intercourse and together with his fellow man should praise, confess and attest God" (*CD* III/4, p. 289). Likewise, Barth notes that what ethics has to contribute, given the Sabbath commandment, is not the formal and legal structures for setting aside a holy day, but "its proper contribution to the problem of Sunday is necessarily the proclamation of the Gospel" (*CD* III/4, p. 66). The space made possible by the Sabbath prohibition of work is unintelligible without the positive activity of proclamation within that space. Witness and worship logically precede speech. They are not just particular uses to which speaking may on occasion be put. Rather, they stand as the activities toward which speaking itself presses and yearns, and thus where it finds its natural home.

Truthfulness is thus a "value" that comes secondarily by way of describing what is happening in the first-order activity of witness. Likewise, true witness allows us to speak intelligibly of *false* witness, something that would otherwise be unavailable. Witness carries with it the goods and goals intrinsic to its practice, which are the background against which it is possible to perceive and determine what counts as endangering those goods and goals. True and false witness are more specific terms than truthtelling and lying, but they are also more basic, because they are not subject to an ideological disguise whereby the content of the speech named by those terms disappears, leaving behind abstract concepts that get used as though they have obvious (or, as for Kant, rational) meanings.

If the truth is going to be told, it will be for its own sake rather than for anything it brings about by telling it. As Barth declares, "The witness and confession claimed from man must always bear the character of an action without an ulterior goal" (*CD* III/4, p. 77). A positive doctrine of truthfulness must do more than give compelling reasons why telling the truth is important. In moving beyond this kind of justification, it is (using Taylor's terms) moving from being an opportunity-concept to being an exercise-concept. We may note that Aquinas called a hypocrite one whose relationship with the truth was defined by instrumentality, one who speaks the truth for the sake of appearance rather than for its own sake.[39] Certainly there are reasons other than hypocrisy that one could give for when to tell the truth or for when it is proper or even necessary not to do so. Kant famously considered whether it is immoral to lie to a murderer re-

39. Aquinas, *ST* II-II.111.3, reply to obj. 1.

garding the whereabouts of the would-be victim you are hiding (he thought it is).[40] A diversity of notions also concerns whether certain false statements qualify as lies or not (including, as before, when told out of ignorance). But this diversity itself differs from the variety of notions that help to decide whether there is falsehood or deception in the first place. Positive truthfulness depends on a background of speech-content that not only gives justification for truthfulness, but that also suggests and even defines or specifies its content.[41] My claim is that this speech-content, at its most basic level, is the testimony of the gospel of Christ, and that telling it is witness. In other words, witness is the practice that makes intelligible the claim that truthfulness is an exercise-concept.

The Christian doctrine of witness marks the beginning of a positive doctrine of truthfulness, because it recognizes that something is worth saying. This is appreciably different from recognizing that there are reasons for saying something, even something that is true. As with positive liberty, positive practices constitute the very notions that otherwise could not be established in their positivity. Positive liberty does not admit to practices that achieve or bring about a liberty that might also be achieved or brought about by other means. This is because liberty is realized precisely in free acts, that is, in acts that are themselves liberty's exercise, as Taylor argues. In the same way, positive truthfulness embodies practices that are themselves determinative of truthfulness and without which truthfulness would not be recognizable as such. Witness descries the grounds for truthfulness within the truthful something of which it speaks. To put it simply, the truth demands truthfulness.

A further way that Christian witness differs from justificatory theories is that the former does not assume that judgments on falsehood can always be made ahead of time. If a taxonomy of falsehood is an insufficient starting point, then it is not possible to take for granted that we will know what falsehood is when we encounter it. We do not know what form it will take, since it has no intrinsic, determinate form (owing to the fact that it is privative of what is true). The witness will live with an uncertainty about where falsehood lies, but with the conviction that bearing true witness is

40. A version of this example goes back to Augustine. Augustine, Aquinas, and Kant all thought one should tell the truth even in this case. Still, they divided types of lies according to taxonomies: Augustine, in *Contra Mendacium,* had eight and Aquinas had three (*ST* II-II.110.2).

41. This is the case even though the specific content of witness resists systematic formalization.

indispensable toward discovering forms of falsehood she thought either did not exist before, or that she may even previously have mistaken for the truth. This surely places the witness in a precarious situation, vulnerable to lies and every kind of deception and falsehood the less she allows her life to be formed according to truthful practices. The will not to be deceived is not sufficient for dwelling within the truth. Witness describes more than a will; it defines a life of motion, of circulating within what is true, whether it is known or unknown, beautiful or horrifying. Its coming to rest in the belief that it has secured truth is a sign that it has in fact abandoned a true life altogether and is now eminently laid open before every thinly disguised deception, ill-equipped to recognize it as such.

*   *   *

Up to this point, this chapter has shown some ways that speaking the truth is qualified ahead of the actual exercise of speaking truly. I have argued that both taking for granted the obviousness of not-lying and elevating the form of assertion are inadequate to account for the content of what one speaks. Oath-taking is a further case: an oath is a kind of prolegomenon to testimony. It is legal and judicial throat-clearing that specifies a particular relationship between truth and power and submits the former to the latter. Recall, though, that there are good reasons for rejecting the prolegomenon on grounds that any explanation of the subsequent discourse is really *part* of that discourse rather than prior to it. Oaths function the same way, as a prior justification and guarantee of what is about to be spoken. Quite apart from the testimony itself, the oath reassures those who will hear it that this is a matter of great seriousness, that there are penalties for speaking falsely, and that this is in some way proof of trustworthiness.

It is worth noting, however, that the truthfulness in which the *oath itself* is spoken cannot be greater than the truth of the testimony it is meant to control. This means that nothing can be said in addition to a true testimony in order to guarantee that it will be true. To express it differently, it is more important to tell the truth than to promise to tell the truth (since even a promise to tell the truth must be told truthfully if it is to have any meaning). When oaths are sworn in courts, the introduction of an allegedly higher standard (symbolized by the oath) that denotes the subsequent possibility of perjury really introduces a *lower* standard for speech that is not spoken under oath. Another way to make the same point is to say that the practice of oath-taking depends on justifying oaths quite apart from justifying truthfulness. A person will generally be persuaded to swear an oath for reasons that are different from the reasons he may have for speaking the truth (such as fear, a desire to please, to escape harm, or to keep one's head). Jesus' teaching on oaths in the Sermon on the Mount (Matt. 5:33-37) even seems to indicate that some often take oaths in order to avoid doing what is promised. Moreover, people who think more is at stake for speaking truthfully when under oath are then less likely to have their characters formed according to the commitment to speak the truth all the time.

Heirs of the Radical Reformation, such as Anabaptists and Quakers, sometimes faced severe opposition for their resistance to oath-taking.[42] Anabaptists in particular found that, by resisting taking oaths, they were resisting the authorities who understood oaths to be a foundation of civil society. This perspective was shared by Reformers such as Luther, Melanchthon, and Heinrich Bullinger.[43] A seventeenth-century Puritan offers a clear example of this view:

> Oaths are necessary for the execution of the magistrate's office and the preservation of human society. For without such oaths the commonwealth hath no surety upon public officers and ministers: nor kings upon their subjects; nor lords upon their tenants; neither can men's titles be cleared in causes civil, nor justice done in causes criminal; nor dangerous plots and conspiracies be discovered against the state.[44]

It is striking that the emphasis here is not that truthfulness is the basis of civil society, but that the oath is. It is the guarantee that is most important because it acknowledges who has authority to punish, who has a right to the truth, and in what setting, on what matters, and so on. An oath pays homage to the one responsible for the security brought by the binding nature of an oath and the punishment that attends to perjury. But as the Anabaptists and others discovered, oaths then become more important than the truth itself. It is easy to commit perjury, but it is very difficult to refuse to swear an oath, especially when one might face being put to death as a

---

42. Alan Kreider, "Christ, Culture, and Truth-telling," *The Conrad Grebel Review* 15, no. 3 (Fall 1997): 207-33.

43. Bullinger called the oath "the bond, which holds together the whole body of the common good of just government" (quoted in Kreider, "Christ, Culture, and Truth-telling," p. 217).

44. Daniel Featly, *The Dippers Dipt* (London, 1646), p. 142 (quoted in Kreider, "Christ, Culture, and Truth-telling," p. 217).

heretic.[45] Against this, those who refused oaths took their understanding of truthful speech from the Sermon on the Mount: "Let what you say be simply 'Yes' or 'No'; anything more than this comes from evil" (Matt. 5:37). Jesus' disciples should not look for ways of making their speech true or certifying it apart from simply speaking truly. An oath is redundant in the face of true testimony. Here again, one encounters the insoluble problem of making something more true than the truth. Oaths condition truthful speech in the same way that theories of truth condition truth. Both rely on what they purport to control. Oaths safeguard the truthfulness of the truth in advance of testimony, betraying a reliance on the power of magistrates — and ultimately the sword — at the expense of the power of a truthfully spoken yes and no.[46]

Oaths are posturing and bluffing. They accomplish nothing because they are merely an exercise of power that only obtains to the extent that testimony is connected to power. Testimony that is free and true will be spoken as such in blithe indifference to what the powerful want to hear. They will rather hear oaths than the truth, and submissive speech rather than critical speech. Where there exists a people determined to speak the truth about all things, uncoerced by the force of punishment or anything else, their freedom and free actions will be as dissident as anything they dare to speak. And if Foucault is right, their freedom and their speaking what is true are much more closely associated than we might think.

45. Kreider, "Christ, Culture, and Truth-telling," p. 218.
46. Some common expressions, such as "and that's the gospel truth," function in the same way. Furthermore, oaths are based on lying. As the Quaker William Penn observed, where there is no lying, there is no need to govern testimony by oaths: "[I]f Christians ought never to lie, it is most certain that they need never to swear; for swearing is built upon lying; take away lying, and there remains no more ground for swearing; truth-speaking comes in the room thereof" (Penn, *A Treatise of Oaths: Containing Several Weighty Reasons Why People called Quakers Refuse to Swear* [1675], in *Selected Works*, vol. 2 [1825], 44, quoted in Kreider, "Christ, Culture, and Truth-telling," pp. 218-19).

CHAPTER 9

Truthfulness and Its Subordinates

In the preceding chapter I surveyed a number of strategies for understanding an ethic of truth-telling according to what I have referred to as negativity. Negative truth-telling is not only prohibitive rather than positive and permission-granting, but it is also formalistic. Oath-taking and Kantian rule-making, for example, have a formal structure that governs speech without becoming entangled in the content of what is spoken. Therefore, they have the effect of subordinating what one says to how one says it and its mode of transmission. My attempt has been to counter these subordinating tendencies with a nonsubordinating account of the ethics of truth-telling that itself arises from what is true. Witness, I argue, is itself a truth-telling practice of determinate and decisive (though never static) content replete with demands on particular moral dispositions that bear on one's relationship with what is real.

There is a further set of accounts that this chapter considers: those for which the truth serves another desirable good. These will be shown to enact their own versions of subordinating content to form. But rather than prioritizing the mode of transmission to the substance of speech, they prioritize the goods that telling the truth may achieve. These have the advantage of making prominent the connection between truth and goodness that is a crucial connection for a project — such as mine — that seeks to associate more closely the gospel's proclamation and the ethics of truth-telling. Truth and goodness are both characteristics of the gospel. Even so, getting this connection right entails avoiding subordinating one to the other, a move not always achieved nor even attempted by the accounts that this chapter surveys. Instead, one finds several ways of instrumentalizing telling the truth for accomplishing other ends.

John Stuart Mill is most commonly associated with this kind of reasoning. For example, he recommends lying to those who are seriously ill.[1] Consequentialism, as a style of ethical reasoning, elevates the *mode* of reasoning above any substantive activity, the assessment of which its tools are meant to enable. It is not itself an activity of substance; it is designed to be of most value, in fact, when it is most distant from them. To the question "What are you doing?" the consequentialist cannot say, "I am engaged in consequentializing." Consequentialism provides no guidance for what one should be doing in one's spare time when one is not engaged in the exercise of consequentialist moral reasoning. Putting it more mildly, the technique of consequentialism does not arise from matters of substance, even though the consequentialist may hold to them, subscribe to them, or otherwise engage in and embody them. Of course, this is a function of the distancing strategies that the Enlightenment sought with such single-mindedness. The objectivity that consequentialism can claim for itself is not only a point of pride but is partly, or even entirely, justification for its superiority over other metaethical modes. Its formalistic character is a necessary aspect of its ability to claim universal application.

With this kind of reasoning, what is true will always be less important than what it can accomplish and what benefits attend to its being spoken. However, what happens when telling the truth turns out to be insufficient for achieving these benefits? Robert Spaemann rightly observes: "To define a thing by its function is to make it in principle replaceable through equivalents."[2] If the truth serves certain purposive ends, is not the truth replaceable by something else that happens to serve the same ends? Are not those ends therefore elevated to a higher importance than the truth, for example, the goodness that is achieved or the happiness of the other party? If so, then instrumentality will govern not only truthfulness but falsehood. The noble liar is morally no different from the noble truth-teller (nobility here being the important characteristic of the action). Reasons for lying become qualitatively indistinguishable from reasons for telling the truth. The subordination is real, and it is in service to other moral concepts. What are they?

A hallmark of consequentialist approaches to telling the truth is the priority of some other good. This prioritizing takes the form of asserting

---

1. John Stuart Mill, *Utilitarianism* (Indianapolis: Hackett, 1979), p. 22.

2. Quoted in Bernd Wannenwetsch, *Political Worship: Ethics for Christian Citizens* (Oxford: Oxford University Press, 2004), p. 22, n. 7.

greater relative importance of some good, such as "goodness" itself. Proclus, commenting on Plato, said: "That which is good is better than the truth," with the implication that falsehood can likewise be justified if it brings about good.[3] Therefore, truthfulness can be no better than falsehood because, depending on the situation, one may make a compelling case for one or the other for attaining goodness. In contrast, Aquinas rejected placing goodness above truth on the grounds that goodness and truth are convertible, a point he attributes to Augustine. Aquinas also agrees with Aristotle that being as such is true and so the divine transcendentals (goodness, beauty, and truth) are convertible with each other.[4] What we say about truth will ultimately take its bearings from the same source as what we say about goodness. While I am sure that this philosophical notion of convertibility can tend toward a great deal of abstraction, it at least signals an aspect of Christian thought that cautions against setting truth and goodness at odds, of being able to say that one is better than the other. After all, few will know how to display a commitment to goodness in the abstract. It is more common to specify particular goods. The most brazen elevation of another good above the truth continues to be found in Joseph Fletcher's *Situation Ethics*. For Fletcher, the most worthy and important good is love. Love is always good, and thus it should function as the governing principle of every moral judgment. Therefore, whatever love dictates in each particular situation is the right action in that situation. According to Fletcher, asking what is true is of little consequence, since "we are to tell the truth for love's sake, not for its own sake. If love vetoes truth, so be it."[5] The argument of this chapter may be seen as an extended counterstatement to Fletcher's: that Christian thought must instead countenance telling the truth precisely for its own sake. Nothing — not even love — can veto the truth without being truer than truth, which is incoherent.[6]

3. Quoted in Sissela Bok, *Lying: Moral Choice in Public and Private Life* (Sussex, UK: Harvester, 1978), p. 266.

4. Aquinas, *ST* I.16.3.

5. Joseph Fletcher, *Situation Ethics: The New Morality* (Philadelphia: Westminster, 1975), p. 65 (hereafter, page references to this work will appear in parentheses in the text). Others use the language of instrumentality more generally: "Truth telling is a means for accomplishing purposes. So is deception" (David Nyberg, *The Varnished Truth: Truth Telling and Deceiving in Ordinary Life* [Chicago: University of Chicago Press, 1993], p. 53). Of course this is right in an empirical sense, but Nyberg endorses forms of instrumental deception.

6. I admit to coming close to something that I am also trying to avoid: the incoher-

On the surface, it may seem as though Fletcher agrees with Aquinas, who taught that lying is a sin because it is "contrary to the love of God and our neighbor."[7] After all, for Aquinas, the reason charity is not specifically enjoined in the Decalogue is that it underlies all of the commandments and would therefore be redundant. But, whereas Aquinas took not bearing false witness against one's neighbor to be an act of charity, Fletcher takes it to be *secondary* to charity: "If a lie is told unlovingly it is wrong, evil; if it is told in love it is good, right." One should, at all costs, avoid assuming that the most legalistic and rigorous formulas — such as "Thou shalt not lie" — are the most morally serious (p. 65). Telling a white lie out of pity is not an evil act that nevertheless might still be justified; it is, for Fletcher, positively good. The same is true of lies told in order to keep a secret, whether from fidelity to a promise one has made or in keeping valuable information from the enemy in wartime or espionage. Several objections are in order.

First, Fletcher mistakenly identifies love as itself a singular good. In this he fails to appreciate a longstanding Christian insistence on charity as the form of all the virtues, one of which is truthfulness. In his formulation, charity is itself a virtue that is now able to *compete* with the others precisely because it is like them in respect of being a virtue. It is true that Fletcher denies making love a virtue: he speaks of it as "the one and only *regulative principle* of Christian ethics" (p. 61). Nevertheless, he defines love as the only thing that is good as such; everything else has extrinsic moral worth depending on whether and how they display love. Opposing love to truth in this way entirely reduces the virtue of truthfulness to love. Aquinas represents a richer tradition that is also more subtle, upholding the variety of virtues, each given form by love. If charity is the form of virtues like truthfulness, there can be no competition between them. Aquinas simply would not have understood Fletcher's attempt to use charity to trump and qualify the command to tell the truth.

Second, Fletcher misunderstands the nature of internal and external

---

ence of proffering truth and truthfulness as themselves goods that are better than goodness. Of course, the gospel proclamation will, as Aquinas teaches, make convertible claims about the gospel's goodness and truth. But I am taking care to avoid instrumentalizing its truth to its goodness (it is a mistake to claim that the gospel is good *because* it is true). The most straightforward way to avoid this is to insist, as I do, on convertibility, thus prohibiting either goodness or truth from gaining the upper hand. But also — and partly owing to convertibility — the gospel's truth will be seen by many to be anything but good in a straightforward or immediate sense.

7. Aquinas, *ST* II.II.110, reply to obj. 2.

goods. He insists that his ethic is "extrinsic," meaning that right and wrong (or good and evil) are merely predicates of actions rather than intrinsic properties (p. 67). Love is to be sought for its own sake and is therefore the only valid, objective universal (p. 64). But loving is only displayed through other acts and does not specify the shape of any of them on its own. This is what Fletcher means by claiming that love is extrinsically achieved. Love is an external good that is achievable either by telling the truth or a falsehood, depending on the situation, rather than an internal good — that is, where the truth is itself good due to convertibility. But practices that wrongly identify internal and external goods can devolve into making competition normative. By contrast to Fletcher, Aristotle took means to be related to ends internally and not externally.[8] Consider an illustration. Games are practices with both internal goods (such as the satisfaction of winning) and external goods (such as fame or money for, say, professional athletes). Internal and external goods usually coexist, meaning that a footballer can enjoy both the thrill of winning, the satisfaction of a well-executed play, *and* the fame and money that this brings.[9] However, when the virtues are separated from the practices they serve, then engaging in the practice becomes consequentially dominated by the external goods it achieves. There is no longer any reason to avoid cheating because, while cheating would violate the achievement of the game's internal goods, it might grant greater access to the external goods. Olympic runners who use steroids in order to run faster violate the virtues of running, but, assuming they are not discovered in such cheating, will have greater access to fame and glory. Over time, the unseating of internal goods threatens the compelling nature of the practice, which then becomes an exercise in *one way* of achieving the desired ends. Fame and glory can be had in many ways, but running the hurdles successfully cannot.[10]

---

8. Alasdair MacIntyre, *After Virtue,* 2nd ed. (Notre Dame, IN: University of Notre Dame Press, 1984), p. 184. I am clearly indebted to MacIntyre in this discussion of internal and external goods.

9. Bernard Williams argues that, in the search for truth, being motivated by fame does not necessarily corrupt the search, so long as one hopes to become famous for having found the truth (Williams, *Truth and Truthfulness* [Princeton, NJ: Princeton University Press, 2002], p. 142). Nevertheless, on this example, fame will still be an external good as long as it is possible to complete a search for truth but not achieve fame. This suggests that "the search for truth" may not name a practice specific enough to know how fame might constitute an internal good (since it is possible to imagine practices in which it does). I suspect that, while the search for truth as such may not be corrupted in such practices, the virtue of truthfulness will be.

10. Less clear-cut, though no less interesting, are debates about whether footballers

One reason external goods are insufficient to sustain a practice lies in the limited availability of those goods. This might seem like a strange suggestion, since I have just noted that external goods are, in a sense, achievable more broadly than just by the particular practice in question. In turn, this might seem to suggest that fame and glory, say, are widely available. But it is in the very nature of these kinds of goods that they have a more limited scope of applicability. They always belong more to some individuals than to others. To the extent that some possess them, others do not, or at least not with the same intensity or quantity.[11] In order for fame to work, some people must have more of it than others. If everyone were just as famous as everyone else, fame itself would be meaningless. Yet this contrasts with a practice's *internal* goods: one runner's skill in the practice of running does not threaten anybody else's. In fact, it builds up the practice of running as a whole by contributing goods of excellence to the pool of collective skill in which all runners participate. Better runners means running itself is made better. It does not mean that every runner runs the same. But this is not the case with external goods. Goods like fame and riches assume a condition of scarce resources, where individuals compete for more. Since it is a competition, there are going to be winners and losers. MacIntyre notes that competition dominates societies that acknowledge only external goods.[12] An example of this is Hobbes's description of the state of nature as one of constant war and "where every man is Enemy to every man."[13]

When practices are determined more by external goods than by internal goods, even those things that were previously structured cooperatively cannot avoid degrading into competition. Cooperation in pursuit of goods internal to practices is no longer necessary in view of attaining external goods that, by definition, yield competition. Here we can see the problem of approaches like Fletcher's, in which the practice of telling the

---

who make racist comments should incur in-game punishment. This forces the question of whether racist speech violates internal or external goods.

11. MacIntyre, *After Virtue*, p. 190.

12. MacIntyre, *After Virtue*, p. 196.

13. Thomas Hobbes, *Leviathan* (London: Penguin, 1985, first published 1651), p. 186. Interestingly, even "warre" for Hobbes is, in a sense, still privative on "a common Power to keep them all in awe" (p. 185). In a related way, individualism indicates that our lives (and specifically our moral language) are governed by external goods. See Jeffrey Stout, *Ethics After Babel: The Languages of Morals and Their Discontents* (Princeton, NJ: Princeton University Press, 2001), p. 291.

truth is instrumentalized and therefore made secondary to what it achieves (although calling Fletcher's account of truth-telling a "practice" may be too generous). This distorts the exercise of the practice in question and even jeopardizes its continued exercise, since external goods are by definition achievable by other means. Truth and love are in competition, since truthfulness is only of value when it is part of an action judged to be loving. Thus is the judgment, as Fletcher claims, extrinsic to considerations such as truth.

In this regard, Xenophon recounts how competition over telling the truth threatened the practice of friendship. Boys were taught that it was right to deceive their friends as long as they might benefit from doing so; they were even encouraged to practice lying to each other in order to sharpen their skills. Over time, the boys took unfair advantage of everyone, including their friends, leading eventually to the need for a law requiring everyone to tell the truth all the time.[14] A separation of truthfulness from friendship imperiled the very notion of justice that led them to commend developing the skill of deception in the first place: "for their own good" lost its meaning when they could no longer identify how truthfulness is a good of friendship. Without truthfulness, the boys could no longer discern those things that were for the good of their friends, and so their attempts at justice became corruptions. In other words, justice ceased being a good internal to friendship, and thus truthfulness and falsehood were seen as serving external goods. Unsurprisingly, friendship then devolved into competition between peers.

*   *   *

If goodness and love are insufficient for giving an account of truth's importance, and for suggesting when and how it should be spoken, MacIntyre's appeal to the maintenance of relationships appears to hold more promise. After all, one lesson to draw from Xenophon is that instrumentalizing truth in order to serve goodness (in his case, one's own good) risks becoming incoherent when what is good is defined so narrowly that it excludes relationships with others. If friendship is itself also an authentic human good, then it will be ill served by other goods that only make contact with it by instrumental means. This is because "friendship" is not really something that we can conceive of apart from how it is served by things

---

14. Xenophon, *The Life of Cyrus The Great* (1.6.31-33).

like trust and truth-telling. Friendship simply *is* how we describe the relationships in which these things are prominent. Speaking the truth for the sake of relationships goes some way toward specifying a practice in which truthfulness is a good. Still, as I hope to demonstrate in what follows, MacIntyre has difficulty exceeding the limitations inherent in appeals to rules and overly formal descriptions of practices. It is worth dwelling on MacIntyre's account because it is so instructive for our purposes.

In his 1994 Tanner Lectures, "Truthfulness, Lies, and Moral Philosophers: What Can We Learn from Mill and Kant?" MacIntyre discusses what Kant and Mill both thought about lying.[15] The reader will recall that Kant forbade all lying on principle as a derogation of the duty all rational beings have, even in the extreme case of lying to protect someone from an aggressor. Unlike Kant, Mill allowed exceptions to the general rule not to tell lies. He based this on determining the effects telling the truth or telling a lie might bring about, such as averting an evil act or not disturbing the happiness of a seriously ill person who is ignorant of her condition.[16]

While MacIntyre finds reasons to be dissatisfied with both Kant and Mill, he nevertheless wants to borrow something from each one. From Kant, MacIntyre borrows the idea of a principle for moral action, except that he does not want to develop such a principle from our status as rational beings, as Kant does. Reason alone does a disservice to our full humanity. Therefore, MacIntyre argues that any legitimate moral principles will derive from our embodied status as persons in relationships. "We begin, that is, from within the social practices, through which we discover, and through which alone we can achieve, the goods internal to those practices, the goods that give point and purpose to those relationships" (pp. 352-53). This is a very MacIntyrian sentence — with its focus on practices and goods internal to those practices. It is also the kind of sentence one might find in his seminal *After Virtue*, with its assertion that we do not know

---

15. Alasdair MacIntyre, "Truthfulness, Lies, and Moral Philosophers: What Can We Learn from Mill and Kant?" in *The Tanner Lectures on Human Values* (Salt Lake City: University of Utah Press, 1995), pp. 309-61. Hereafter, page references to this work appear in parentheses in the text.

16. H. Tristram Engelhardt shows that medicine, in fact, functions as an enduring metaphor for guiding decisions about when to use deception (Engelhardt, *The Foundations of Christian Bioethics* [Exton, PA: Swets and Zeitlinger, 2000], pp. 354-66). Engelhardt cites Eastern saints and mystics in support of selective lying in the pursuit of a person's spiritual welfare and salvation, consciously opposing the train of thought in which the West has generally followed Augustine.

which goods are worth pursuing (or even counted as goods at all) except within purposive activities and practices that aim at some kind of achievement. Also characteristic of MacIntyre is its focus on the moral agent as someone who is not merely an autonomous individual, but a person in a community whose moral life is pervaded and constituted by relationships with others.[17] Both of these observations accord with my arguments for a positive notion of truthfulness. Truthfulness not only serves my relationships with others, but it is at least partly what makes them relationships in the first place.

Nevertheless, MacIntyre then makes a series of quite uncharacteristic moves. He considers what he takes to be two strong objections to the rule against lying. The first is that nonlying absolutists are equivalent to pacifists who cannot avoid being moral free-riders in societies where their own lives are "sustained by systematic uses of coercion and lying" (p. 350). It is morally disreputable to insist on being more principled than one's society can reasonably bear alongside its own commitment to survive as a society. Insisting on it alienates one from the community that is otherwise necessary for one's life to be morally coherent.

A second objection is that certain concrete cases seem to require violence and lies to maintain relationships of trust with those who are vulnerable. A Dutch housewife who hides her Jewish neighbor's child, after the mother has been taken away to a concentration camp, lies to the Nazis at her door when they inquire whether all the children in the house are hers. A Massachusetts single mother kills her estranged and violent former lover when he threatens her child. It is striking that both of these examples involve the frailty of mothers and children against men, and that both involve violence. In fact, the second example is not actually about lying at all. (I will return to the association between lying and violence later.)

MacIntyre is not opposed to setting out a rule when it comes to not lying. However, he thinks that whatever rule we have must also allow for the exceptions and objections he lists. He is careful to say that we should not follow Kant or Mill either in making a rule absolutely prohibitive or in making exceptions to otherwise absolute rules. Instead, the objections should be part of the rule itself, meaning that, like Fletcher, one may on occasion point to a specific lie as itself a positive and unequivocal good. The

17. "It is in general only within a community that individuals become capable of morality" (MacIntyre, "Is Patriotism a Virtue?" in *Liberalism, Volume 3*, ed. Richard J. Arneson [Aldershot, UK: Edward Elgaar Publishing, 1992], p. 253).

Dutch housewife and the Massachusetts single mother need to be seen as upholding the rule when they lie, rather than breaking it, even in a justified way. Therefore, MacIntyre offers this rule:

> Uphold truthfulness in all your actions by being unqualifiedly truthful in all your relationships and by lying to aggressors only in order to protect those truthful relationships against aggressors, and even then only when lying is the least harm that can afford an effective defense against aggression.

MacIntyre glosses the rule by saying that it "is one to be followed, whatever the consequences, and it is a rule for all rational persons, as persons in relationships" (p. 357). He also notes that, although neither Kant nor Mill would be happy with this rule, it owes quite a lot to insights from both of them.

It is necessary to raise some questions about MacIntyre's rule, first by suggesting why it is not true to the best of his projects, and then arguing why such a rule suffers from difficulties that become prominent when one tries to accommodate it within Christian native practices.

To begin with, MacIntyre's rule is disappointing on MacIntyre's own grounds. What has happened to the things he is most known for, namely, virtues and practices? Since when do we look to MacIntyre for providing ethical rules? After all, what is distinctive about MacIntyre's retrieval of Aristotle in his wider corpus is precisely the unseating of the moral authority of rules. In *After Virtue,* he notes that "perhaps the most obvious and astonishing absence from Aristotle's thought for any modern reader [is]: there is relatively little mention of rules anywhere in the *Ethics.*" Instead, what Aristotle points to, and what MacIntyre more commonly commends, is the need to develop the habits of judgment for "do[ing] the right thing in the right place at the right time in the right way," all of which is irreducible to rule-making and rule-enforcing.[18] It is not that rules cannot on occasion function as guides to behavior; they clearly can, underwriting Aristotle's arguments for laws in the attainment of virtue.[19] But on their own, that is, divorced from the *telos* of human life and human flourishing — what is life *for*? — rules become arbitrary and negative.

It is certainly a strength of MacIntyre's rule on truth-telling that it attempts to take into account both teleology (life is about truthful relation-

18. MacIntyre, *After Virtue,* p. 150.
19. Aristotle, *Nicomachean Ethics,* Book 10.

ships) and the need to move past negative prohibitions ("uphold truthful-ness . . ." rather than "do not lie"). Nevertheless, one might still have expected no rule at all; instead, one might expect a discussion of a practice that requires a particular relationship to telling the truth in order to achieve the goods internal to that practice. MacIntyre might have elabo-rated a practice that forms habits and skills of practical reason for negoti-ating unforeseeable situations according to the virtue of truthfulness. Maybe scientific research, cultural criticism, or friendship could be seen as practices that require telling the truth about what is the case. The concom-itant virtue to these practices would be truthfulness. MacIntyre does occa-sionally mention truthfulness as a virtue, first in summarizing Aquinas on the subject, and then in a discussion of Mill (pp. 315, 330). Yet, insofar as he means for his rule to be connected to the virtue of truthfulness, the latter is clearly secondary to both rules and practices (p. 354).

Moreover, it is not clear that the virtue of truthfulness is what you would get by following MacIntyre's rule. After all, in order to protect the child in her care, the Dutch housewife would need to lie convincingly to the Nazi at the door. How would she have become accomplished at lying? Should she, like the boys in Xenophon's account, practice lying so that she can uphold relationships of trust when the time comes? Even though Mac-Intyre's rule is meant to encompass both the positive directive to tell the truth and the exceptions to it, it is not clear that the virtues necessary to follow the rule are free from contradiction. Is it possible to cultivate the virtues necessary for maintaining trust and also to cultivate the virtues necessary to deceive? Augustine was concerned that telling a lie for some good distorts one's relationship with the truth.[20] It dislodges us from an intimate kinship with a true life and keeps us from being at home in it. Apart from these specific concerns, however, consider how MacIntyre in-tends for rules to work.

For MacIntyre, rules function to articulate the content of virtues, and to the extent that they are embedded in the practices of a particular tradition, they are evident to the so-called "plain person" as natural law.[21]

---

20. Augustine, *Contra Mendacium*, xiv, 7. See also J. L. Garcia, "Lies and the Vices of Deception," *Faith and Philosophy* 15, no. 4 (October 1998): 531; see also Rosalind Hursthouse, *On Virtue Ethics* (Oxford: Oxford University Press, 1999), p. 85.

21. MacIntyre discusses the moral philosophy of "plain persons" in Alasdair MacIn-tyre, "Plain Persons and Moral Philosophy: Rules, Virtues and Goods" in *The MacIntyre Reader,* ed. Kelvin Knight (Notre Dame, IN: University of Notre Dame Press, 1998), pp. 136-52.

This evident-ness can be deceiving if the rules are taken as givens by moral philosophers who intend to express how the virtues of a given tradition govern action, since it might be wrongly assumed that rules, rather than virtues, actually govern action. Neither rules nor virtues can be reduced to theory; rather, both arise out of the social practices and relationships that engender them. Contrary to Kant, MacIntyre's concept of the duty to obey a rule does not depend on a *theory* about rules and why they should be obeyed (such as in the fulfillment of duty), since the allegiance to follow *some particular rules* will always be more fundamental to the life of a particular community than their allegiance to follow rules as such. This is the element that allows for talk of rule-following without appeal to a formalistic quality of rules as such. It matters what the rules are. It is possible to ask of any rule: Does it accord with and engender virtues that accomplish the good of this people (and to the extent that this is defensible, *all* people, since surely no people will think that what is good for themselves is not also good for everyone[22])?

The answers to this and related questions about the normativity of rules will not come from moral theory, but from the life of the community and its relationships. This does not mean that there is no place for rules. It only means that rules will be practice-dependent rather than theory-dependent. MacIntyre emphasizes that someone who helps members of a community theorize about — and rationally attempt to justify — their community's ways of living will "*first* have to enter into cooperative relationships *already* informed by allegiance to just those rules for which she or he aspired to provide a justification. Hence, allegiance to these particular rules has to precede any set of arguments, any theorizing."[23]

Rules will play a more significant part in the moral formation of the young or of those who join the community at a later point in life. They will be followed by rote when the virtues required to act according to the rules by habit have not yet been developed. But over time, rules will become less

22. MacIntyre makes this point in response to the detachment that would be required in order to be a moral relativist or, in Richard Rorty's terms, an ironist (Rorty, *Contingency, Irony, and Solidarity* [Cambridge: Cambridge University Press, 1989]). "The protagonists of those viewpoints which generate large and systematic disagreements, like the members of moral communities of humankind in general, are never themselves relativists. And consequently they could not consistently allow that the rational justification of their own positions is merely relative to some local scheme of justification" (MacIntyre, "Moral Relativism, Truth and Justification," in *The MacIntyre Reader*, p. 204).

23. MacIntyre, "Plain Persons and Moral Philosophy," p. 143 (emphasis added).

and less central to the practice of the virtues as the virtuous person develops habits of action and embodied dispositions that enable him to go beyond the rules to then make judgments about what to do in situations that are not controlled by strict rule-following. But even at this later stage in moral development, the rules remain. Only now, one of the things that has been learned is that rules can never exhaustively address every situation, but they are (paradoxically) still essential to the practices that appeared to be enabled by the dispositions stimulated by the initial rule-following. Furthermore, it is important that rules be exceptionless, because the following of a rule is a learned skill about how it applies in one situation as opposed to another. Rather than learning the exceptions to rules, one learns how to match exceptionless rules to situations, as MacIntyre's rule scrupulously endeavors to make apparent. Likewise, developing these skills does not imply that the need for rules has come to an end. To put it simply, the more the rules are followed, the less they are required. For, in the course of following them, one learns that it is possible to surpass them; but one surpasses them only having depended on them, and thus does so by depending on them.

Even though Wittgenstein may not have had Aristotle in mind when he discussed rules in his *Philosophical Investigations,* he meant to argue against Kant — as does MacIntyre.[24] Wittgenstein notes that understanding rule-following involves coming to terms with a paradox by which what constitutes following a rule according to one interpretation may then easily constitute breaking that same rule according to a different interpretation. While one solution to this paradox would be simply to make more elaborate interpretations, he maintains that doing so only leads to an infinite regress and an infinite number of interpretations. Instead, there must be "a way of grasping a rule which is *not* an *interpretation,* but which is exhibited in what we call 'obeying the rule' and 'going against it' in actual cases."[25] There must be a socially shared practice or custom that secures the meaning of the rule so that there can then be such a thing as following it (or breaking it). The most genuine explanations of what is going on in rule-following will thus be descriptions of a practice: We do such-and-such.[26] We are in-

24. Wittgenstein also meant to correct his view of language presented in the *Tractatus.* Wittgenstein considers rule-following in *Philosophical Investigations,* trans. G. E. M. Anscombe (New York: Macmillan, 1953), secs. 198-202.

25. Wittgenstein, *Philosophical Investigations,* sec. 201.

26. The "we" is also important since "it is not possible to obey a rule 'privately': otherwise thinking one was obeying a rule would be the same thing as obeying it" (Wittgenstein, *Philosophical Investigations,* sec. 202). In this section I am indebted to John Churchill's

culcated into abiding by a particular rule, then, by participating in public activities or sets of practices that allow us to "get it" or "catch on" to the rule's meaning. John Churchill summarizes Wittgenstein on this point: "At the root of every practice is a way of operating that we learn not by having it explained and justified to us, but by simply doing it, or by being trained into it."[27] In pointing to the practice, one does not supply a *reason*, but a *cause*.

> A cause may explain how it came about that *this* is the way the practice goes, but that sort of explanation does nothing to provide a normative account of why it *should* go so rather than in some other way. Why is *this* the right way of following the rule? Finally the answer has to be, as Wittgenstein emphasizes over and over again, a gesture toward the fact that it just *is* the right way. "What is 'learning a rule'? — *This*. What is 'making a mistake in applying it'? — *This*. And what is pointed to here is something indeterminate. . . . *This* is how we think. *This* is how we act. *This* is how we talk about it."[28]

It is possible to overdraw how Wittgenstein's position helps to explain MacIntyre's.[29] Yet it is sufficient to underscore how rules are neither fundamental nor dispensable in the pursuit of virtuous practices. Wittgenstein only calls this a paradox in order to indicate how it appears from a perspective that straightforwardly takes rules to be one or the other (either fundamental or dispensable), a prejudice shared by both Kant's moral philosophy and Wittgenstein's own earlier positivism.

The objection I wish to make to MacIntyre's truth-telling rule is that in this instance he has not really moved past Kant as much as one might expect based on what he says elsewhere about rule-following (and if we

---

analysis in "Wonder and the End of Explanation: Wittgenstein and Religious Sensibility," *Philosophical Investigations* 17, no. 2 (April 1994): 388-416 (esp. pp. 398-99).

27. Churchill, "Wonder and the End of Explanation," p. 401.

28. Churchill, "Wonder and the End of Explanation," p. 402. The internal quotes are from Wittgenstein, *On Certainty,* trans. Denis Paul and G. E. M. Anscombe (New York: Harper and Row, 1969), sec. 28, and *Zettel,* trans. G. E. M. Anscombe (Oxford: Blackwell, 1981), sec. 309. See also Wittgenstein, *Philosophical Investigations,* sec. 198, for the distinction between cause and reason.

29. Indeed, they may disagree over the extent to which the explanation of a cause counts as a description of a practice normative for all human attainment of the good. It may be that Wittgenstein's comments on innate, and therefore common, human behavior is parallel to MacIntyre's account of Aquinas on natural goods. However, a discussion of this would take us too far afield.

can take him to be more or less Wittgensteinian on this point). Even though he focuses on relationships rather than on rationality for determining the character of the moral agent, he does not allow for the particular nature of those relationships to bear on his rule. He asks a good question: "Why within our relationships . . . is truthfulness important and why ought lying to be prohibited?" (p. 353). But he then goes on to answer it of relationships in general and in the abstract, which again is unexpected on MacIntyrian grounds. He might have been expected to conclude that relationships need truthfulness in part because of the nature of those particular relationships. After all, there are some people who do not want others to lie in their defense, and this for reasons that arise out of the substance of what these particular relationships take to be most important.[30]

This problem is parallel to the problem (suggested above) with assuming that truthfulness is enjoined simply in the use of speech. Despite the insufficiency of the Kantian reliance on the givenness of a morality inherent in speech-as-such or, as we have seen, assertion-as-such, MacIntyre persists in appealing to it in another iteration as rational-relationships-as-such. If we have learned from MacIntyre to question the soundness of appeals to reason qua reason, are we to contradict our repaired intuitions by assuming that "rational relationship" denotes something consistent and stable? If so, we may wonder whether he longs for a modicum of the very universality of Kantian ethics that he is famous for critiquing. So long as relationships are evacuated of their constitutive content by being made to function as a theoretical trope in a universally applicable rule, MacIntyre continues to discharge a traditionless ethic or, as John Milbank accuses, an ethic without custom.[31]

---

30. The tension between rights and security in post-9/11 America is an obvious parallel, as Wendell Berry highlights. "Since September 11, far too many public voices have presumed to 'speak for us' in saying that Americans will gladly accept a reduction of freedom in exchange for greater 'security.' Some would, maybe. But some others would accept a reduction in security (and in global trade) far more willingly than they would accept any abridgment of our Constitutional rights" (Berry, "Thoughts in the Presence of Fear," *Orion Magazine* (Autumn 2001): http://www.orionmagazine.org/index.php/articles/article/214.

MacIntyre's account of truthfulness is slightly more promising in *Dependent Rational Animals: Why Human Beings Need the Virtues* (Chicago: Open Court, 1999), chap. 12. He speaks about "concealing from view the nature of our relationships" to others as an offense against truthfulness (p. 151). But even in this later treatment of the topic, he fails to indicate that the nature of our relationships might actually bear on our understanding of truthfulness itself.

31. John Milbank, *Theology and Social Theory: Beyond Secular Reason* (Oxford:

MacIntyre's rule depends on properly assessing the nature of the relationships of trust that we are told we must uphold. But this, in turn, depends on seeing truthfully those relationships for what they are. MacIntyre
says that we need a discipline corresponding to psychoanalysis that will save
us from the distortions and fantasies that we would rather believe than admit that we believe fantasies. (This is why, in this book, *seeing* precedes *testifying.*) MacIntyre has in mind a discipline that is not academic but that is
"in our everyday lives and relationships," something to retrain our tendencies to misrepresent reality according to our otherwise unexamined need to
have our anxieties and wishfulness mollified (pp. 354-55). Nevertheless,
MacIntyre does not supply us with a discipline that can do this, and it is not
clear that psychoanalysis is able to do the work he thinks it does, since one
suspects that it can both produce and rely on its own distortions. Alternatively, as I have been arguing, we do better to consider how truth-telling
might itself be a practice: the Christian practice of bearing witness to the
gospel. This would suggest that Christians need not look first to a rule governing truth-telling, because they have been given a truth-telling task.

*   *   *

I have argued throughout these chapters that bearing witness to the gospel is
a practice. But, unlike scientific research or cultural criticism, the practice itself has substantive content. It has words to say and claims to make along the
lines that Jesus is Lord and that God raised him from the dead. Of course,
Christians have found a thousand different ways of saying this, and so claiming that the gospel constitutes content is not a way of dictating in advance
which specific words should be said. Other practices (psychoanalysis, cultural criticism) may *require* telling the truth by holding up that requirement
as a means to an end, a way of achieving goods of excellence. Witness differs

Blackwell, 1990), p. 329. Milbank makes a similar point in discussing MacIntyre's appeal for
"thick" virtues such as truth and justice over against "thin" virtues such as tolerance or respecting liberty. The thick virtues arise from particular notions of the good life and not from
attempts to disabuse, say, consensus-making appeals of such contingent content. Milbank
argues that this strategy, while surely on the right track, opens itself to a contradiction. Particular notions of the good provide the means for deciding what counts as a virtue and what
does not. However, when it tries to justify the promotion of thick virtues in general, it cannot help making general appeals that violate — or at least render unnecessary and arbitrary
— the particular (Milbank, *Being Reconciled: Ontology and Pardon* [London: Routledge,
2003], p. 166).

in being itself a practice of telling the truth. Two comments are necessary concerning how witness as truth-telling problematizes MacIntyre's rule on substantive — rather than formal — grounds. After all, if anyone is to make the case that witness is a truth-telling practice, it requires that the substance of the gospel, the message it bears and claims to be true, obtains in the shape of the argument, that is, in what it assumes, presupposes, allows for, and so on. My intention here is to be suggestive rather than exhaustive.

First, I have already noted that MacIntyre's two exceptions that compelled the language of aggression in his rule have to do with the threat of violence. One of them, the Massachusetts single mother, is purely about violence and protection and not actually about lying at all. Moreover, the reference to pacifists and absolutist truth-tellers as free-riders makes the same point: violence and lying can be justified in principle because of one's duty to uphold rational relationships, both personal and societal. This is MacIntyre's point, which, of course, is not particularly novel since many of the academic arguments used to justify war have also been used to justify lying. For example, Aquinas thought that deceiving the enemy in a just war is just and that therefore ambushes in a just war should not be called lying, or even deception.[32] Versions of MacIntyre's Dutch housewife and the Nazi story go all the way back to Augustine, not always to justify lying (which Augustine condemned), but often to justify killing in war for the defense of the weak. The relationship between deception and violence is perhaps even more complex. I suspect that the reason lying to Nazis is often taken to be a clear and compelling test case of protecting the weak is that it simultaneously relies on and justifies the apparently noble use of force by nations. This is most evident when such debates have the potential, among the victors of certain wars, to justify those wars. One might ask how these examples would function differently if Germany had not been defeated. At any rate, MacIntyre follows a clear logic in which violence is justified in reaction to the threat of violence, just as the use of deception is justified in response to threatened rational relationships.

Though this is not the place to argue the nonviolence of the gospel in a sustained way, I simply want to gesture in that direction in order to show difficulties with this way of linking speech and killing. As a paradigm for truth-telling, Christian witness contradicts the assumptions that lead to this association with violence. The proclamation of the gospel is a declaration that God raised Jesus from the dead; the judgment that condemned

32. Aquinas, *ST* II-II.40.3.

Jesus, as well as the violence done to him, was overturned in God's larger judgment, vindication, and glorification of Christ. The gospel does not block the aggressor by withholding the truth, but speaks the truth that, in its substance, is precisely about how God has overcome aggression, not through lies or violence, but through death and resurrection. The cross is how God deals with evil. This is why the paradigmatic witnesses are martyrs: their deaths are *part of* the truth they tell, since their dying is continuous with their speaking about the truth and hope of resurrection that enables them to face risk. On MacIntyre's grounds, it is not clear that martyrdom is possible. In fact, I may be obligated to retreat from speaking the truth in order to preserve my availability for those with whom I have otherwise truthful relationships.[33] Indeed, the fact that some may die because of the Christian determination to speak the truth — including those who do not share that determination — is an old idea.

Second, MacIntyre relies on a distinction between those who are inside and those who are outside my relationships, emphasizing the duty I have to protect those who are inside. Those who are outside a particular set of relationships do not constitute a threat to it until they aggress against it, at which point someone who is part of that set of relationships is duty-bound to protect it. But what if my relationships are not the final good, but only derive from another good, a good that does not distinguish between what is mine and what is not mine? Or what if it makes that distinction in an entirely different way? Lying to aggressors sounds altruistic, but the logic only works if those I am duty-bound to protect are *my* children or in some other sense *mine*.[34] Christian witness problematizes this. After all,

---

33. However, elsewhere MacIntyre seems to allow for martyrdom: "[M]y allegiance to the community and what it requires of me — even to the point of requiring me to die to sustain its life — could not meaningfully be contrasted with or counterposed to what morality required of me. Detached from my community, I will be apt to lose my hold upon all genuine standards of judgment" (MacIntyre, "Is Patriotism a Virtue?" p. 254). But it is likely that martyrdom is far from MacIntyre's mind and that the one who dies for the community is a warrior whose death comes by fighting rather than a martyr who dies by not fighting. This recalls Milbank's critique of MacIntyre's reliance on antique virtue, which is the virtue of warriors (Milbank, *Theology and Social Theory*, pp. 332-36). In fact, MacIntyre appears to be arguing that there is not simply a morality that governs whether or not to kill and die for the survival of my community, but that my doing so in fact undergirds the very possibility of morality. I think there are good reasons to agree that this is true of a community that is able to produce martyrs but untrue of a community that produces warriors.

34. See John Howard Yoder, *What Would You Do? A Serious Answer to a Standard Question* (Scottdale, PA: Herald, 1983), p. 20.

what if I also have duties to my enemies, such as loving them? What if even aggressors do not finally fall outside of the sphere of relationships I have? These are not, of course, relationships based on trust and truthfulness, but does this mean that therefore I have no relationship with them?

MacIntyre rightly rejects Kant, but his rejection is not thoroughgoing enough. He preserves the duty of truthfulness, shifting it only from speech to rational relationships. The logical priority of relationships takes trust to be fundamental, but only because such relationships already exist. While we might say that they are characterized by trust and are therefore derivatively constituted by truthfulness, we could not say that they exist on the basis of any particular truth. Because witness is part of a mission that aims at refashioning old enmities through baptism, then its speaking is not only directed to and for those who may lie outside already existing relationships of trust; but overcoming the boundary between stranger and friend is also, in fact, the very substance of what is proclaimed. If Christians proclaim that Christ has broken down the wall between Jew and Gentile and hence between every other analogous natural relationship (Eph. 2:14-16), then the rationale for deciding when to tell the truth cannot depend on upholding this difference. This is the case even when the difference comes in other forms, such as public and private, which is problematized with respect to the Christian *oikos* and polis.[35] The truth itself has implications for how it gets told because the truth of the gospel changes the nature of relationships.[36] Duty in the gospel is not only to those who are inside my relationships and already share my life, but crucially to those who are outside by virtue of the gospel being news, that is, something others (those outside) will not know unless they are told it.[37] In the end, MacIntyre cannot escape the implication that truthfulness is really all about me and what is mine.

35. Bernd Wannenwetsch has successfully argued this point in *Political Worship: Ethics for Christian Citizens*, trans. Margaret Kohl (Oxford: Oxford University Press, 2004), pp. 133-59, noting that the family of God is not in conflict with heavenly citizenship: "[T]he call to discipleship relativizes the obligations of the life previously lived in the *oikos* (that is, relates them to the kingdom), but without disparaging these spheres of life in principle" (p. 133). Because of that relativization, those spheres are no longer determinative for Christian ethics.

36. We might, therefore, accept MacIntyre's rule but note that, because of how the gospel changes relationships, much of it is simply moot.

37. Even so, otherness as such makes no moral claim on Christians, which is to say that there is no moral status to "other," but only to specific "others." This I have argued in part I.

Finally, it remains to respond to an objection that says that Christian witness, while perhaps a helpful illustration, is fairly limited in its helpfulness and should only be considered as a special case rather than determinative or paradigmatic for truth-telling more generally. This is most likely what MacIntyre would say. A version of this says that even though discipleship may not be an ethical technique, that it does not function instrumentally for goods other than the ones it advances through its own exercise, this does not mean we cannot have ethical techniques for other things. The problems with this objection are twofold. First, it assumes a radical discontinuity between the life of the disciple as disciple and the life of the disciple as rational being, suggesting a low view of Christian identity. I have been arguing that the Christian life, understood according to its highest loyalties and actions, should refigure all of the others. Saying as much is just as distant from the claim that Christianity provides all moral answers up front (or even along the way) as it is from the idea that it is an exception to what can be discovered and known through other means. Second, it assumes that the truth of the gospel is on the same horizon as the truth of all other kinds of discourse, so that we can say that the gospel is true just as it is true that I had eggs for breakfast. Against this, the lordship of Christ requires a theological realism that takes theological truth to be more real, more true, and more basic than all other truths. Though it is not always obvious or provable, these other truths (such as eggs for breakfast) are nevertheless derivatively and analogically related to the truth of the evangel. If the gospel is true, it does not only make a claim about its most obvious reference — the lordship of Christ — since the lordship of Christ, if true, changes absolutely everything else in the whole universe.

If the root of Christian ethics is Christian discipleship, it is first a way of life and only secondarily submits to theorizing. Therefore, asking about the practices of the moral life signals a vital corrective to traditional ethical modes (such as deontology and consequentialism, but also principles and rules). But, of course, as I have repeatedly emphasized, it then matters *which* practice is being considered, since just talking about practices in general (even if it is relationships in general) is not enough. The problem I have tried to diagnose in MacIntyre's lectures on truthfulness and lies is precisely his inability to get closer to the ground than practices-in-general. What is clear from his lectures is that he wants to talk about things like having trust in relationships but, because he cannot identify a truth-telling practice, he cannot say much about why trust is important — that is, in which practice it is a good.

Even though having relationships might be thought of as a practice, because I might prefer to have friends who lie to me about myself in order to reinforce my self-deception, it is not clear that this practice is sharp enough for the work MacIntyre wants it to do. Christian witness is a practice that contains within itself both a command to speak the truth and the conditions that not only make that speech authentic but make the speakers witnesses, that is, disciples.

CONCLUSION

The Fragility of Truth

Christian witness is eminently vulnerable, exposed, laid bare before the exigencies and strains of the world. It abjures prior rational justifications of both its central premises and its exercise as a mode of knowledge at risk of disqualification against the demands of modern epistemology. This is why I have argued the inadequacy of accounts of Christian witness that rely on reasons and of accounts of truth-telling that rely on not lying, natural law, oath-taking, and rule-following. I have proposed that it is better to think of the activity of witness as a practice that engenders truthfulness over against some of the problems with practicing truthful relationships-as-such. It is appropriate to conclude by considering also the *fragility* of that practice. Even though the truth may be so compelling that it must be told among those who believe it, the compelling nature of true testimony is another matter. Those who hear the testimony about Christ are not only not compelled by the witnesses to believe it, but such testimony, in being true, is exposed to the vulnerability that comes from not having recourse to the security that comes with telling half-truths.

The truth is vulnerable because it can only be one thing and is always in danger of being edged out by falsehood, which can be anything else (its only limitation being that it not be the truth). This led Hannah Arendt to conclude that the truth is fragile and falsehood is robust.[1] Falsehoods are always versions of the truth, but the reverse is not the case. The truth-teller is thus at a disadvantage, being unable to shape his speech to fit with the

1. Hannah Arendt, "Truth and Politics," in *The Portable Hannah Arendt,* ed. Peter Baehr (London: Penguin, 2000), pp. 545-75.

expectations and hopes of the audience as the liar does. There is no guarantee that the truth will be plausible, because plausibility only trades on
what has been known before. Because it is so implausible, the resurrection
of Christ can only be known by witnesses. It is difficult to persuade others
to believe something that is unlikely, particularly without the aid of coercion. This is not only the case with what is true, of course, because many
people are coerced into believing what is false.

Consider further the moral status of noncoercion relative to truth.
Richard Rorty thinks that it is irrelevant whether people are coerced to believe what is true or what is false since coercion is corrupt in either case.
When George Orwell's character O'Brien, in *1984*, coerces Winston into
believing that two plus two equals five, Rorty adduces that a consideration
of "truth and falsity drop out."[2] There would be no moral difference if
Winston were being coerced into believing something that is true. However, in a way that is similar to my argument in chapter 6, Bernard Williams does not think that noncoercion may be separated quite so easily
from considerations of truth or falsity. He argues that what makes coercion wrong is not merely that one's belief is imposed on another, since,
without truth, it is not possible to know what constitutes humiliation, deg-
radation, horror, and so on. Rorty's dependence on a negative doctrine of
liberty leads him to a negative (or worse) doctrine of truthfulness.
Winston writes in his diary: "Freedom is the freedom to say that two plus
two equals four. If that is granted, all else follows."[3]

For Rorty, what is salient here is that, under torture, one becomes irrational in the specific sense of being unable to offer reasons for some beliefs that fit together with one's other beliefs. He scrupulously wants to
avoid the idea that it means losing contact with reality since what is real
(like what is true) is a construction and to think otherwise is to hold on to
an outmoded equation of what is real with what is divine. Killing God was,
for Nietzsche, the most momentous thing humans have accomplished,
even though facing the unsettling fact that what is real is no longer an-
chored in divine constancy is extremely difficult to embrace. So what now?
Without God, Rorty must find reasons other than truth and falsity to con-
demn coercion. Coercion to the point of inhibiting the construction from

2. Richard Rorty, *Contingency, Irony, and Solidarity* (Cambridge: Cambridge University Press, 1989), p. 179.
3. Quoted in Bernard Williams, *Truth and Truthfulness* (Princeton, NJ: Princeton
University Press, 2002), p. 146.

holding together is the reason that now, presumably after killing God, "cruelty is the worst thing we do."[4] Yet, if freedom is freedom for truth, then, according to how Williams reads Orwell, coercion is manifestly wrong because it hinders realizing the purpose of freedom, understood as much more than simply freedom from coercion. I argued along these lines in chapter 8 (with the help of Charles Taylor).

In part, the very ability to make a moral judgment against coercion relies on something like the ability to claim that, irrespective of the ways that power is wielded, "coercion is wrong" is still true. More to the point, Orwell has O'Brien inducing a *false* belief precisely in order to highlight the way torture erects a fantasy that itself dissolves one's ability to distinguish what is true from what is false. Torture alienates from reality the one being coerced and deprives her of the capacity for true belief.[5] This is what signals the ultimate triumph of totalitarian power: not an alternative construction that imposes itself under a disorienting coercion, but a fantasy world in which the exercise of power confounds one's relationship with what is real. It is here, in the coercion itself rather than in the condemnation of it, that truth and falsity truly drop out. I consider it a weakness of Williams's account, however, that he fails to move beyond his own theoretical defense of positive liberty and truthfulness. He rightly says that freedom must be freedom *for truth;* but he differs from the argument I have presented, primarily in chapter 7 (with the help of Karl Barth), in relying on a formalistic notion of what is true.

My account goes further than Williams's does in adducing freedom as not merely a good according to which one may be free for what is true, but as a characteristic of truth's exercise — of speaking it, for example — precisely on account of what is true *in particular,* what is actually spoken. Likewise, though coercion may function to make someone believe what is false, it may also estrange her from her own freedom to lie. As Arendt reports elsewhere, many have believed it impossible to invent a lie while being tortured (the Greek word for "torture" is derived from *necessity*).[6] If this is the case, it supports Williams against Rorty, since surely the inability to lie derives from one's vertigo in the face of what is true, as I have argued in chapter 8. The freedom to invent a lie is indistinguishable from the free-

4. Rorty, *Contingency,* p. 173.

5. Williams, *Truth and Truthfulness,* pp. 147-48.

6. Hannah Arendt, *The Human Condition,* 2nd ed. (Chicago: University of Chicago Press, 1998), p. 129, n. 78.

dom to believe what is true. It is only because of the latter that it is possible to speak about such freedom as a good. And if the freedom to speak the truth is to be considered more than simply the freedom to make noise, as Stanley Fish insists, then it surely matters what one speaks. But introducing questions of content at this level illuminates precisely what makes truthfulness so fragile.

Rorty agrees with Nietzsche that the contingent nature of reality both flows from and demands the rejection of everything suprahistorical, timeless, and oriented toward transcendence. By dislodging freedom from truth, he is able to commend a certain liberal form of politics that does not depend on anything greater than consent; it does not require the people to agree on what is true (or, as Rorty might prefer, what is *True*). They may nevertheless agree that it is good to be free in the more limited sense of being free from coercion. In disagreeing with Rorty (and other theorists of liberalism), must one necessarily affirm his antithesis? Attempting to tell a history of truth through the concept of *parrhēsia*, Foucault certainly thought he was being faithful to Nietzsche: truth is a matter of genealogy, history, and moral and political activity rather than a strictly philosophical matter of knowing and being. But Foucault's account involves a strong association of freedom with truth (though not in the sense that Rorty rejects). Truth is realized primarily in the active telling of the truth; and the persistence of those who insist on speaking the truth is what constitutes the freedom of that speech (as I have argued in chapter 4). So, despite their vast differences in other respects, I notice a family resemblance on these matters between Foucault, Barth, and Williams. I find in them resources for navigating between the shoals of Rorty and a certain Nietzschean preoccupation, on the one hand, and the treasured aspirations of the Enlightenment, on the other.

Among the many places where Christian thought will surely part ways with Nietzsche, I do not think that his inability to be an ally in fashioning a democratic order (as Rorty worries) is one of them. In fact, if Foucault is correct, there is a form of democracy that, in its dependence on truth-telling, is both much older than modern, liberal forms and also at crucial points decidedly at odds with them. Particularly in its understanding of freedom as a moral activity rather than a condition ensured by sovereignty, the democracy that Euripides saw steadily slipping away from Athens is not easily accommodated within a liberal framework, especially as one could argue that that framework resembles the very reliance on sovereign and institutional forms to which Athens was fated. Foucault certainly had no interest in buttressing liberal democracy for another related reason: he must have lamented the way liberal societies are not only inimical to engendering virtue of any kind (let alone *parrhēsia*), but appear specifically designed with this in mind. What makes the virtues so difficult to acquire in a liberal ethos is the way they depend on the habits and practices that give rise to them, things that in the name of uniting a diverse society typically receive scant attention for reasons that my brief exposition of Rorty makes plain. My engagement with MacIntyre in chapter 9 acknowledges this state of affairs even while I press for a more particular, theological description of truth-telling rooted in Christian practice, rather than what amounts to only a slight improvement over the non-virtue-based accounts MacIntyre is otherwise determined to surpass.

Therefore, in arguing in chapter 5 that Christianity, at its core, in fact celebrates and enjoins a set of parrhesiastic practices, I make room for a kind of democracy that Foucault might have understood but would not have approved of. He might have understood how witness is parrhesiastic and how the democracy it countenances is nonsovereign; but he would not have approved of its Christianity. Rorty would disapprove of its illiberal form, its association of truth and truth-telling with freedom. Nietzsche would have recognized what it owes to perhaps Foucault's most Nietzschean impulse: that the will to truth is more important than truth. Williams would have appreciated the close association of truth with freedom.

Even so, what is distinctive about the Christian inflection I have outlined on these themes involves the additional step that none of these thinkers countenanced, namely, that the truth proclaimed as God's truth is Christ himself, and this Christology reshapes the entire field. Christianity does not only produce a people determined to speak the truth about whatever happens to be the case; but the faithful, who adore God with their speech and also speak to others about God's glorious acts, adore God through their proclamation of the gospel. God in Christ precedes Christians in this, because Jesus does not merely disclose truths about the Father but *is* the Father's communication to us. In Christ, the Word became flesh (John 1:14), and God became a concrete, material word-presence among his creation. This lies behind all preaching of the gospel, as the gospel does more than communicate through its speaking: it is crucial that it be able to claim to actually *deliver* Jesus himself as God's Word. Christ's witnesses, therefore, as church, are agents of Jesus-talk even while, as the body of Christ, they are in their speaking actually nothing less than the way that Jesus witnesses *to himself* as the good news of God.

This certainly yields a very distinctive parrhesiastic practice, which I explicated in chapter 6 (with the help of John Howard Yoder). Christians ultimately have no reason to share in a Nietzschean anxiety about transcendence. Even so, there is something eminently terrestrial about Christian witness: historical, material, creaturely, temporal, human. It does not seek to rise above the conditions of its own existence. It looks to disclose Jesus as risen Lord in ways that demand nothing less than the very terrestrial ability to point to the historical events through which the Son reveals the Father. Witnesses are appointed to bear testimony about things that they believe but may not fully understand.

> Go and tell John what you hear and see: the blind receive their sight and the lame walk, lepers are cleansed and the deaf hear, and the dead are raised up, and the poor have good news preached to them. (Matt. 11:4-5)

> He is not here; for he has risen, as he said. Come, see the place where he lay. Then go quickly and tell his disciples that he has risen from the dead, and behold, he is going before you to Galilee; there you will see him. (Matt. 28:6-7)

These are the kinds of commissions made to Christ's witnesses. Their truth-telling practices are more narration than explanation. They may proclaim the resurrection of Christ without knowing with precision what a resurrection is. "Christ was dead and now is alive" is a confession of historical contingencies. Witnesses are not swayed to police their confessions before the world on account of the implausibility of what they have seen. I have argued that what they have seen in fact demands a particular knowing, believing, and speaking posture. As terrestrial, the details of the Christian story will be no less contingent than the contingency of creation itself. Contingency, though, is always fragile. As Wittgenstein said, it is like our life — because the lives of creatures are contingent. When we despise the one, we despise the other.

*   *   *

As Arendt teaches, the sheer contingency of what is the case works against the one who comes forward to declare it. But one thing the liar cannot do is substitute what is the case with what is not; he cannot *make* the truth false, though he will try everything short of it. The truth-teller is even more limited since there is nothing whatsoever to change. Arendt claims that this indicates that truth-telling is hence a nonpolitical or antipolitical act, isolating the truth-teller from the normal realm of political discourse. The liar is political by being a person of action who attempts to change the world.[7] The truth-teller, on the other hand, must be content not to change the world since his ability to tell the truth is preserved only so long as he refuses to act out of self-interest.

Politically, Arendt identifies two kinds of lies: the traditional lie and the modern lie. The traditional lie is just a one-off lie, for example, a "secret" fed to the enemy. But traditional lies are politically ineffective because, in order for them to work, they need to rely too much on the surrounding truths. It becomes easy to spot the holes in a fabric. In order for a deliberate lie to avoid being dismissed out of hand, it will need to be convincing and plausible, something best done by encircling it with a great deal of truth. Yet this is also its precise weakness. Lies told to the enemy about the location of our weapons, for example, are easily found to be lies because too many other things that impinge on those particular false claims are known to be true. With the traditional lie, not only is the truth hidden and secret, but the lies told are also hidden and secret, because they are meant for small-scale audiences. This secrecy limits their effectiveness again, since any action taken on the basis of a secret, traditional lie will always be relatively tentative and small in scope. This accounts for the casuistic appeal of small-scale examples such as Nazis at the door, as opposed to the large-scale ones that place Nazis there at the door in the first place and convince them to knock on it.

In contrast to the traditional lie, the modern lie operates openly on a mass scale. It no longer deals with secrets, but with what is widely known.[8] It fashions another reality, another fabric where the holes either are not so easily spotted or are thought necessary — and thus are willingly accepted. This is propaganda and image-making, large-scale deception that makes it

---

7. Arendt is not cynically claiming that all politicians are corrupt, but that politics seeks to achieve the same kind of change that lying does. Still, as Jean Bethke Elshtain remarks in *Who Are We? Critical Reflections and Hopeful Possibilities* (Grand Rapids: Eerdmans, 2000), we are now even more given over to the idea that truth and falsehood have no purchase in the political realm than when Arendt wrote her essay (p. 137). If this is true, then the real danger lies not with the cynic's misplaced oppositional confidence but with the inability to imagine that a purportedly amoral politics presents a threat.

8. Arendt, "Truth and Politics," p. 565.

difficult to say exactly where the deception is happening, since it is so pervasive. Arendt notes that the concentration camps of Nazi Germany were well known, but it was taboo to discuss them. Nationalistic rhetoric in America about liberty, justice, and freedom, when it is impervious to critique, does not mean that it is difficult to show how these noble ideals fail to correspond to the American reality. It means that the image the ideals collectively generate is one that in turn engenders an extremely strong will, among those who cling to it so tenaciously, to believe that it is true. The myth is untouchable *because* it is otherwise so obviously vulnerable and fragile. "They have not died in vain" is often believed so strongly because it is so clearly false: they *have* died in vain; they accomplished nothing; we cannot bring them back; and we cannot bear the thought that all we have are our memories of them and our commitments to remember them in certain ways. The modern lie is elaborate, intransigent, widely dispersed, and receives support that is just as wide. Its falsehood is so popular and generates such enthusiasm for it that it is not generally necessary to try to prove that it is true. The modern lie thus enjoys a much more open operation than does the traditional lie.[9]

Nevertheless, no image can last very long. It must constantly be repaired and safeguarded against the stubbornness of facts. But this means that the fabric of the false image ends up being counterproductive in the long run, as the citizens grow weary of the categories "true" and "false." Arendt thinks that there is no remedy for this dyspeptic cynicism. Nevertheless, if the image is slow to crumble, there may always be rogue citizens.

If the biggest threat to the traditional lie is the enemy spy who discovers a nugget of truth, then the biggest threat to the modern lie is "those inside the group itself who have managed to escape its spell and insist on talking about facts or events that do not fit the image."[10] The difference is

---

9. I want to be clear about Arendt's purpose in this essay. She is concerned that factual truths continue to be spoken: that the Holocaust happened, that Germany invaded Belgium, etc. It is a concern about how history is remembered and told, how that history may be misrepresented for political purposes, and with what consequences for the future. Her concern is not primarily with philosophical truth (all men are mortal) or so-called religious truth (Jesus is Lord), though she admits that much of what she says also applies to these others. For example, one thing all truth has in common is that it can be destroyed by persuasion and violence (Arendt, "Truth and Politics," p. 570). I would add that the Christian claim that Jesus is Lord suffers a severe distortion once it takes on the qualities of a concept rather than a set of contingent, historical claims.

10. Arendt, "Truth and Politics," p. 568, 567. Recall the discussion in part II about the inadequacy of Foucault's exaltation of the Cynics and Cynic protest.

that the threat has moved from outside to inside, from the enemy abroad to the citizen at home. Nevertheless, the citizen who speaks the truth is still, in some crucial sense, *outside.* After all, the only important sense in which the citizen can be outside the spell of the image is by first being potentially enthralled by it. Those enthralled by it are the same ones responsible for upholding it and passing it along as they come to believe the very lies they tell. But rogue citizens are not easily enthralled. They would rather face painful — even unbearable — truths than live a lie. They quickly disclaim all responsibility for propping up an order that requires casting spells over what the people believe. They are unimpressed by imposing images. They gratefully take the world as it is if the only way to make it better is by making it less than real.

We have finally arrived again at some of the central questions that have occupied us throughout this book. What enables some citizens to escape the spell of the image, evade the modern lie, and continue talking about the facts of the past? How do they resist? What is the shape of these people? What are they engaged in? What are their virtues and practices? These questions have animated these chapters. As with the immediately foregoing argument, Arendt suggests that idealists who decry lying on principle (what I have called negative truth-telling) are not a serious threat since such moralizing can easily be accommodated within the false image. In the same way, any regime can tolerate a certain amount of debate concerning "the issues" so long as the respective positions (such as left and right) sedulously busy themselves with alternative perspectives on this or that aspect of the established narrative in such a way that it never occurs to them to raise more fundamental questions.

Arendt teaches that something additional is necessary. Even though the truth is impotent in an open contest with power, the contingency of factual truth need not be a liability: "Who says what is . . . always tells a story, and in this story the particular facts lose their contingency and acquire some humanly comprehensible meaning."[11] It is true that the modern lie of mass manipulation also exploits this by telling a false story, stringing together otherwise true facts into a fabric that, as a whole, distortedly narrates the facts. The answer to propaganda is not just more facts, but a true story.[12] Nevertheless, a false fabric is unstable precisely be-

---

11. Arendt, "Truth and Politics," p. 572.

12. Slavoj Žižek faults Noam Chomsky for merely focusing on exposing people to the facts at the expense of challenging the false narrative in which the facts take their places

cause of the stubbornness of the facts it attempts to disguise. True stories, on the other hand, have no need to disguise the facts; they are free to highlight them. Therefore, the ability of some rogue citizens to resist the modern lie resides in their practice of persisting in telling true stories, that is, in testifying.

I have attempted in this book to look with ethical seriousness at the fact that Christians are a people who are commanded to tell true stories about Jesus Christ, to bear true witness. I have shown that, in order to do so successfully, they must take up the mantle of discipleship and refuse the totalizing vision that attempts to smooth over fragile, contingent facts and disabuse distorted knowledge, not achieving this through greater objectivity but through the embodied love of Christ and his contingent creation. In chapter 1, I followed Gregory of Nyssa's close association of seeing with both following and desire, where the desire to see God is fulfilled in the disciples' following, though it is also a nonseeing of God, inasmuch as beholding does not bring satiety or any other reason for turning away. Chapter 3 developed the way that this distinctive discipleship vision funds an alternative to the terrors of the Enlightenment through the ways that Murdoch and Nussbaum insist that love yields its own knowledge. I pressed their insights further in order to enfold the object within this love for a people whose witness is of something particular. Furthermore, the boldness of witness is correlative of a witnessing people's ability to resist the lies that rely on sovereignty for justifying their existence. Both boldness and resistance accompany the eschatologically oriented patience of this people's true speech. Finally, in the absence of reasons that might be given for practicing speech that holds onto the fragility of true realities, there is

---

(Doug Henwood, "Interview with Slavoj Žižek " in *The Anti-Capitalism Reader: Imagining a Geography of Opposition,* ed. Joel Schalit [New York: Akashic Books, 2002], pp. 77-78). Even though it is clear to me that Chomsky is full of facts that most Americans do not know, I think Žižek is right that, for example, history is a story rather than simply one thing after another. Nevertheless, I also think he underestimates how much another narrative is still at work for Chomsky (perhaps despite Chomsky's own declarations to be telling only the facts). One need only notice that the reality that some celebrate Chomsky and others revile him has very little to do with whether the facts he presents are correct. It certainly has much more to do with whether people approve of how his facts challenge the stories they tell themselves about reality. For example, do Americans want to believe that their country is a terrorist state, as Chomsky insists? It seems to me that the will to believe this is more fundamental than the facts he provides to back up the claim. Just as surely, for some, the effect is the opposite: their reality-stories may too quickly accommodate and overdetermine the facts he presents. Our wills can be too strong, just as they can be too weak.

only the bodily presence and activity of this people whose existence owes to nothing more than sheer promise.

Is Arendt right, however, to say that liars are people of action and truth-tellers are not? Is it the case that truth-telling cannot change the world? For Christian thought, these questions point again ultimately and ineluctably to the martyrs. Christians will want to say of their fallen fellow disciples that they have not died in vain. But these convictions are not part of an untouchable myth like the modern lie, whose falsehood is actually a strength, trading on matching the will for fantasy with what is easy to believe. As first citizens of the renewed polis who proclaim the truth from within the eschatologically primary *ekklēsia,* speaking freely and without fear, martyrs witness to a truer politics. They witness to the establishment of a new political order that would rather suffer for the truth than survive through lies. The deaths that silence martyrs do not silence their true witness. As the paradigmatic witnesses, martyrs are also the paradigmatic antipoliticians, since they do not try to change the world (they are Barth's "mere witnesses"), but only witness to how the world has already been changed. This is the Christian witnesses' agenda and joy. It is their toil and rapture.

Bibliography

Anderson, Benedict. *Imagined Communities: Reflections on the Origin and Spread of Nationalism.* Rev. ed. New York: Verso, 1991.

Anscombe, G. E. M. "Modern Moral Philosophy." *Philosophy* 33, no. 124 (January 1958).

Aquinas, Thomas. *Summa Theologica.* Translated by Fathers of the English Dominican Province. Allen, Texas: Christian Classics, 1981.

Arendt, Hannah. *Crises of the Republic.* New York: Harcourt Brace and Company, 1972.

———. *The Human Condition.* 2nd ed. Chicago: University of Chicago Press, 1998.

———. "Truth and Politics." In *The Portable Hannah Arendt,* edited by Peter Baehr. London: Penguin, 2000.

Aristotle. *Nichomachean Ethics.* Translated by Terence Irwin. Indianapolis: Hackett, 1999.

Arneson, Richard J., ed. *Liberalism, Volume 3.* Aldershot: Edward Elgaar Publishing, 1992.

Augustine. *City of God Against the Pagans.* Edited and translated by R. W. Dyson. Cambridge: Cambridge University Press, 1998.

———. *Confessions.* Translated by Henry Chadwick. Oxford: Oxford University Press, 1998.

———. *Confessions.* Translated by William Watts. Loeb Classical Library. Cambridge, MA: Harvard University Press, 1946.

———. *Contra Mendacium.* Translated by H. Browne. Nicene and Post-Nicene Fathers, vol. III, edited by Philip Schaff. Edinburgh: T. & T. Clark, 1988.

———. *De Trinitate.* Translated by Edmund Hill. New York: New City Press, 1998.

———. *On Christian Teaching.* Edited and translated by R. P. Green. Oxford: Oxford University Press, 1997.

———. *The Soliloquies of St. Augustine.* Translated by Rose Elizabeth Cleveland. Boston: Little, Brown, 1910.

Baehr, Peter, ed. *The Portable Hannah Arendt.* London: Penguin, 2000.

Barber, Daniel. "The Particularity of Jesus and the Time of the Kingdom: Philosophy and Theology in Yoder." *Modern Theology* 23, no. 1 (January 2007): 63-89.

Barth, Karl. *Anselm: Fides Quaerens Intellectum.* Translated by Ian W. Robertson. Richmond, VA: John Knox, 1960.

———. *The Christian Life: Church Dogmatics IV,4 Lecture Fragments.* Translated by Geoffrey W. Bromiley. Grand Rapids: Eerdmans, 1981.

———. *Church Dogmatics, Volumes I-IV.* Translated by G. W. Bromiley et al. Edinburgh: T. & T. Clark, 1956-1975.

———. *Dogmatics in Outline.* Translated by G. T. Thomson. London: SCM, 1968.

———. *The Epistle to the Romans.* Translated by Edwyn C. Hoskyns. Oxford: Oxford University Press, 1968.

———. *Ethics.* Translated by G. W. Bromiley. Edinburgh: T. & T. Clark, 1992.

———. *The Knowledge of God and the Service of God According to the Teaching of the Reformation.* London: Hodder and Stoughton, 1938.

———. *Natural Theology: Comprising "Nature and Grace" by Professor Dr. Emil Brunner and the Reply "No!" by Karl Barth.* Translated by Peter Fraenkel. London: Geoffrey Bles, 1946.

Barton, Gregory A. *Empire Forestry and the Origins of Environmentalism.* Cambridge: Cambridge University Press, 2002.

Bauckham, Richard. *Jesus and the Eyewitnesses: The Gospels as Eyewitness Testimony.* Grand Rapids: Eerdmans, 2006.

———. *The Theology of the Book of Revelation.* Cambridge: Cambridge University Press, 1993.

Bauerschmidt, Frederick Christian. "Aquinas." In *The Blackwell Companion to Political Theology,* edited by Peter Scott and William T. Cavanaugh. Oxford: Blackwell, 2004.

Berkhof, Hendrikus. *Christ and the Powers.* Translated by John Howard Yoder. Scottdale, PA: Herald, 1977.

Berlin, Isaiah. *Four Essays on Liberty.* Oxford: Oxford University Press, 1969.

Bernauer, James. *Michel Foucault's Force of Flight: Toward an Ethics for Thought.* London: Humanities Press International, 1992.

Bernauer, James, and David Rasmussen, eds. *The Final Foucault.* London: MIT Press, 1988.

Berry, Wendell. "The Futility of Global Thinking." In *Learning to Listen to the Land,* edited by Bill Willers. Washington, DC: Island Press, 1991.

———. *Life Is a Miracle.* Washington, DC: Counterpoint, 2000.

———. "The Whole Horse." In *The Art of the Commonplace: The Agrarian Essays of Wendell Berry,* edited by Norman Wirzba. Washington, DC: Counterpoint, 2002.

Biggar, Nigel. *The Hastening That Waits: Karl Barth's Ethics.* Oxford: Clarendon, 1993.

Bok, Sissela. *Lying: Moral Choice in Public and Private Life.* Hassocks, Sussex: Harvester, 1978.

Bonhoeffer, Dietrich. *Ethics.* Translated by Neville Horton Smith. London: Touchstone, 1995.

Bouchard, Donald F., ed. *Language, Counter-Memory, Practice: Selected Essays and Interviews.* Ithaca, NY: Cornell University Press, 1977.

Bounds, Elizabeth M. *Coming Together/Coming Apart: Religion, Community, and Modernity.* London: Routledge, 1996.

Bourdieu, Pierre. *Outline of a Theory of Practice.* Translated by Richard Nice. Cambridge: Cambridge University Press, 1977.

Braaten, Carl E. "Sins of the Tongue." In *I Am the Lord Your God: Christian Reflections on the Ten Commandments,* edited by Carl E. Braaten and Christopher R. Seitz. Grand Rapids: Eerdmans, 2005.

Braaten, Carl E., and Christopher R. Seitz, eds. *I Am the Lord Your God: Christian Reflections on the Ten Commandments.* Grand Rapids: Eerdmans, 2005.

Brueggemann, Walter. *Theology of the Old Testament: Testimony, Dispute, Advocacy.* Minneapolis: Fortress, 1997.

Buechner, Frederick. *Telling the Truth.* New York: HarperCollins, 1977.

Burdon, Christopher. *Stumbling on God: Faith and Vision through Mark's Gospel.* Grand Rapids: Eerdmans, 1990.

Burrell, David. *Aquinas: God and Action.* Notre Dame, IN: University of Notre Dame Press, 1979.

Busch, Eberhard. *The Great Passion: An Introduction to Karl Barth's Theology.* Translated by Geoffrey W. Bromiley. Grand Rapids: Eerdmans, 2004.

Byrskog, Samuel. *Story as History — History as Story: The Gospel Tradition in the Context of Ancient Oral History.* Tübingen: Mohr Siebeck, 2000.

Calvin, John. *Institutes of the Christian Religion.* Edited by John T. McNeill. Translated by Ford Lewis Battles. Library of Christian Classics, vols. XX and XXI. London: SCM, 1960.

Candler, Peter McCray. *Theology, Rhetoric, Manuduction: On Reading Scripture Together on the Path to God.* Grand Rapids: Eerdmans, 2006.

Caputo, John D., and Michael J. Scanlon, eds. *God, the Gift, and Postmodernism.* Bloomington: Indiana University Press, 1999.

Cartwright, Nancy. *The Dappled World: A Study of the Boundaries of Science.* Cambridge: Cambridge University Press, 1999.

Cavanaugh, William T. "Killing for the Telephone Company: Why the Nation-State Is Not the Keeper of the Common Good." *Modern Theology* 20, no. 2 (April 2004): 243-74.

Cavell, Stanley, et al. *Philosophy and Animal Life*. New York: Columbia University Press, 2008.

Churchill, John. "Wonder and the End of Explanation: Wittgenstein and Religious Sensibility." *Philosophical Investigations* 17, no. 2 (April 1994): 388-416.

Clarke, Howard. *The Gospel of Matthew and Its Readers: A Historical Introduction to the First Gospel*. Bloomington: Indiana University Press, 2003.

Clough, David. *Ethics in Crisis: Interpreting Barth's Ethics*. Aldershot, UK: Ashgate, 2005.

Coles, Romand. "The Wild Patience of John Howard Yoder: 'Outsiders' and the 'Otherness of the Church.'" *Modern Theology* 18, no. 3 (July 2002): 305-31.

De Certeau, Michel. *The Practice of Everyday Life*. Translated by Steven F. Randall. Berkeley: University of California Press, 2002.

DeMan, Paul. *Allegories of Reading*. New Haven: Yale University Press, 1979.

Deleuze, Gilles. *Cinema 2: The Time-Image*. Translated by Hugh Tomlinson and Robert Galeta. London: Athlone, 1989.

———. *Foucault*. Translated by Séan Hand. London: Athlone, 1988.

Derrida, Jacques. *Margins of Philosophy*. Translated by Alan Bass. Sussex, UK: Harvester, 1982.

———. "On the Gift." In *God, the Gift, and Postmodernism,* edited by John D. Caputo and Michael J. Scanlon. Bloomington: Indiana University Press, 1999.

Dreyfus, Hubert L., and Paul Rabinow. *Michel Foucault: Beyond Structuralism and Hermeneutics*. 2nd ed. Chicago: University of Chicago Press, 1983.

Eagleton, Terry. *After Theory*. New York: Basic Books, 2003.

———. *The Illusions of Postmodernism*. Oxford: Blackwell, 1996.

———. "Mystic Mechanic." *Times Literary Supplement* (April 29, 2005): 10.

Ellison, Louise. *The Adversarial Process and the Vulnerable Witness*. Oxford: Oxford University Press, 2001.

Elshtain, Jean Bethke. *Who Are We? Critical Reflections and Hopeful Possibilities*. Grand Rapids: Eerdmans, 2000.

Engelhardt, H. Tristram. *The Foundations of Christian Bioethics*. Exton, PA: Swets and Zeitlinger, 2000.

Feyerabend, Paul. *Against Method*. 3rd ed. London: Verso, 1993.

Fish, Stanley. *There's No Such Thing as Free Speech*. Oxford: Oxford University Press, 1994.

Fitzgerald, John T., ed. *Friendship, Flattery, and Frankness*. Leiden: Brill, 1996.

Fletcher, Joseph. *Situation Ethics: The New Morality*. Philadelphia: Westminster, 1975.

Flynn, Thomas. "Foucault as Parrhesiast." In *The Final Foucault,* edited by James Bernauer and David Rasmussen. London: MIT Press, 1988.

Fodor, James. *Christian Hermeneutics: Paul Ricœur and the Refiguring of Theology*. Oxford: Clarendon, 1995.

Foucault, Michel. *The Archaeology of Knowledge.* Translated by Rupert Swyer. New York: Pantheon, 1972.

—. *Discipline and Punish: The Birth of the Prison.* Translated by Alan Sheridan. New York: Vintage, 1995.

—. *Fearless Speech.* Edited by Joseph Pearson. Los Angeles: Semiotext(e), 2001.

—. *Foucault Live (Interviews, 1961-1984).* Edited by Sylvere Lotringer. Translated by Lysa Hochroth and John Johnston. New York: Semiotext(e), 1989.

—. *The History of Sexuality 1: The Will to Knowledge.* Translated by Robert Hurley. London: Penguin, 1978.

—. *The History of Sexuality 2: The Use of Pleasure.* Translated by Robert Hurley. London: Penguin, 1984.

—. Introduction to *On the Normal and the Pathological,* by Georges Canguilhem. Translated by Carolyn R. Fawcett. Boston: D. Reidel, 1978.

—. *Language, Counter-Memory, Practice.* Edited by Donald F. Bouchard. Ithaca, NY: Cornell University Press, 1980.

—. "On the Genealogy of Ethics." In *Michel Foucault: Beyond Structuralism and Hermeneutics.* 2nd ed. Edited by Hubert L. Dreyfus and Paul Rabinow. Chicago: University of Chicago Press, 1983.

—. "The Order of Discourse." In *Untying the Text: A Post-Structuralist Reader,* edited by Robert Young. London: Routledge and Kegan Paul, 1981.

—. *The Order of Things: An Archaeology of the Human Sciences.* Translated by Alan Sheridan. London: Routledge, 2002.

—. "Polemics, Politics, and Problematizations: An Interview." In *The Foucault Reader,* edited by Paul Rabinow. New York: Pantheon, 1984.

—. "Prison Talk." In *Power/Knowledge: Selected Interviews and Other Writings 1972-1977,* edited by Colin Gordon. New York: Pantheon, 1980.

—. "Sexuality and Solitude." *London Review of Books* 3, no. 9 (21 May–3 June 1981): 3-7.

—. "Theatrum Philosophicum." In *Language, Counter-Memory, Practice: Selected Essays and Interviews,* edited by Donald F. Bouchard. Ithaca, NY: Cornell, 1977.

—. "Truth and Power." In *Power/Knowledge: Selected Interviews and Other Writings 1972-1977,* edited by Colin Gordon. New York: Pantheon, 1980.

—. "What Is Critique?" In *The Politics of Truth,* edited by Sylvere Lotringer. Los Angeles: Semiotext(e), 1997.

Frankfurt, Harry. *On Bullshit.* Princeton, NJ: Princeton University Press, 2005.

Galloway, Lincoln E. *Freedom in the Gospel: Paul's Exemplum in 1 Cor 9 in Conversation with the Discourses of Epictetus and Philo.* Paris: Peeters, 2004.

Garcia, J. L. "Lies and the Vices of Deception." *Faith and Philosophy* 15, no. 4 (October 1998): 514-37.

Geertz, Clifford. "Anti-relativism." *American Anthropologist* 86 (1984): 263-78.

Georgi, Dieter. *Theocracy in Paul's Praxis and Theology.* Minneapolis: Fortress, 1991.

Godsey, John D., ed. *Karl Barth's Table Talk.* Edinburgh: Oliver and Boyd, 1963.

Goleman, Daniel. *Vital Lies, Simple Truths: The Psychology of Self-Deception.* London: Bloomsbury, 1997.

Gordon, Colin, ed. *Power/Knowledge: Selected Interviews and Other Writings 1972-1977.* New York: Pantheon, 1980.

Griffiths, Paul J. *Lying: An Augustinian Theology of Duplicity.* Grand Rapids: Brazos, 2004.

Griffiths, Paul J., and Reinhard Hütter, eds. *Reason and the Reasons of Faith.* New York: T. & T. Clark, 2005.

Gunton, Colin, and Robert W. Jenson. "The *Logos Ensarkos* and Reason." In *Reason and the Reasons of Faith,* edited by Paul J. Griffiths and Reinhard Hütter. New York: T. & T. Clark, 2005.

Harrison, Robert Pogue. *Forests: The Shadow of Civilization.* Chicago: University of Chicago Press, 1992.

Hart, David Bentley. *The Beauty of the Infinite: The Aesthetics of Christian Truth.* Grand Rapids: Eerdmans, 2003.

Harvey, David. *The Condition of Postmodernity: An Enquiry into the Origins of Cultural Change.* Oxford: Blackwell, 1990.

Hauerwas, Stanley. *Dispatches from the Front: Theological Engagements with the Secular.* Durham, NC: Duke University Press, 1995.

———. "Pacifism: Some Philosophical Considerations." *Faith and Philosophy* 2, no. 2 (April 1985): 99-104.

———. *The Peaceable Kingdom: A Primer in Christian Ethics.* Notre Dame, IN: University of Notre Dame Press, 1983.

———. *Performing the Faith: Bonhoeffer and the Practice of Nonviolence.* Grand Rapids: Brazos, 2004.

———. *Sanctify Them in the Truth: Holiness Exemplified.* Nashville: Abingdon, 1998.

———. *Truthfulness and Tragedy.* Notre Dame, IN: University of Notre Dame Press, 1977.

———. *Vision and Virtue: Essays in Christian Ethical Reflection.* Notre Dame, IN: University of Notre Dame Press, 1981.

———. *With the Grain of the Universe: The Church's Witness and Natural Theology.* Grand Rapids: Brazos, 2001.

Hauerwas, Stanley, and Philip D. Kenneson. "The Church and/as God's Non-Violent Imagination." *Pro Ecclesia* 1, no. 1 (Fall 1992): 76-88.

Hauerwas, Stanley, Chris K. Huebner, Harry J. Huebner, and Mark Thiessen Nation, eds. *The Wisdom of the Cross: Essays in Honor of John Howard Yoder.* Grand Rapids: Eerdmans, 1999.

Hauerwas, Stanley, Nancey Murphy, and Mark Nation, eds. *Theology Without*

Foundations: Religious Practice and the Future of Theological Truth. Nashville: Abingdon, 1994.

Henwood, Doug. "Interview with Slavoj Žižek." In *The Anti-Capitalism Reader: Imagining a Geography of Opposition,* edited by Joel Schalit. New York: Akashic Books, 2002.

Hobbes, Thomas. *Leviathan.* London: Penguin, 1985 (first published 1651).

Horkheimer, Max, and Theodore W. Adorno. *Dialectic of Enlightenment.* Edited by Gunzelin Schmid Noerr. Translated by Edmund Jephcott. Stanford: Stanford University Press, 2002.

Hovey, Craig. "Democracy Beyond Democracy." *Theology Today* 61, no. 3 (October 2004): 355-59.

———. "Forester, *Bricoleur,* and Country Bumpkin: Rethinking Knowledge and Habit in Aquinas's Ethics." *Scottish Journal of Theology* 59, no. 2 (July 2006): 159-74.

———. *Nietzsche and Theology.* New York: T. & T. Clark, 2008.

———. *To Share in the Body: A Theology of Martyrdom for Today's Church.* Grand Rapids: Brazos, 2008.

Howes, David. *Sensual Relations: Engaging the Senses in Culture and Social Theory.* Ann Arbor: University of Michigan Press, 2003.

Hoy, David Couzens, ed. *Foucault: A Critical Reader.* Oxford: Blackwell, 1986.

Huebner, Chris K. "Can a Gift Be Commanded? Theological Ethics Without Theory by way of Barth, Milbank and Yoder." *Scottish Journal of Theology* 53, no. 4 (2000): 472-89.

Hursthouse, Rosalind. *On Virtue Ethics.* Oxford: Oxford University Press, 1999.

Hütter, Reinhard. "Hospitality and Truth: The Disclosure of Practices in Worship and Doctrine." In *Practicing Theology: Beliefs and Practices in Christian Life,* edited by Miroslav Volf and Dorothy C. Bass. Grand Rapids: Eerdmans, 2002.

Jenson, Robert. *Systematic Theology,* vol. 1: *The Triune God.* Oxford: Oxford University Press, 1997.

———. *Systematic Theology,* vol. 2: *The Works of God.* Oxford: Oxford University Press, 1999.

Jones, L. Gregory. "Truth and Lies." *The Christian Century* (March 11, 1998).

Jonsen, Albert R., and Stephen Toulmin. *The Abuse of Casuistry: A History of Moral Reasoning.* Berkeley: University of California Press, 1989.

Kant, Immanuel. *Kant's Political Writings.* Edited by H. S. Reiss. Cambridge: Cambridge University Press, 2003.

———. *The Metaphysics of Morals.* Translated and edited by Mary Gregor. Cambridge: Cambridge University Press, 1996.

Kaufmann, Walter, ed. and trans. *The Portable Nietzsche.* London: Viking Penguin, 1968.

Kenneson, Philip D. "There's No Such Thing as Objective Truth, and It's a Good

Thing, Too." In *Christian Apologetics in the Postmodern World,* edited by Timothy R. Phillips and Dennis L. Okholm. Downers Grove, IL: InterVarsity Press, 1995.

Kittel, Gerhard, and Gerhard Friedrich, eds. *Theological Dictionary of the New Testament.* 10 vols. Translated by Geoffrey W. Bromiley. Grand Rapids: Eerdmans, 1964-76.

Knight, Kelvin. *The MacIntyre Reader.* Notre Dame, IN: University of Notre Dame Press, 1998.

Kofman, Sarah. *Nietzsche and Metaphor.* Translated by Duncan Large. London: Athlone, 1993.

Kreider, Alan. "Christ, Culture, and Truth-telling." *The Conrad Grebel Review* 15, no. 3 (Fall 1997): 207-33.

Lincoln, Andrew T. *Truth on Trial: The Lawsuit Motif in the Fourth Gospel.* Peabody, MA: Hendrickson, 2000.

Lohfink, Gerhard. *Does God Need the Church? Toward a Theology of the People of God.* Translated by Linda M. Maloney. Collegeville, MN: Liturgical Press, 1999.

Long, D. Stephen. *The Goodness of God: Theology, Church, and the Social Order.* Grand Rapids: Brazos, 2001.

Lotringer, Sylvere, ed. *The Politics of Truth.* Los Angeles: Semiotext(e), 1997.

Loughlin, Gerard. *Telling God's Story: Bible, Church, and Narrative Theology.* Cambridge: Cambridge University Press, 1996.

Lovibond, Sabina. *Realism and Imagination in Ethics.* Oxford: Basil Blackwell, 1983.

Luther, Martin. *Kleiner Katechismus.* Cited in Robert Jenson, *Systematic Theology,* vol. 2: *The Works of God.* Oxford: Oxford University Press, 1999.

———. "Treatise on Good Works." In *The Christian in Society I.* Luther's Works, vol. 44. Translated by W. A. Lambert. Philadelphia: Fortress, 1966.

MacIntyre, Alasdair. *After Virtue.* 2nd ed. Notre Dame, IN: University of Notre Dame Press, 1984.

———. *Dependent Rational Animals: Why Human Beings Need the Virtues.* Chicago: Open Court, 1999.

———. "Is Patriotism a Virtue?" In *Liberalism, Volume 3,* edited by Richard J. Arneson. Aldershot, UK: Edward Elgaar Publishing, 1992.

———. "Moral Relativism, Truth and Justification." In *The MacIntyre Reader,* edited by Kelvin Knight. Notre Dame, IN: University of Notre Dame Press, 1998.

———. "Plain Persons and Moral Philosophy: Rules, Virtues and Goods." In *The MacIntyre Reader,* edited by Kelvin Knight. Notre Dame, IN: University of Notre Dame Press, 1998.

———. *Three Rival Versions of Moral Enquiry: Encyclopedia, Genealogy, and Tradition.* Notre Dame, IN: University of Notre Dame Press, 1990.

———. "Truthfulness, Lies, and Moral Philosophers: What Can We Learn from

Mill and Kant?" In *The Tanner Lectures on Human Values,* vol. 16. Salt Lake City: University of Utah Press, 1995.

————. *Whose Justice? Which Rationality?* Notre Dame, IN: University of Notre Dame Press, 1984.

Malherbee, Abraham, and Everett Ferguson, ed. and trans. *Gregory of Nyssa: The Life of Moses.* Classics of Western Spirituality. New York: Paulist, 1978.

Marrow, Stanley B., SJ. "*Parrhēsia* and the New Testament." *The Catholic Biblical Quarterly* 44, no. 3 (July 1982): 431-46.

Marshall, Bruce D. *Trinity and Truth.* Cambridge: Cambridge University Press, 2000.

McCabe, Herbert. *God Matters.* London: Continuum, 2005.

McClendon, James. *Systematic Theology.* 3 vols. Nashville: Abingdon, 1986-2000.

Merquior, J. G. *Foucault.* London: Fontana, 1991.

Milbank, John. *Being Reconciled: Ontology and Pardon.* London: Routledge, 2003.

————. *Theology and Social Theory: Beyond Secular Reason.* Oxford: Blackwell, 1990.

————. *The Word Made Strange: Theology, Language, Culture.* Oxford: Blackwell, 1997.

Milbank, John, and Catherine Pickstock. *Truth in Aquinas.* London: Routledge, 2001.

Mill, John Stuart. *Utilitarianism.* Indianapolis: Hackett, 1979.

Murdoch, Iris. *Existentialists and Mystics: Writings on Philosophy and Literature.* Edited by Peter Conradi. New York: Penguin, 1999.

————. *Metaphysics as a Guide to Morals.* New York: Penguin, 1994.

————. *The Sovereignty of Good.* London: Routledge, 2002.

Musurillo, Herbert, ed. and trans. *From Glory to Glory: Texts from Gregory of Nyssa's Mystical Writings.* London: John Murray, 1961.

Nehamas, Alexander. *Nietzsche: Life as Literature.* London: Harvard University Press, 1985.

Niebuhr, H. Richard. *The Responsible Self: An Essay in Christian Moral Philosophy.* Louisville: Westminster John Knox, 1999.

Nietzsche, Friedrich. *The Antichrist.* In *The Portable Nietzsche,* edited and translated by Walter Kaufmann. London: Viking Penguin, 1968.

————. *Beyond Good and Evil.* Translated by R. J. Hollingdale. London: Penguin, 1990.

————. *The Birth of Tragedy.* Translated by Ronald Speirs. Cambridge: Cambridge University Press, 1999.

————. *Ecce Homo.* Translated by R. J. Hollingdale. London: Penguin, 1992.

————. "Fragment on Ethics, 1868." In *The Portable Nietzsche,* edited and translated by Walter Kaufmann. London: Viking Penguin, 1968.

————. *The Gay Science.* Translated by Josefine Nauckhoff. Edited by Bernard Williams. Cambridge: Cambridge University Press, 2001.

————. *Human, All Too Human.* In *The Portable Nietzsche,* edited and translated by Walter Kaufmann. London: Viking Penguin, 1968.

————. *On the Genealogy of Morality.* Translated by Carol Diethe. Cambridge: Cambridge University Press, 1994.

————. "From 'On Truth and Lie in an Extra-Moral Sense.'" In *The Portable Nietzsche,* edited and translated by Walter Kaufmann. London: Viking Penguin, 1968.

————. *Philosophy and Truth: Selections from Nietzsche's Notebooks of the Early 1870's.* Edited and translated by D. Breazeale. Amherst, NY: Humanity Books, 1999.

————. *Thus Spoke Zarathustra.* In *The Portable Nietzsche,* edited and translated by Walter Kaufmann. London: Viking Penguin, 1968.

————. *Twilight of the Idols, or How One Philosophizes with a Hammer.* In *The Portable Nietzsche,* edited and translated by Walter Kaufmann. London: Viking Penguin, 1968.

————. *The Will to Power.* Translated by Walter Kaufmann and R. J. Hollingdale. Edited by Walter Kaufmann. New York: Vintage, 1968.

Northcott, Michael. *The Environment and Christian Ethics.* Cambridge: Cambridge University Press, 1996.

Nussbaum, Martha C. *The Fragility of Goodness: Luck and Ethics in Greek Tragedy and Philosophy.* Updated ed. Cambridge: Cambridge University Press, 2001.

————. *Love's Knowledge: Essays on Philosophy and Literature.* Oxford: Oxford University Press, 1990.

Nyberg, David. *The Varnished Truth: Truth Telling and Deceiving in Ordinary Life.* Chicago: University of Chicago Press, 1993.

O'Donovan, Oliver. *Desire of the Nations: Rediscovering the Roots of Political Authority.* Cambridge: Cambridge University Press, 1996.

Ollenburger, Ben C., and Gayle Gerber Koontz, eds. *A Mind Patient and Untamed: Assessing John Howard Yoder's Contributions to Theology and Peacemaking.* Telford, PA: Cascadia, 2004.

Ochs, Peter. Review of *With the Grain of the Universe,* by Stanley Hauerwas. *Modern Theology* 19, no. 1 (January 2003): 77-88.

Pannenberg, Wolfhart. *Systematic Theology.* Translated by Geoffrey W. Bromiley. Grand Rapids: Eerdmans, 1991.

Phillips, Timothy R., and Dennis L. Okholm, eds. *Christian Apologetics in the Postmodern World.* Downers Grove, IL: InterVarsity Press, 1995.

Pinches, Charles R. *Theology and Action: After Theory in Christian Ethics.* Grand Rapids: Eerdmans, 2002.

Placher, William. *Unapologetic Theology: A Christian Voice in a Pluralistic Conversation.* Louisville: Westminster/John Knox, 1989.

Plato, *Phaedrus.* Translated by Harold Fowler. Loeb Classical Library. Cambridge, MA: Harvard University Press, 1982.

————. *The Republic.* Translated by Richard W. Sterling and William C. Scott. New York: W. W. Norton and Company, 1985.

Pohl, Christine. *Making Room: Recovering Hospitality as a Christian Tradition.* Grand Rapids: Eerdmans, 1999.

Preston, Richard. "Climbing the Redwoods." *The New Yorker* (February 14 and 21, 2005): 212-25.

Rabinow, Paul, ed. *The Foucault Reader.* New York: Pantheon, 1984.

Ricoeur, Paul. *Essays in Biblical Interpretation.* London: SPCK, 1981.

Rogers, Eugene F., Jr. *Thomas Aquinas and Karl Barth: Sacred Doctrine and the Natural Knowledge of God.* Notre Dame, IN: University of Notre Dame Press, 1995.

Rorty, Richard. *Contingency, Irony, and Solidarity.* Cambridge: Cambridge University Press, 1989.

————. "Foucault and Epistemology." In *Foucault: A Critical Reader,* edited by David Couzens Hoy. Oxford: Blackwell, 1986.

————. *Philosophy and the Mirror of Nature.* Princeton, NJ: Princeton University Press, 1979.

Rose, Gillian. *Mourning Becomes the Law: Philosophy and Representation.* Cambridge: Cambridge University Press, 1996.

Roy, Arundhati. *Field Notes on Democracy: Listening to Grasshoppers.* Chicago: Haymarket, 2009.

————. *War Talk.* Cambridge, MA: South End, 2003.

Said, Edward. "Foucault and the Imagination of Power." In *Foucault: A Critical Reader,* edited by David Couzens Hoy. Oxford: Blackwell, 1986.

Schalit, Joel, ed. *The Anti-Capitalism Reader: Imagining a Geography of Opposition.* New York: Akashic Books, 2002.

Schlier, Heinrich. *"parrhēsia."* In *Theological Dictionary of the New Testament.* 10 vols. Edited by Gerhard Kittel and Gerhard Friedrich. Translated by Geoffrey W. Bromiley. Grand Rapids: Eerdmans, 1964-76.

Scott, James C. *Domination and the Arts of Resistance: Hidden Transcripts.* New Haven: Yale University Press, 1990.

————. *Seeing like a State: How Certain Schemes to Improve the Human Condition Have Failed.* New Haven: Yale University Press, 1998.

Scott, Peter, and William T. Cavanaugh, eds. *The Blackwell Companion to Political Theology.* Oxford: Blackwell, 2004.

Seligman, Adam. *The Idea of Civil Society.* Princeton, NJ: Princeton University Press, 1992.

Sider, J. Alexander. "Constantinianism Before and After Nicea: Issues in Restitutionist Historiography." In *A Mind Patient and Untamed: Assessing John Howard Yoder's Contributions to Theology and Peacemaking,* edited by Ben C. Ollenburger and Gayle Gerber Koontz. Telford, PA: Cascadia, 2004.

Smith, James K. A. "Questions about the Perception of 'Christian Truth': On the

Affective Effects of Sin." Essay presented at the American Academy of Religion, Philadelphia, 2005.

Stout, Jeffrey. *Democracy and Tradition*. Princeton, NJ: Princeton University Press, 2003.

———. *Ethics After Babel: The Languages of Morals and Their Discontents*. Princeton, NJ: Princeton University Press, 2001.

Szakolczai, Arpad. *The Genesis of Modernity*. London: Routledge, 2003.

Taylor, Charles. "Foucault on Freedom and Truth." In *Foucault: A Critical Reader*, edited by David Couzens Hoy. Oxford: Blackwell, 1986.

———. *Philosophy and the Human Sciences*. Philosophical Papers 2. Cambridge: Cambridge University Press, 1985.

———. *Sources of the Self: The Making of the Modern Identity*. Cambridge, MA: Harvard University Press, 1989.

Toole, David. *Waiting for Godot in Sarajevo: Theological Reflections on Nihilism, Tragedy, and Apocalypse*. Boulder, CO: Westview, 1998.

Toulmin, Stephen. *Cosmopolis: The Hidden Agenda of Modernity*. Chicago: University of Chicago Press, 1990.

Trites, Allison A. *The New Testament Concept of Witness*. Cambridge: Cambridge University Press, 1977.

Tyler, Anne. *A Patchwork Planet*. New York: Ballantine, 1998.

Van Unnik, W. C. *Sparsa Collecta: The Collected Essays of W. C. van Unnik*, vol. 2. Leiden: Brill, 1980.

Volf, Miroslav. *Exclusion and Embrace: A Theological Exploration of Identity, Otherness, and Reconciliation*. Nashville: Abingdon, 1996.

———. "Johannine Dualism and Contemporary Pluralism." *Modern Theology* 21, no. 2 (April 2005): 189-217.

Volf, Miroslav, and Dorothy C. Bass, eds. *Practicing Theology: Beliefs and Practices in Christian Life*. Grand Rapids: Eerdmans, 2002.

Walzer, Michael. "On the Role of Symbolism in Political Thought." *Political Science Quarterly* 82, no. 2 (June 1967): 191-204.

———. "The Politics of Michel Foucault." In *Foucault: A Critical Reader*, edited by David Couzens Hoy. Oxford: Blackwell, 1986.

Wannenwetsch, Bernd. *Political Worship: Ethics for Christian Citizens*. Translated by Margaret Kohl. Oxford: Oxford University Press, 2004.

———. "You Shall Not Kill — What Does It Take? Why We Need the Other Commandments If We Are to Abstain from Killing." In *I Am the Lord Your God: Christian Reflections on the Ten Commandments*, edited by Carl E. Braaten and Christopher R. Seitz. Grand Rapids: Eerdmans, 2005.

Weaver, Alain Epp. "Unjust Lies, Just Wars?" *Journal of Religious Ethics* 29, no. 1 (2001): 51-78.

Webb, Stephen H. *The Divine Voice: Christian Proclamation and the Theology of Sound*. Grand Rapids: Brazos, 2004.

Wells, Samuel. *Improvisation: The Drama of Christian Ethics.* Grand Rapids: Brazos, 2004.

Wengst, Klaus. *Pax Romana and the Peace of Jesus Christ.* Philadelphia: Fortress, 1987.

Werpehowski, William. "Ad Hoc Apologetics." *Journal of Religion* 66 (July 1986): 282-301.

Willers, Bill. *Learning to Listen to the Land.* Washington, DC: Island Press, 1991.

Williams, Bernard. Introduction to *The Gay Science,* by Friedrich Nietzsche. Cambridge: Cambridge University Press, 2001.

————. *Truth and Truthfulness.* Princeton, NJ: Princeton University Press, 2002.

Williams, Rowan. *On Christian Theology.* Oxford: Blackwell, 2000.

————. "What Does Love Know? St. Thomas on the Trinity." *New Blackfriars* 82 (2001): 260-72.

Winter, S. C. "*Parrhēsia* in Acts." In *Friendship, Flattery, and Frankness,* edited by John T. Fitzgerald. Leiden: Brill, 1996.

Wirzba, Norman, ed. *The Art of the Commonplace: The Agrarian Essays of Wendell Berry.* Washington, DC: Counterpoint, 2002.

Wittgenstein, Ludwig. *Culture and Value.* Translated by Peter Winch. Oxford: Basil Blackwell, 1980.

————. *On Certainty.* Translated by Denis Paul and G. E. M. Anscombe. New York: Harper and Row, 1969.

————. *Philosophical Investigations.* Translated by G. E. M. Anscombe. New York: Macmillan, 1953.

————. *Remarks on the Foundations of Mathematics.* Rev. ed. Edited by G. H. von Wright, R. Rhees, and G. E. M. Anscombe. Translated by G. E. M. Anscombe. Cambridge, MA: MIT Press, 1983.

————. *Tractatus Logico Philosophicus.* Translated by D. F. Pears and B. F. McGuinness. London: Routledge, 2001.

————. *Zettel.* Translated by G. E. M. Anscombe. Oxford: Blackwell, 1981.

Wolfe, Cary. "Exposures." In *Philosophy and Animal Life,* edited by Stanley Cavell et al. New York: Columbia University Press, 2008.

Wolin, Sheldon. *Politics and Vision.* Rev. ed. Princeton, NJ: Princeton University Press, 2004.

Yoder, John Howard. *Christian Attitudes Toward War, Peace, and Revolution.* Grand Rapids: Brazos, 2009.

————. "Christianity and Protest in America." Unpublished essay delivered at Emory University Law School, 1991.

————. "Ethics and Eschatology." *Ex Auditu* 6 (1990): 119-28.

————. *The Jewish-Christian Schism Revisited.* Edited by Michael G. Cartwright and Peter Ochs. Grand Rapids: Eerdmans, 2003.

————. "Meaning After Babble." *Journal of Religious Ethics* 24, no. 1 (Spring 1996): 125-38.

—————. "On Not Being Ashamed of the Gospel: Particularity, Pluralism, and Validation." *Faith and Philosophy* 9, no. 3 (July 1992): 285-300.

—————. *Nevertheless: The Varieties and Shortcomings of Religious Pacifism.* Rev. and expanded ed. Scottdale, PA: Herald, 1992.

—————. *The Original Revolution: Essays on Christian Pacifism.* Eugene, OR: Wipf and Stock, 1998.

—————. "'Patience' as Method in Moral Reasoning: Is an Ethic of Discipleship 'Absolute'?" In *The Wisdom of the Cross: Essays in Honor of John Howard Yoder,* edited by Stanley Hauerwas, Chris K. Huebner, Harry J. Huebner, and Mark Thiessen Nation. Grand Rapids: Eerdmans, 1999.

—————. *The Politics of Jesus.* 2nd ed. Grand Rapids: Eerdmans, 2000.

—————. *The Priestly Kingdom: Social Ethics as Gospel.* Notre Dame, IN: University of Notre Dame Press, 1984.

—————. "Reinhold Niebuhr and Christian Pacifism." *Mennonite Quarterly Review* 29 (April 1955): 101-17.

—————. *The Royal Priesthood: Essays Ecclesiological and Ecumenical.* Edited by Michael G. Cartwright. Scottdale, PA: Herald, 1998.

—————. "Walk and Word: The Alternatives to Methodologism." In *Theology Without Foundations: Religious Practice and the Future of Theological Truth,* edited by Stanley Hauerwas, Nancey Murphy, and Mark Nation. Nashville: Abingdon, 1994.

—————. *The War of the Lamb.* Edited by Glen Stassen, Mark Thiessen Nation, and Matt Hamsher. Grand Rapids: Brazos, 2009.

—————. *What Would You Do? A Serious Answer to a Standard Question.* Scottdale, PA: Herald, 1983.

Young, Robert, ed. *Untying the Text: A Post-Structuralist Reader.* London: Routledge and Kegan Paul, 1981.

Index